Ani's
RAW FOOD
ESSENTIALS

Recipes and Techniques
for Mastering the
Art of Live Food

Ani's RAW FOOD ESSENTIALS

Ani Phyo

Da Capo
LIFE LONG

A MEMBER OF THE
PERSEUS BOOKS GROUP

Designed by Pauline Neuwirth
Set in 10 point Din by the Perseus Books Group

Cataloging-in-Publication data for this book is available from the Library of Congress.

First Da Capo Press edition 2010
ISBN: 978-0-7382-1377-4

Published by Da Capo Press
A Member of the Perseus Books Group
www.dacapopress.com

Note: The information in this book is true and complete to the best of our knowledge. This book is intended only as an informative guide for those wishing to know more about health issues. In no way is this book intended to replace, countermand, or conflict with the advice given to you by your own physician. The ultimate decision concerning care should be made between you and your doctor. We strongly recommend you follow his or her advice. Information in this book is general and is offered with no guarantees on the part of the author or Da Capo Press. The author and publisher disclaim all liability in connection with the use of this book. The names and identifying details of people associated with events described in this book have been changed. Any similarity to actual persons is coincidental.

Da Capo Press books are available at special discounts for bulk purchases in the United States by corporations, institutions, and other organizations. For more information, please contact the Special Markets Department at the Perseus Books Group, 2300 Chestnut Street, Suite 200, Philadelphia, PA, 19103, or call (800) 810-4145, ext. 5000, or e-mail special.markets@perseusbooks.com.

10 9 8 7 6

I dedicate this book to our children.
May we work together to uncover the truth
about food; to continue improving our
health through organic gardening and
whole food nutrition; to inspire our friends,
family, and communities to live a life they
love; and to heal our earth.

CONTENTS

INTRODUCTION

When I first started on my path to live foods, I was amazed by the potential—there are so many things you can do with raw fruits and vegetables. Even seemingly "hands-off" foods, such as pizza or pasta, could be made using fresh, uncooked ingredients. I'm not a formally trained chef; I came to raw foods from a simple and practical hands-on perspective. I wanted delicious, healthy foods that were fast and easy. My recipes are simple and can easily be made more complex by adding sauces and serving beautifully.

Over the past fifteen years, I've gone from making the simplest raw meals to starting my own raw foods company, SmartMonkey Foods. I've always focused on fast, fresh, unfussy—and ultimately, delicious—food. Along the way, I've developed some more complicated recipes but always keep an eye on what is quick to assemble and use seasonal ingredients whenever possible. I've designed these recipes with simplicity in mind, based on how I feed my busy self. Most recipes require only a few easy-to-find ingredients that are blended or processed quickly. Most of the recipes are ready to eat right away.

This book is for anyone who's new to raw foods—if you're curious and not sure where to start, I'll tell you what utensils you need and which ingredients to stock in your essential raw pantry. You'll also learn a lot of basic techniques—from how to split a fresh coconut to working with a dehydrator (and how to experiment if you don't own your own Excalibur Dehydrator just yet!). If you've been around the raw foods block a few times, you'll find some new tips to make your time in the kitchen less complicated and more enjoyable, as well as recipes you can use as templates to develop your own unique raw foods kitchen. It's easy—and the rewards are endless.

ONE SMALL STEP

It seems every person I meet is eager to live healthier, greener, fitter, leaner, and happier. But many people have the misconception that to be healthy, they need to invest a lot of time and energy. I'm going to break it all down for you to help you get healthy the fast, easy, and delicious way. It's simple to do when we start by taking small steps, one at a time. Each little bit adds up over time to make a difference.

We all would benefit from eating more unprocessed whole foods—fresh, unheated fruits, vegetables, nuts, and seeds are what the FDA calls "superfoods," which have been shown to increase our overall health. Superfoods help us ward off diseases and illness, give us more energy and stamina, keep us at our ideal body weight, and help us look and feel our best.

LIVING WELL

Raw food is more than just a diet. It's an entire philosophy and way of life. Eating more fresh organic ingredients affects the way we look, how we feel, and how we interact with other life and planet Earth.

Whole, fresh, unheated, unprocessed, organic fruits, vegetables, nuts, and seeds are rocket fuel for our body. This turbo-charged, nutrient-dense food fills us up with the vitamins, minerals, amino acids, and enzymes our body needs to hum like a well-oiled machine.

Raw foods and sunshine give me energy, mental clarity, focus, and help me to be more productive.

A properly fueled brain can take charge and orchestrate the trillions of cells in our body to fight illness and disease. As our health and stamina increase, we may shed unwanted extra pounds, our complexion may clear up . . . all while we tread lightly on our planet. And, when we feel great, anything is possible!

My recipes are designed to help you enjoy more healthy, whole, fresh food, which is the key building block for living life well.

MY RAW FOOD JOURNEY

Most of my youth was spent in the Catskill Mountains, living on a large plot of land where my family grew our own organic produce. We didn't have candy, sugar, soda, or processed foods in my house growing up. I ate a lot of Korean food, which, like most Asian food, is traditionally wheat and gluten free. Like most traditional foods, Korean food is whole and unprocessed. And a majority of Korean food is vegan, raw, and fermented.

My father was a raw fooder, and mono dieted frequently. He'd eat a whole bell pepper like an apple, and I had thought this was because he was from the "Old Country." That era of raw foods is what I now label "Raw Food 1.0." Raw food was eaten functionally back then, because it was good for you, not necessarily for taste.

My parents, having come from what was considered a third-world country in those days, were frugal. Having grown up poor, Koreans were good at conserving and using less . . . which are essential for treading lightly on our planet and living eco-green.

Although I grew up in a raw foods family, my eating habits changed when I got to college: the dining halls were full of new types of food, such as fried cheese, pasta, cake, and cookies. I loved trying all these new tastes. Unfortunately, I was eating mostly white flour, sugar, and dairy, and this newfound "diet" took its toll. I gained the Freshman 15 in just a few months' time and my cholesterol was almost at 300, which is too high for anyone. My mom put me back on a vegan, whole food diet—and immediately, my cholesterol dropped. I began exercising again. That was the turning point on my path back to an active, healthy lifestyle.

After college, I discovered vegan raw foods in San Francisco. A friend took me to a raw restaurant that had delicious food served like I'd never experienced before. It was what I call "Raw Food 2.0" and was beautiful, delicious, and healthy.

I had so much energy after my first Raw Food 2.0 meal, I couldn't sleep. I felt fine the next day and carried on with work as if I'd rested. Soon, I began to eat more of this raw gourmet food for energy, stamina, mental clarity, and focus. I could work more efficiently, be more productive, feel great, and sleep less without getting sick. I began making and incorporating more gourmet raw foods into my diet, and the people around me were interested in learning more. When I moved to Los Angeles for work a few years later, a few other raw chefs and I offered weekly dinners around town; their popularity grew quickly. This was when I realized I wanted to focus only on raw foods to help people and our planet.

It Just Takes Practice

A KEY TO living well is consistency and daily practice, not extremes. Extremes cause stress mentally, emotionally, physically, and spiritually. Consistency, on the other hand, practiced repeatedly over time, becomes a good habit.

A mentor once recommended having a daily practice. That practice may take the form of reading the latest industry news for fifteen minutes daily, or walking for thirty minutes every day.

Let's say walking for thirty minutes burns 150 calories. That's 1,050 calories a week. If it takes burning 3,500 calories to lose one pound, then in just over three weeks, you'll have lost one pound. It adds up over time.

Having a consistent practice will build self-esteem, and when you're fueling your body with ultimate superfoods, you'll feel great. You'll shine from the inside out with health.

My daily practice is to slow down and relax more.

MODERATION AND GRATITUDE

I developed a line of prepared packaged foods under the name SmartMonkey Foods, eventually also launching a line of fruit and nut bars. To focus on my raw foods business, I moved to Portland, Oregon, for four years.

Portland was cold and damp probably ten months out of the year, with gorgeous summers, wild blackberries, and no humidity. Eating all uncooked, cold, damp foods in that cold, damp climate took its toll on me over time without my even realizing it.

I didn't listen to my friends who told me to consider the climate in relation to my diet—that I couldn't eat the same way in the cold months in Portland as I did in warm

Los Angeles. I was into being fully raw, and it worked for me for a while. What I learned wasn't that it's impossible to be 100 percent raw in a cold climate; rather, that it's important to find what works for each of us. We all come from different ethnic backgrounds, have a unique genetic makeup, and have grown up and live in various climates.

When people ask me how important it is to be 100 percent raw, I remind them to have an attitude of gratitude instead. We are lucky to have the option to decline food because it's not raw, organic, or vegan, for example, while people in other parts of our world are starving. If someone makes a meal filled with good intentions that happens to not be all organic or raw, it may just be healthier to choose to accept it graciously, rather than being extreme. Extremes cause stress.

There are many days when I enjoy all raw foods, especially if I'm really busy or it's super hot outside. But, on cold, overcast, damp days, I may crave a hot soup, and so I'll have one.

I've actually found as I've let go of my reins of extremeness, people are more open and willing to try my style of eating and living. The pressure to be 100 percent perfect is gone. Instead, having gratitude for the foods I have to eat helps me make the right choices.

We are indeed privileged to have the choice to decline food that is not organic, vegan, or fresh. We are blessed. Let's remember to give thanks for this. On your own path, you may want to go 100 percent raw, or you may find it's best for you to try adding raw dishes to your diet daily or weekly. What's important to remember is that you don't need to be rigid and you don't have to go to extremes. The recipes in this book were created with those thoughts in mind.

ECO-GREEN LIVING AND LONGEVITY

Eating raw foods increases our health, no doubt. But to increase longevity even further, it's important to consider our overall well-being. To increase my overall health and longevity, I make sure to live eco green and toxin free, I enjoy an active lifestyle, I choose natural beauty and eco fashion, I work on being happy, and I eat my delicious, whole, fresh, raw foods.

TOXIN-FREE LIVING

Toxins in our living and working environments can be decreased by using toxin-free cleaners, choosing organic materials for furnishings whenever possible, and opening windows to air rooms. The EPA estimates indoor air can have two to five times more pollution than outside air.

Nontoxic Cleansers

TO AVOID nerve-damaging chemicals such as the butyl cellosolve and ammonia found in conventional cleaners, just make your own with ingredients you already have in your kitchen.

GLASS CLEANER
¼ cup vinegar
½ tablespoon eco liquid soap or detergent
2 cups water

Place all ingredients in a spray bottle, and use to clean glass.

ALL-PURPOSE CLEANER
½ cup vinegar
¼ cup baking soda
½ gallon water
Essential oils, for scent (optional)

Place all the ingredients in a bucket, mix, and use to clean most surfaces.

MOLD BUSTER AND ASTRINGENT
1 teaspoon tea tree oil
1 cup water

Mix the tea tree oil and water in a spray bottle. Shake to blend. Spritz on an item such as fabric and leave on; do not rinse. Line dry. I even use this to give my dog a quick bath when she gets into something dirty.

TO UNBLOCK SLOW DRAINS
1 gallon water
½ cup salt

Heat the water and salt to almost boiling and pour it down your drain. If you have a major blockage, you'll need to snake your drain instead.

Or, try using baking soda and vinegar to unblock your drain.
½ cup baking soda
½ cup white vinegar
1 quart water

Pour the baking soda down the drain. Then pour the vinegar down the drain. It will fizz. Lastly, pour the water down the drain to flush.

I love my dress made from a Baltimore Orioles jersey.

In Korea, shoes are left at the door, which avoids tracking in residual pesticides. I use a HEPA filter vacuum to filter out dust, bacteria, pollen, and dog dander from my pooch, Kanga. My shower curtains are PVC-free to avoid toxins that can disrupt my hormones, and I have green plants that help clean and filter my indoor air. A NASA study found plants remove 96 percent of harmful carbon monoxide from a closed room.

Toxin-free living also means abandoning toxic thoughts. A positive outlook makes it easier to feel happier. Focus on what you want, and don't waste energy worrying about what you don't want.

ACTIVE LIFESTYLE

Our body was designed to run away from predators in the wild, and to gather our food. Today, we work all day at our desk in an office and buy our food at the market. So, it's important to include cardio, stretching, and weight-bearing exercises, to build strong, lean muscles and a healthy body that's less prone to injury and pain.

I've got to sweat every day to detox and clean myself from the inside out—even if it means going to a sauna on days when I've got less energy. Meditation is exercise for my brain muscle, and I do my best to meditate, even if only for five minutes, every morning upon rising and every evening before bed.

ECO BEAUTY AND FASHION

Eating more whole, fresh, organic foods increases overall health from the inside out to give us a glow of health. In Los Angeles, we have clothing recycling stores, where you can trade about three stylish fashion items for credit toward another item in the store. I love shopping at these fashion recycleries and find one-of-a-kind gems that create my fashion statement. Plus, it's a cost-effective way to get new clothes. When buying new clothing, I do my best to choose organic fabrics that help me avoid chemicals on my skin.

Research has found toxic chemicals called parabens, used as preservatives in makeup, shampoos, deodorants, and nail polish, in cancer cells. Choosing poison-free beauty options will decrease your exposure to toxic chemicals that build up on your body over time. Our skin is our largest organ, and what we put on it is the same as if we are drinking or eating the substance. I make sure everything I put on my body is safe to eat, such as lemon juice to lighten, and coconut oil and jojoba oil to moisturize my hair and skin.

Take time out for our friends, family, and pooches.

HAPPINESS

When we feel happy, we are less stressed, and our overall sense of well-being is increased. I've found being happy takes practice, but the rewards are endless. Happy people win favors, receive kind gestures, laugh more, have fewer wrinkles, and even make others smile.

Even though I eat a nutrient-rich diet of fresh, organic, whole foods, I still have days when I need to work on feeling happy. It helps me to make a list of ten to twenty blessings I'm thankful for today. I may be grateful for something as basic as a new day, a good night's rest, a strong body, a beating heart, and my family and friends. I try not to think about what I don't have, once had, or wish I had, and focus on this moment and all that's good in my life.

To increase happiness, be kind, take a minute to help someone out, and give compliments freely. Give it a try, and you'll see how good it makes you feel. Spend more time with your family. Our family and friends are the most important thing in life. At the end of your life, you won't wish you'd worked harder, or made more money. You'll wish you'd spent more time with the people you love.

I haven't had a TV in years, and I avoid gossip. Living without these leaves me with more time to make nourishing food, meditate, contemplate, and feel gratitude and bliss. And, I make sure to give my dog, Kanga, as much love as possible.

GREEN EATING

What we choose to eat has the largest impact on our planet, and the right foods can help us feel and look our best. By enjoying more organic raw foods, we're contributing to a green planet by decreasing the production and use of toxic chemicals and their contamination of our natural environment. We ingest less poisonous chemicals, and place less stress on our immune system. We provide nutrient-rich food to fuel our optimal physical, mental, and emotional performance.

When I started eating more whole foods, I noticed an immediate decrease in kitchen garbage, as most of it comes from food packaging. The stuff we throw away is what we're paying for . . . the packaging, printing, manufacturing, warehousing, refrigeration, and distribution. After all this has been paid off, there's not much money left for the actual ingredients in the food. This is why most processed, packaged, and prepared foods are full of chemical flavors, colors, and empty calories created to make actual food ingredients go further. Another reason for enjoying more whole, fresh, raw foods straight from the source.

RAW FOODS 2.0

My style of Raw Foods 2.0 includes fruits, vegetables, nuts, and seeds. Most are never heated or cooked, and if heated, the temperature never goes above 104°F. I believe anything hotter than 104°F begins to damage the nutrients and enzyme activity in our food. Research has shown nutrients are damaged and destroyed as food is heated and cooked. I've heard some people heat raw foods up to as high as 110° or 118°F, and you'll hear varying numbers. I believe anything hotter than 104°F damages enzymes and nutrients, because 104°F is hot when I touch it and feels as if it's damaging my skin.

Whole, unprocessed, fresh fruits, vegetables, nuts, and seeds are mixed together in a blender or food processor, or simply tossed together in a bowl, to create delicious, nutrient-rich dishes that taste better than the cooked versions. Good for you and good for the planet, my recipes support eco-green living, health, and overall well-being.

I consider my food to be living foods, which is a bit different from the "classic" definition of raw foods. A dehydrated cracker can be raw but has less enzyme activity, so its shelf life is longer than, say, a living apple, which contains water and enzymes and will ripen more and more over time until it eventually composts back into the earth. I recommend enjoying dehydrated foods in moderation, and drinking plenty of water with it to keep hydrated. Remember, water is the basis of all things living.

I prefer soaking all my nuts and seeds, and even sprouting them, whenever possible. It can be challenging to soak and sprout when busy or traveling, though, so I do the best I can each day. Personally, I don't eat much dehydrated food. But these foods are definitely fun to eat and are a great way to transition away from wheat, breads, and crackers. Dehydrated treats are a good way to incorporate more raw foods into any diet.

CHOOSE ORGANIC AND LOCAL

To keep the level of toxins inside my body to a minimum, I enjoy organics whenever possible. Because I live in Los Angeles, where organics are widely available, it's easy for me to choose local, which ensures I eat produce when it's in season and at its peak in nutritional profile and flavor. I shop at farmers' markets as much as possible, which keeps money in my local community.

Genetically modified foods (GMOs) have been altered by science to be resistant to pests and to produce greater crop yields, artificially. GMO foods contain less nutrients, so you're actually getting less for your money. They are far from natural or healthy and it's wise to avoid them.

My garden produces vegetables faster than I can eat or give them away.

Here are some tips for reading the PLU codes on fruit and vegetable labels.

► a four-digit number means the item is conventionally grown.
► a five-digit number beginning with 9 means it's organic.
► a five-digit number beginning with 8 means it's been genetically modified.

WHAT'S A "RAW FOODER"?

Definitions of a "raw fooder" varies from someone who eats 50 percent raw 100 percent of the time, to eating 80 percent raw and 20 percent cooked in a day, to eating only 100 percent raw. I want to encourage you to find whatever works for you and fits your lifestyle. You'll be undoing any good effects of eating healthy if you're stressing out about what you can and cannot eat. How much raw food you eat may also change with the seasons, with what's happening in your life at the moment, and over time as your body changes. Keep in mind, health is a lifelong pursuit.

LEAN AND GREEN, FROM THE INSIDE OUT

Eliminating food from my diet leaves me with a sense of deprivation. Instead, I prefer *including* more healthy, guilt-free, weight-loss-promoting, and eco-green ingredients into each meal. Over time, more of the good stuff we include leaves less and less space for the less-valuable, less-nutrient-dense, less-healthy foods, without having to try to eliminate them. What is bad for us gets elbowed out naturally.

As we increase the amount of nutrient-dense foods into any diet, the amount of vitamins, minerals, enzymes, and antioxidants we feed our body increases, and the healthier we become. The water and fiber from fresh, whole fruits, vegetables, nuts, and seeds shower and sweep our insides clean, detoxifying us in a healthy way from the inside out.

RESEARCHERS AT UNIVERSITY of California in San Diego have found eating red meat and dairy products increases inflammation in the body because our body doesn't recognize molecules from other animals, since they're not human, and treats animal molecules as invaders. This increases inflammation throughout the body. As we displace those ingredients with more whole, fresh, fruits, vegetables, nuts, and seeds, our body becomes less swollen. It looks tighter and leaner and helps us lose unwanted extra pounds.

GET YOUR SHINE ON

Today's fashion is driven by the look of natural beauty and lighter cosmetics. The healthier our body becomes, the more we obtain clear skin, shiny hair, strong nails, bright eyes, and more energy.

Our skin is our largest organ, and its health reflects the purity of our body on the inside. Eating healthy raw foods will give you the shine of glowing skin and the radiance of overall vitality and natural beauty.

PART 1

THE
BASICS

1

TOOLS AND INGREDIENTS

KITCHEN TOOLS

It's easy to set up a raw food kitchen. Most tools are the same as in a conventional cooked kitchen, minus the pots and pans. A few must-have items will make it easy to start making my recipes, and a few other nice-to-have items that aren't necessary will make kitchen play even more enjoyable and fun.

MUST-HAVES

Two raw food tools to start with in your kitchen are a food processor and a blender. To make some of the recipes in this book, you'll also need a dehydrator, which is used to make crackers, biscuits, cookies, and pancakes. (In chapter 2, you'll learn how to use a conventional oven to experiment with dehydrating.) And, you'll at least need a knife, bowl, and measuring spoons and cups.

FOOD PROCESSOR

 A food processor chops dry and low-moisture ingredients, such as nuts and vegetables. You could instead chop by hand with a knife, but a food processor will save you heaps of time.

HIGH-SPEED BLENDER

 I recommend saving money to buy just one high-speed blender. I have the Vitamix, which will last me a lifetime. It's powerful and pulverizes nuts, seeds, and vanilla beans whole. A blender is used with liquid to make mylks, smoothies, soups, and sauces.

TRIBEST PERSONAL BLENDER

 A smaller blender is great for traveling, and the Tribest Personal Blender is priced lower and makes a great first blender. It comes with a grinding blade, so you can grind your nuts and seeds before blending to create a smoother texture while decreasing strain on your blender's motor.

EXCALIBUR DEHYDRATOR

 A dehydrator is used to dry at low temperatures and simulates sun drying. My dehydrator brand of choice is the Excalibur Dehydrator. It comes with four to nine 14-inch-square shelves plus heatproof Paraflexx liners, and I recommend getting a model with a built-in timer.

KNIFE

 Obtain several knifes of various sizes. I prefer ceramic knives because they never need sharpening and the oxidation of cut vegetables and fruits is slower than when cut with a metal knife. You can find these on my Web site, www.AniPhyo.com/store.

MIXING BOWLS

Larger mixing bowls make it easier to toss ingredients without making a mess outside your bowl. I have an assortment of different-size mixing bowls in my kitchen and have found that it's useful to have at least three bowls of varying sizes handy.

MEASURING CUPS AND SPOONS

You'll need measuring cups and spoons to get the right proportions of ingredients into your recipes. There's a slight difference between wet and dry measuring cups that matter more when working with wheat flours. I use both wet and dry interchangeably. I have a 4-cup wet measuring cup with a handle and spout, plus the standard ¼-, ⅓-, ½-, and 1-cup dry measuring cups.

NICE-TO-HAVE

I love kitchen toys, and the following items are definitely fun to have, if not absolutely necessary to begin making and enjoying the recipes in this book. These tools will make it easier to create new textures and will speed up your prep time.

SPIRALIZER

 Some of the noodle recipes use a spiralizer to create thin angel hair–type vegetable noodles. You can slice noodle shapes with a knife until you get your hands on a spiral slicer, available online at www.AniPhyo.com/store.

MANDOLINE SLICER

 A mandoline slicer helps slice vegetables very thinly, giving you consistent slices. You can slice the old-fashioned way, using a knife, too.

CITRUS JUICER

 A citrus juicer helps extract more juice from your lemons and limes than if you squeezed them by hand.

VEGETABLE JUICER

 Only a few recipes require vegetable pulp, left over from juicing carrots. You can always visit a juice bar to ask for pulp if you don't want to buy a juicer.

WHISK

 A whisk is used to mix liquids evenly. You can also use a fork for a similar effect.

ICE-CREAM SCOOPER

 An ice-cream scooper makes it easy to portion and shape batter for cookies and other sweets, as well as ice kream.

GRINDER

 A grinder helps make a powdered meal out of nuts and seeds. Your Personal Blender will come with a grinder top. Your high-speed blender may have a dry container to use for grinding. Or, you can grind in your liquid high-speed blender container, though it will dull the blades over time. You can buy already ground almond and flax meal, too.

STRAINING SIEVE

 A sieve makes it easy to strain solids out of your liquid. I prefer a metal sieve for seeds, soaked rice, and soaked quinoa, and a smaller plastic sieve for my kefir grains.

LEMON ZESTER

 This tool makes fun, long, curly strands of citrus zest. You can zest a piece of fruit with a planer or grater.

COOKIE CUTTERS

 Cookie cutters help form cookies and mini cakes. You can always use your hands, and kids can help make fun shapes, too.

COCKTAIL SHAKER

 Cocktail shakers are fun to have, especially when making elixirs for dinner parties. You can use a jar with a tight lid to seal and shake, then a strainer, instead.

MASON JARS

 Mason jars are good containers for making my raw fermented vegetables. But any glass jar with a lid will work, too.

BAKING, PIE, OR TARTLET PAN

 Baking pans help shape and hold cakes, pies, and tartlets. You can always use a plate and form shapes with your hands.

RUBBER SPATULA

A spatula makes it easier to scrape up all batter off the edges of your food processor, bowl, or blender. I also like scrapers, a semicircular spatula without a handle, for scraping bowls.

GLOVES

 When using your hands, wearing disposable plastic or latex gloves will keep food from sticking to you, and they're more hygienic.

Spend Time in Your Own Kitchen, Rather Than in a Restaurant

RESTAURANTS MAY KNOW how to make food taste good, but they don't care about your health. Take time to prepare more of your own meals at home, and take snacks and lunch to your workplace. This will save you a bunch of money, and you might find yourself losing weight while looking and feeling better, too.

SHOPPING

I prefer buying seasonal food because it's at its peak in nutritional content and flavor, so I get more for my money. Local food travels less and is handled less, lowering the chances for contamination and food-borne illness.

I love shopping at my local farmers' markets. The produce arrives superfresh, straight from the farm, usually picked just a few hours before. You'll notice how much longer this food keeps, compared with what you'd buy at a regular grocery store. This means less spoilage and less money wasted.

Buying directly from farmers means you're bulk buying without packaging. This helps you tread lightly on our planet by using less resources. And if you bring your own bags, you'll be helping that much more. Paper, plastic, and packaging prices are soaring due to the increase in gas prices, contributing to rising food costs.

I choose organic whenever it's available, which means I'm investing in the future of our planet and my health. Disease is caused by the toxins we put into and onto our body and eating organic lowers this toxic load. Prevention is the lowest-cost way to save money in the long run.

Grocery stores put items on sale weekly at a really low price to bring customers into their store. If you have the time, it's worth it to do your shopping at several different stores, to save money by buying sale items.

THE ESSENTIAL RAW PANTRY AND FRIDGE

Here is a list of basic items I keep in my pantry and fridge. You can use this as your shopping list, to make it easy to stock your kitchen with everything you'll need to make the recipes in this book.

Fresh fruits and veggies, on the other hand, are specific to each recipe and should be purchased at time of use. This will also encourage you to be creative and use these recipes as a template for new dishes.

I store shelf-stable items, such as dried spices and herbs, nuts, and seeds, in my pantry. I store food with a shorter shelf life, such as flaxseeds and fresh produce, in my fridge.

THE ESSENTIAL RAW PANTRY

NUTS
I buy nuts in bulk a pound at a time and store them in glass jars, as I use them up quickly. You can also store them in your fridge or freezer to slow their turning rancid.

Almonds, whole and meal	Coconut, dried and shredded	Sunflower seeds
Brazil nuts	Pecans	Walnuts
Cashews	Pistachios	

SEEDS
I buy bulk raw seeds by the pound, when available, and store my seeds in glass jars. It makes it easy to see what's inside. In case you haven't yet discovered chia seeds and buckwheat groats, they are available at natural food co-ops and health food stores, and online at my store at www.AniPhyo.com/store.

Buckwheat groats	Pumpkin seeds	Sunflower seeds
Chia	Quinoa	Wild rice
Hemp seeds, also called hemp nuts	Sesame seeds	

CEREAL
Oats are gluten free, but some are processed with wheat. If you're allergic to gluten, check with your oat source to learn how it's processed. I purchase raw whole oats by the pound. Oats are cooked during processing, so look for the label "raw" rather than "steel-cut" or "rolled" oats.

Oats, whole

DRIED FRUITS

I buy the following fruits by the pound and in bulk when available, except where noted. Cacao is raw, unprocessed fruit of the cacao tree and is where all chocolate comes from.

Carob is an alternative to chocolate that's caffeine free and has a malt flavor.

Goji berries, small red berries from Asia, used traditionally in Chinese medicine, are high in vitamin C and taste sweet.

Dates ripen on the tree, and I prefer them fresh. But they are also available dried, too.

Cacao powder	Cranberries	Mangoes
Cacao nibs	Dates	Raisins
Carob powder	Goji berries	Sun-dried tomatoes

OILS

Oils are used to give a smooth consistency and add flavor. I prefer toasted sesame oil, which is obviously not raw, for adding Asian flavor to a recipe. I use such a small amount, it's worth the rich flavor it adds for me. You can choose raw sesame oil instead, if you prefer. Some natural food stores sell oils in bulk, and I like to take in my own glass jars to collect it. Be sure to store sesame oil in the fridge, as it can go rancid quickly.

Coconut oil	Sesame oil, toasted
Olive oil, extra-virgin, cold pressed	

SEA VEGETABLES

Sea vegetables come from the ocean. They're full of minerals and iodine to feed our thyroid and help regulate our metabolism. Nori sheets are flattened seaweed laver used to make maki rolls. Kelp is pressed into noodle shapes to make nutritious kelp noodles that have only 6 calories a serving. There are many other seaweeds, such as *hijiki*, *arame*, and different lavers, which vary in color, texture, and flavor. Most are dried, and you reconstitute them by soaking them in water before using. I include nori, kelp, and *wakame* here because they're the most common and easiest to find at natural food stores and online.

Kelp noodles	Nori sheets	Wakame

SWEETENERS

Agave and yacón are both low-glycemic sweeteners that are supposedly safe for diabetics. Yacón has even less sugar and calories than does agave, is deep in color, and has a rich consistency and a molasses flavor. Stevia is a plant whose leaves are dried and ground into a powder. Supposedly stevia doesn't even register in the body as a sugar at all and may even lower blood sugar levels. It has little calories and is considered noncaloric. I like to use stevia in smoothies, but sparingly, as it has a strong flavor. If you prefer to use maple syrup, choose grade B, which is less processed and contains more nutrients than grade A does. It's definitely cooked but provides a wonderful, unique flavor. Another cooked sweetener popular in the macrobiotic world is brown rice syrup, made from cooked rice inoculated with enzymes, which ferment to turn the starches in the rice into sugars.

Agave syrup	Maple syrup, grade B	Yacón syrup
Brown rice syrup	Stevia powder	

DRIED HERBS, SPICES, AND FLAVORS

I make sure to always have at least a cup of the following dried herbs and spices on hand in my spice rack. Well, except for whole vanilla bean, which can be expensive. I just keep a few of them on hand in a sealed jar to retain moisture. I buy these in bulk when available and store them in small glass jars. Nutritional yeast has a cheeselike flavor, is grown for its nutritional value, and provides B vitamins 1, 2, 3, 6, and 12. It's different from brewer's yeast, which is a by-product of breweries and distilleries. You can find it in most health food stores, larger chain health food stores such as Whole Foods, or online.

Almond extract	Cumin, ground	Thyme, dried
Black pepper	Nutritional yeast	Vanilla extract, alcohol-
Cayenne, ground	Oregano, dried	free, and/or vanilla
Chipotle chile, ground	Rosemary, dried	beans
Cinnamon, ground	Sage, ground	
Coriander, ground	Sea salt	

THE ESSENTIAL RAW FRIDGE

These are the items I like to keep stocked in my fridge to make it easy to whip up any recipe in a snap. The following items all have a relatively long shelf life. Fresher vegetables and fruits, I like to buy as needed and as in season, per whatever recipe I'm making.

NUTS AND SEEDS

I buy flaxseed and meal by the pound. I buy tahini, which is mulled sesame seeds, and almond butter by the jar and store them in the fridge to extend their shelf life. Look for the label "raw," as these are usually made with toasted seeds and almonds. Other fun butters to explore are made from other nuts and seeds such as pumpkin, cashew, walnut, and pecan. I include tahini and almond butter because they are the most common and easiest to find. Thai baby coconuts can be found at most natural food stores and co-ops. I like to buy them by the case of nine at the natural food store or at an Asian market. They keep for a couple of weeks.

Almond butter   Tahini
Flaxseed and meal   Thai young coconuts

CONDIMENTS

Condiments will keep indefinitely, so I have these in my fridge at all times. I'd recommend starting out with the smaller sizes to see which you like the taste of best. They go a long way. Bragg Liquid Aminos is a gluten-free salty sauce similar to soy sauce but has a slightly different flavor and is supposedly raw. Nama Shoyu is a raw soy sauce that has not been pasteurized. Miso contains probiotics and is a fermented and cultured food. Miso comes in different flavors, including white, red, and brown. White is the mildest and easiest to use, because it doesn't affect the color of your recipes. I like to buy apple cider vinegar containing the filament "culture" inside it to show it's raw, alive, and full of probiotics and enzymes. Store all condiments in your fridge.

Apple cider vinegar   Miso, unpasturized, white
Bragg Liquid Aminos   Nama Shoyu

FRUITS

Olives will keep for up to six months or longer in your fridge. I prefer black olives because they are the most common to find online and occasionally at health food stores. Buy them pickled, using sea salt rather than table salt. Sea salt is raw and healthier for us because it is dried ocean water; table salt is chemically created. I always keep at least a pound of dates on hand. Shelf life in the fridge is up to six months, or one year frozen. They dry out, so keep them sealed. I store four or five lemons and a few limes in the fridge, as they keep for a couple of weeks; and a couple of avocados, which will last for a week or more in the fridge. Buy other fresh fruits as needed per recipe.
Avocados

Black olives
Lemons
Limes

Medjool dates
Other in-season fresh fruits

VEGETABLES

Onion and garlic will keep for weeks, so I always have them in my produce drawer. Jalapeño will keep for a week or two, and I keep one or two on hand. I always buy whatever greens look great at the farmers' market, then figure out what to make when I get them home. Or, you can also buy greens as needed per recipe.

Garlic
In-season greens and lettuces as
    needed, such as collard, kale, and
    romaine

Jalapeño
Onion, red
Onion, yellow

FRESH HERBS

When in season, fresh herbs are always the way to go. They will only keep for a week at most, so buy as needed per recipe. Use half the amount of dried when out of season, since dried is stronger than fresh.

In-season fresh herbs, as needed, such as basil, thyme, and rosemary

HOW TO USE THIS BOOK

I'll give you the basic tools you need, along with the essential understanding of how to create interesting textures and delectable flavors, so you can start creating your own unique recipes.

I've spent fifteen years learning about the art of live foods, and one of the things I've discovered is that anyone can learn to make delicious raw foods that are simple to prepare yet sophisticated in flavor and presentation.

BACK TO THE BASICS

In this book I'll tell you all you need to know to enjoy making fast, easy, delicious, healthy food . . . every day. Once you get down the basics, you can then explore swapping out ingredients, adding spices and flavors, and even adding sauces and additional recipes to create increasingly complex dishes.

I start out each chapter or section with a series of "basic" recipes that are pared down to the fewest ingredients possible. Next, I include "basic plus" recipes by adding ingredients to a "basic" recipe, to show you how easy it is to create new flavors and variations. I also provide other recipes designed to help inspire you to explore and experiment, to create your own personalized recipes. Look for my SmartMonkey to point out my simple basic recipes.

I will show you that you don't need to spend hours in the kitchen to prepare sophisticated, delicious, healthy food. It can be done quickly and easily.

NUT ALLERGIES

This book uses nuts and seeds extensively, though there are some nut-free recipes. If you're allergic to nuts, this may not be the best book for you.

IN LOVE AND COMMITTED

Once you've fallen in love with making and eating raw foods, you may want to venture deeper and deeper into the world of dehydration and fermentation. I've included a dehydration chapter full of easy-to-make foods that require several hours of patience as they dry, before you can eat them. But still, the prep time remains short and fast. Recipes that require dehydration include breads, pizza crust, chips, vegetables, wraps, pancakes, and jerky.

Cultured foods are extremely beneficial for any diet. I include pickled vegetable recipes for making sauerkraut, cucumber pickles, and Korean-inspired kimchi, and also a cultured drinks chapter where I'll show you how to make probiotic drinks such as kefir and kombucha. These recipes are easy to make but require time to brew and ferment.

RESOURCES

At the end of this book, I provide additional resources for green living, my recipes and online uncooking videos, ingredients, and kitchen tools.

TRANSITIONING TO AND FROM COOKED FOOD

All natural food starts out raw, whether eaten immediately or cooked and eaten later. When you make my food, you can enjoy it right away without having to cook it. However, if you are just starting with raw foods or maybe it's a chilly day and you want something that's warm, you may decide you want to cook or heat my recipes, such as a soup, burger, sauce, or pizza, after it's been prepared. Feel free to change my recipes to suit your liking, even if it means heating or cooking them. At least the ingredients started with all fresh, whole food, and preferably organic ingredients. So, it's still a very healthy option free of fillers, chemical flavors, or artificial colors snuck in along the way.

You'll see places throughout this book with a cooked-food icon. This is where I recommend transitional ways of enjoying more raw foods. For example, eat my Sun Burgers on a sprouted whole-grain bun, roll up my wraps in a spelt or whole-grain tortilla on the outside, or toss a raw sauce or cheeze over cooked rice noodles.

If adding a bit of cooked food to my recipes helps you to enjoy more raw foods, then I think that's great! Remember to have gratitude, be happy, and celebrate life.

SPIRALIZER

 LEMON ZESTER

 MANDOLINE SLICER

 COOKIE CUTTER

 CITRUS JUICER

 COCKTAIL SHAKER

 VEGETABLE JUICER

 MASON JAR

 WHISK

 BAKING TRAY, PIE, OR TARTLET PAN

 ICE CREAM SCOOPER

 CHOCOLATE MOULD TRAY

 GRINDER

 GLOVES

 SIEVE

 TRANSITIONAL COOKED FOOD

 FOOD PROCESSOR

TIP ICONS

Throughout this book, I've included tips to help make things easier while inspiring you to live life greener and happier.

 WELL-BEING TIP

 GENERAL TIP

 GREEN LIVING TIP

 BASIC RECIPE

2

RAW BASICS AND TECHNIQUES

Dehydrating, Soaking and Sprouting, Fermentation and Pickling, and Substitutions

The essential information in this chapter will have you quickly on your way toward dehydrating, to make delicious flatbreads to use in the same way as you would any toast. I'll show you how easy it is to soak and sprout nuts and seeds, too.

I'll help you start making your own fermented vegetables, using cucumbers to make pickles that will help add probiotic goodness to your diet, so you can absorb more nutrients from the food you eat. I'll also explain how to make substitutions of your favorite ingredients.

Later, in chapter 3, I'll be showing you how to make cultured drinks such as kombucha and kefir. Drinking probiotics works wonders for your digestion and is the easiest way to get more healthy bacteria into your body.

DEHYDRATION

In hot, dry climates such as a desert, food can be laid out under the sun to dry. For the rest of us who don't live in a desert, a dehydrator allows us the flexibility to dry

all year round, with the ability to control the temperature and length of drying time. Dehydrators act as the sun does to dry and preserve foods such as sun-dried tomatoes, raisins, fruit leathers, and jerkies.

A dehydrator is an enclosed container, such as a box, which has a heating element to warm at low temperatures whatever has been placed inside. A fan blows this warm air across the surface of food, which has been placed or spread on lined mesh trays to dry.

Although dehydrating isn't necessary to the raw diet, it will help you create a unique baked or fried texture. You can make crackers, breads, pizza crusts, chips, fried onions, scones and biscuits, pancakes, and even bacon. In this chapter, I'll show you how to make three easy flatbreads with a texture similar to a cracker. They can be used like toast to make sandwiches, as croutons crumbled onto your salad and soup, and as a pizza crust topped with sauce and cheeze.

Don't have a dehydrator? Don't worry—I'll offer tips on transitioning and easy ways to learn about dehydrating before you invest in your own machine. You can familiarize yourself with these essentials and then move on to the recipes, or you can go straight to the rest of the recipes. All of these basics are cross-referenced throughout the book. I hope you enjoy these essentials from my kitchen.

THE EXCALIBUR DEHYDRATOR

I use an Excalibur Dehydrator. I've tried many dehydrators over my lifetime, and keep coming back to the Excalibur. I have a nine-tray model in my home, just for myself. You can choose from as few as four trays, to as many as nine. I like having nine trays because I like to make large batches of crackers, pizza crusts, and cookies, especially during the holiday season. Nine trays give me space to make a couple of trays of cookies, a few trays of breads and crackers, a few trays of wrappers, and a couple of trays of Buckwheat Crispies, all at the same time.

I've been using my nine-tray Excalibur Dehydrator at home and in my commercial kitchens for over a decade, and they've made food for thousands of people. I love Excalibur's large, 14-inch-square mesh trays. Unlike other dehydrators that have an air channel and hole in the center of each tray, Excalibur's solid trays allow me to dry large pieces of bread, wrappers, and big round pizza crusts.

Excalibur offers reusable Paraflexx nonstick sheets that fit perfectly over each tray. These liners support my eco-green lifestyle because I don't have to waste parchment paper.

I recommend choosing a dehydrator with a timer, for convenience. The timer control is built right into the box frame and makes it easy to set your drying time, to prevent over- or underdrying. Each model also has a temperature-control dial, not simply an on-off switch.

For more information on the Excalibur Dehydrator, visit www.excalibur dehydrator.com.

DEHYDRATION TIPS

Dehydration is our raw equivalent of baking in the cooked world. As with cooking, you don't want to overbake your food, or it will become too dry. For best results, you need to consider your climate and the outside temperature and humidity, when you use a dehydrator. Here are a few tips:

DON'T OVERDEHYDRATE

How quickly you plan to eat your treats will determine how long you should dry them. The longer you dehydrate your food, the drier and crisper it gets, and the longer its shelf life. But when I make dehydrated snacks such as a pizza crust or corn tortillas that I know will disappear in a day or two, I choose to leave them a bit less dehydrated, so they will be a little softer. This saves electricity, too. The only items you'll definitely want to dry all the way are the crispy chips, or any fresh herbs that you wish to preserve (underdehydrating them could contribute to their growing moldy when stored). If you do accidentally overdehydrate your food, you can rehydrate it by spritzing it with water with a spray bottle.

MORE FULL, MORE TIME

If I'm going to dehydrate, I make sure to fill as many dehydrator trays as I can. However, note that the more your dehydrator is filled, the longer it will take to dry, because more total moisture needs to be extracted and evaporated.

CLIMATE

The temperature and moisture around your dehydrator will effect the drying time. Drying times will be briefer in hot, dry climates and will be longer in cold damp climates.

BATCH VOLUMES

In general, to make a cracker or crust, you want to spread 2 to 3 cups of batter per 14-inch-square Excalibur Dehydrator tray.

ROTATE BACK TO FRONT, TOP TO BOTTOM

The Excalibur Dehydrator has a fan in the back of the unit, so I like to rotate the trays from back to front as well as from top to bottom. This is not completely necessary, since the Excalibur is designed to dry evenly; it's just a habit I've acquired over the years that's especially useful when not fully drying out my food.

DOUBLING AND TRIPLING RECIPES

I recommend doubling and tripling these recipes, and you'll see that making larger volumes doesn't take much more time than a single batch does. Preparation is simple and fast, and cleanup is the same whether you make one batch or five. The only extra ingredient you need is patience, since you have to wait anywhere from 3 to 12 hours for your food to dry before eating.

IF YOU DON'T HAVE A DEHYDRATOR . . .

In my world, live foods are not heated above 104°F; a dehydrator with a temperature control will allow you to maintain the proper heat, to preserve the enzymes in your food. However, I know that not everyone is going to immediately go out and get an Excalibur! While a raw foods lifestyle means not using your oven, if you're new to raw foods and are curious about dehydrating, you can use your big kitchen appliance to experiment with the following simple steps:

Preheat the oven to 140°F or set at the lowest setting. The temperature controls aren't as fine especially at lower heat ranges, but just do the best you can for now.

Line cookie sheets with parchment paper. Spread your batter on the lined cookie sheets and place them in your oven. Prop the oven door open with a butter knife or a chopstick. This method will take a long while to dry. But is a good way to test out the recipes before investing in a dehydrator. Although letting the heat escape is generally not a great idea in terms of conservation, you can use this method sparingly, and hopefully you'll be inspired to invest in a dehydrator.

FLATBREADS

Unlike traditional bread that has wheat and gluten, these dehydrated breads are gluten and wheat free and are made with flaxseeds, a great source of omegas and fiber. Crisp crackers, flatbreads, and moist biscuits have flax meal as their common binding ingredient; this is mixed with seasonings, vegetables, and buckwheat to make different textures and flavors.

Two to three cups of "dough" are blended or processed and then spread evenly across a 14-inch-square Paraflexx-lined Excalibur Dehydrator tray, to make nine slices of "bread."

These recipes serve to introduce you to dehydrating; you'll see recipes for other dehydrated foods throughout the book, as well as recipes that use these breads. Feel free to experiment to get just the consistency you want; for sandwiches, you may want a bread that has a bit more firmness; for pizza, one that has a bit more give. It's all up to your preference and cravings.

RYE FLATBREAD

The olive oil and fiber from celery make for a soft, flexible bread. And the cacao really makes it taste like and look the same color as a dark rye bread.

The caraway plant resembles a carrot plant, with feathery leaves. Caraway fruits, which we call seeds, have an aniselike favor, and I use them to make my rye bread. You can substitute fennel seed for the caraway.

$1^3/_4$ cups chopped celery

2 tablespoons olive oil

2 tablespoons cacao or carob powder

$1^1/_2$ cups flax meal

$1^1/_2$ cups filtered water

1 tablespoon caraway seeds

Place the celery, olive oil, cacao, flax meal, and water in a high-speed blender, and blend until smooth.

Spread the dough on one 14-inch-square Paraflexx-lined Excalibur Dehydrator tray. Sprinkle with caraway seeds and press them lightly into the dough.

Dehydrate at 104°F for 4 to 6 hours. Flip directly onto mesh tray. Peel away Paraflexx sheet. Score it into nine slices. Dehydrate for another 4 to 6 hours, or until desired consistency.

ZUCCHINI BREAD

MAKES 9 SERVINGS

This is a soft bread that combines zucchini and almond meal with the flax meal. The olive oil and squash's cellulose fiber make this a lighter bread that stays moist and pliable.

2 cups chopped zucchini

$1/_4$ cup extra-virgin olive oil

1 teaspoon sea salt

1 cup almond meal

1 cup flax meal

Place the zucchini, oil, and salt in a food processor, and process into a puree. Add the almond meal and flax meal, and process into batter.

Spread the batter evenly on one 14-inch-square lined Excalibur Dehydrator tray. Dehydrate at 104°F for 6 to 8 hours. Flip directly onto mesh tray, peeling away the Paraflexx, and dehydrate for another 4 to 6 hours. Note that the bread will remain moist and flexible.

SUNFLOWER BREAD
MAKES 9 SERVINGS

This hearty yet soft bread is made with sunflower seeds, flax meal, and celery.

> 1½ cups chopped celery
> 3 tablespoons sunflower seeds
> 1½ cups flax meal
> 1 to 1¼ cups water, as needed

Place the celery in a food processor and process into small pieces. Add the sunflower seeds and process into small pieces. Add the flax meal and water, and mix well, using only enough water to make a spreadable batter.

Spread the batter evenly on one 14-inch-square lined Excalibur Dehydrator tray. Dehydrate for 4 hours at 104°F degrees. Flip and peel off the Paraflexx, then place back on the liner and score into nine slices with a butter knife. Be careful not to cut through the mesh. Dehydrate for another 2 to 4 hours, or to desired consistency.

SOAKING AND SPROUTING
The easiest way I soak is to simply place nuts and seeds into at least double the amount of filtered water overnight. In the morning, I rinse the nuts and seeds well and discard the soaking water. If you really want to get into it, there are specific soaking times for different seeds and nuts, but I like taking the easiest route possible.

I find it easiest to drain soaked nuts and seeds through a fine-mesh sieve after rinsing. To sprout them, I'll keep them in the sieve, balanced over a bowl or container, until I see a small tail starting to sprout. Depending on the nut or seed, this can take from hours to days. I run water over the sieve to rinse the nuts or seeds a few times throughout the day.

The benefits to soaking and sprouting is that this begins the germination process in the dormant nut or seed, making it easier to digest and converting the carbohydrates to protein. When I'm traveling and on the road, it's impossible for me to soak or sprout, so I'll forego it then, and do the best I can when I'm at home.

Ideally, you want to soak all nuts and seeds before using them in your recipes. But again, do the best you can. I find that lately I have less time for soaking and sprouting than I used to.

I take the easy route and soak the nuts and seeds overnight. If you want to follow more specific instructions, here's a general chart to work from:

SEED OR NUT	DRY AMOUNT	SOAKING TIME	SPROUTING TIME	SPROUTED YIELD
Almonds	1 cup	8–10 hours	1–2 days, if sproutable	2 cups
Pecans, Walnuts	1 cup	4–6 hours	1–2 days	2 cups
Cashews	1 cup	4–6 hours	1–2 days, if sproutable	2 cups
Buckwheat	1 cup	6 hours	2 days	2 cups
Pumpkin Seeds	1 cup	6–8 hours	1 day	2 cups
Sesame Seeds (Hulled Only)	1 cup	4–6 hours	1–2 days	1 cup
Sunflower Seeds	1 cup	6–10 hours	1 day	2 cups
Flax Seeds	1 cup	4–6 hours	1 day	2 cups
Oat Groats	1 cup	6 hours	2 days	2 cups
Quinoa	1 cup	2–3 hours	1–2 days	3 cups
Wild Rice	1 cup	9 hours minimum, up to 48 hours	3–5 days	2 cups

FERMENTING AND PICKLING

Pickling is a way to preserve food and creates a tangy flavor that is a tasty accompaniment to any dish, including sandwiches, wraps, rice, and even salads. It creates healthy bacteria during the fermentation process, which will aid your digestion so you can absorb more nutrients from the food you eat.

Fermenting drinks is another beneficial way to get more of those good-for-us bacteria into your body; again, I'll show you how to make fermented drinks in the next chapter.

The following recipe is an easy vinegar-free pickle dish made with a salt brine. It'll be ready to eat in one day. For an even speedier pickling time, I include a vinegar recipe in chapter 5, along with many other pickled vegetable recipes.

SLICED CUCUMBER PICKLES

MAKES ABOUT 1 CUP

PICKLING TIME: 1 DAY

Cucumber is softened in salt and lemon juice, then set aside for a day to pickle.

> 1 cup cucumber, peeled, cut into ¼-inch-thick rounds
>
> 1 teaspoon sea salt
>
> 2 tablespoons lemon juice

In a nonreactive mixing bowl, toss the ingredients together. Place in a pickle press, under pressure. Or, place a plate over your mixture in the bowl, and stack heavy plates on top of it. Set aside at room temperature for 1 day.

Will keep in the fridge for several days.

VARIATION: Add 2 tablespoons of fresh dill, or other dried or fresh herbs and spices, to the basic recipe to make additional flavors.

SUBSTITUTIONS

I encourage you to substitute your favorite ingredients whenever your heart desires. You may want to substitute a sweetener such as maple syrup for agave, or dried herbs for fresh (two to one), or collard for romaine lettuce, or almonds for Brazil nuts.

Notice the consistency and flavor when making substitutions. If substituting dates for agave, for example, you'll want to add a bit more water, as dates are a solid fruit and agave is a syrup.

Remember, when using whole food ingredients, no two dates are identical in nature, for example. One may be moister and softer, whereas the next is drier and less sweet. Use your own judgment to adjust levels of spice, flavor, sweetness, and/ or moisture to create the exact flavor profiles and consistencies you love.

Here's some example sweetener substitutions:

> Agave for maple syrup, or vice versa 1:1
>
> A pinch of stevia powder to 1 tablespoon of agave syrup
>
> 2 pitted Medjool dates and 3 tablespoons of water to 1 tablespoon of agave syrup

PART 2

THE RECIPES

3
DRINKS

ALTHOUGH DRINKS MAY seem to be a no-brainer in relation to a raw foods diet, there are nuances of flavor and nutrients, as well as a huge array of possibilities. Even more traditional dairy-laden beverages can be converted to a great raw drink with some creative yet easy-to-find ingredients. Raw drinks can be mastered when we focus on flavors, colors, and consistencies inspired by traditional nonraw versions.

Drinking is the easiest way to get nutrient rich foods into your diet. Add a smoothie, mylk, shake, or elixir to any meal for a blast of instant antioxidants, vitamins, minerals, and enzymes. The water and fiber in my drinks will fill you up while detoxing you from the inside out and will even help you eat less.

Smoothies, mylks, and shakes are made by putting fruits and/or nuts into a high-speed blender and blending them until smooth. Adding ice will create a cold, slushy texture. And using your high-speed blender will give the drink a smooth texture plus

Not All Calories Are Created Equal

CALORIES IN raw foods are different from the calories that come from cooked food. An ordinary iced coffee shake usually will have many more calories than my raw Matcha Shake, but for the sake of this comparison, let's say they have the same number of calories.

Most of the calories from the traditional coffee shake come from refined white sugar and dairy milk. Neither offer any nutritional value, and the dairy raises our cholesterol, depletes our calcium, and places a strain on our heart. Both sugar and dairy cause an allergic response in the body, as well as swelling that makes us feel and look bloated.

My Matcha Shake, on the other hand, is sweetened with dates, which is a whole fruit full of vitamins and such minerals as iron and potassium. My mylk is made from almonds, which is an FDA superfood that lowers cholesterol and gives us vitamins and minerals for healthy skin and hair, in addition to antioxidants to fight free-radical damage.

create bubbles on top, similar to a light cappuccino froth. If you don't have a high-speed blender, you may want to first grind your whole nuts into a powder before placing in your blender, to create a smoother consistency. I'll start you off with three different Basic Smoothie recipes and one Basic Nut Mylk recipe, then I will show you how to create new flavors from there.

Sun teas are antioxidant rich and are made by brewing water in a glass jar with tea bags in the sun. As with traditionally cooked teas, you can add mylk to make a latte.

 ## BASIC FRUIT SMOOTHIE
MAKES 4 CUPS

Blend up your favorite fruit into a delicious, nutritious smoothie. Choose agave syrup or dates to sweeten, and adjust to your desired level of sweetness. Adding dates will give your smoothie more body, because dates are a whole fruit with fiber. Dates are caramel in color, so they will darken your smoothie. Agave syrup, on the other hand, is good to use for a lighter consistency and lighter color.

> 4 cups fruit, such as sliced banana, cubed pineapple or persimmon, or blueberries
>
> ¼ cup agave syrup, or ⅓ to ½ cup pitted dates, packed, as desired
>
> 2 cups filtered water
>
> Ice (optional)

Place all the ingredients in a high-speed blender and blend until smooth.

Add ice, if using, and blend to mix well. Serve immediately.

Will keep for 1 day in the fridge.

Sweeten with Stevia

FOR THE first many years of being 100 percent raw, I always stuffed myself full and never worried about calories. Recently, I've started to keep count of what I'm eating and have been reminded that most calories do come from sweets such as fruit and agave syrup.

For a noncaloric and nonglycemic alternative sweetener, replace dates and agave with a tiny bit of stevia powder instead. Stevia goes a long way, so use sparingly and see if you like the taste.

BASIC GREEN SMOOTHIE

MAKES 4 CUPS

I've been blending greens for years, but this particular style of blending half fruit with half greens was introduced by Victoria Butenko and is relatively new in the raw food world. To get more greens into any diet, use fruit to help mask some of the more intense "green" flavors. Masking the color by using a darker fruit such as blueberries will help when feeding to kids. And, you can always include an additional sweetener, such as a pinch of stevia, for flavor, if desired.

> 2 cups chopped greens, such as romaine lettuce, kale, or collards
>
> 2 cups fruit, such as sliced banana, cubed mango, or blueberries
>
> 2 cups filtered water, as desired

Place all the ingredients in a high-speed blender and blend until smooth.

Will keep for 1 day in the fridge, but best enjoyed immediately.

SUGGESTIONS: Start with milder-tasting greens and stronger-flavored fruits. Although you can use kale, chard, and collards, their flavors are strong and harder to mask. Try these combos:

> 2 cups chopped spinach with 2 cups sliced bananas
>
> 2 cups chopped spinach with 2 cups cubed pineapple
>
> 2 cups chopped romaine lettuce with 2 cups cubed mango

BASIC KREAMY FRUIT SMOOTHIE

MAKES 4 CUPS

Blending nuts creates a creamy consistency, so adding them to your smoothie will add more body, richness, and a creamy color, too.

Once blended, add one to two cups of ice and blend, to add a frosty chill.

3 cups fruit, such as sliced banana, cubed pineapple or persimmon, blueberries, or açaí

$\frac{1}{2}$ cup nuts or seeds, such as pumpkin seeds, almonds, or pecans

$\frac{1}{4}$ cup agave syrup, or $\frac{1}{3}$ to $\frac{1}{2}$ cup pitted dates, packed, as desired

2 cups filtered water

Ice (optional)

Place all the ingredients in a high-speed blender and blend until smooth.

Add ice, if using, and blend to mix well. Serve immediately.

Will keep for 1 day in the fridge.

GENERAL TIP:
When Using Frozen Fruit

I LIKE TO freeze my fruit when it starts getting too ripe and will use it in my smoothies. When using frozen fruit, you may need to add additional water to achieve your desired consistency. Once blended, I like to add 1 to 2 cups of ice to add more of a chilled, frosty texture.

 # PERSIMMON SMOOTHIE

MAKES 4 SERVINGS

If you've never had a persimmon, this beautiful, bright orange smoothie is a wonderful introduction. The recipe calls for Fuyu persimmons, the flatter ones that look like orange tomatoes, rather than the pointed ones.

Choose Fuyu persimmons that are soft to the touch and ripe, rather than too firm. I like choosing persimmons that have the richest orange color.

1 recipe Basic Kreamy Fruit Smoothie (page 34) made with Fuyu persimmons and cashews

1 vanilla bean, or 1 tablespoon alcohol-free vanilla extract

1 cup ice

Place all the ingredients in a high-speed blender and blend until smooth. Enjoy immediately.

Will keep for 2 days in the fridge.

MANGO-GOJI-LIME SMOOTHIE

MAKES 4 SERVINGS

A beautifully bright orange smoothie packed with vitamin C and antioxidant-rich mango and goji berries, kissed with a slight tartness of lime. I always prefer using fresh, but frozen mango will work, too.

> 1 recipe Basic Fruit Smoothie (page 31) made with mango and agave syrup
>
> ¼ cup lime juice (from 1 lime)
>
> ¼ cup goji berries

Follow the instructions for the Basic Fruit Smoothie, adding the lime juice and goji berries as you blend it. Enjoy.

Will keep for 2 days in the fridge.

STRAWBERRY LIQUADO

MAKES 4 SERVINGS

Here is a light, refreshing, and cool strawberry bliss that's great on a hot summer day at the beach or by the pool. The blend of strawberries and ice, sweetened with agave, is inspired by Mexican *aquas frescas* I discovered on visits to Puerto Escondido.

> 1 recipe Basic Fruit Smoothie (page 31) made with strawberries and agave syrup
>
> ¼ cup lime juice (from 1 lime)
>
> 2 cups ice

Follow the directions for Basic Fruit Smoothie recipe, adding the lime juice. Add the ice and blend.

Best if served immediately, but will keep for a day or two in the fridge.

Smoothie for Your Body

THIS IS A quadruple alpha-beta hydroxy acid body scrub you can apply while relaxing by the pool or ocean. The beta hydroxy acid in strawberries cleans away the dirt layer on skin, while the stronger alpha hydroxy acids of grape, apple, and orange get into the pores to dissolve dead skin cells and exfoliate. This lets all that new, fresh, clean skin you've been building come out to the surface. Show it off!

1½ cups strawberries
1 cup grapes
1 apple, cored and quartered
1 orange, peeled, seeded, and quartered

Place all the ingredients in a high-speed blender and blend until smooth.

Apply to your face and body and leave on for 20 minutes. Rinse off in an outdoor shower or the ocean. Enjoy your smooth, clean, fresh skin.

APRICOT ROOIBOS FLURRY

MAKES 4 SERVINGS

Rooibos, a red bush tea from Africa, is the centerpiece of this creamy mylk tea. Rooibos is packed with antioxidants that attack free radicals, limiting their damaging effects and delaying our aging process. It also contains alpha hydroxy acid and zinc, to combat acne and give us healthy, clear, smooth skin.

2 rooibos tea bags
3¼ cups filtered water
1 cup halved, pitted fresh apricots, or ½ cup dried apricots
½ cup cashews
¼ cup pitted dates, packed
1 cup ice

Place the tea bags in a glass jar and add the water; cover. Place the jar in the sun for several hours to brew. If you choose to brew the tea in boiling water, you'll need to let it cool to room temperature before using.

Combine the brewed tea, apricots, cashews, and dates in a high-speed blender and blend until smooth. Add the ice and blend to mix well.

Best served immediately, but will keep for a couple of days in the fridge.

The Beauty of Rooibos

ROOIBOS CONTAINS ALPHA hydroxy, a mild acid that dissolves dry skin for exfoliation without the need for scrubbing. Full of antioxidants, it rejuvenates and revitalizes our skin by helping to decrease inflammation, calm stressed-out skin, increase elasticity, increase circulation, and restore the skin's suppleness.

Apply soaked rooibos tea bags directly to skin irritations such as itches, sunburns, rashes, and acne, and on dry spots on your knees, elbows, and heels.

Put used rooibos tea bags in the fridge or freezer and use on your tired or red eyes to sooth and relax.

ALMOND-BUTTERED BANANA FREEZE

MAKES 4 SERVINGS

This refreshingly light, smooth almond mylk is made by blending bananas with almond butter and a hint of cinnamon. Almonds provide calcium, protein, and vitamin E, and bananas are loaded with potassium. This easy smoothie is a great postworkout fuel—it helps increase circulation and blood flow to stressed muscles, while building lean muscle tissue. The drink is sweetened with yacón syrup, a low-calorie, low-glycemic sweetener that tastes like caramel and molasses. If you don't have yacón handy, you can use agave syrup.

>   2 bananas, sliced
>   ¼ cup almond butter
>   2 tablespoons yacón or agave syrup
>   ¼ teaspoon ground cinnamon
>   3 cups filtered water
>   1 cup ice

Combine the banana, almond butter, yacón syrup, cinnamon, and water in a high-speed blender and blend until smooth. Add the ice and blend to mix well.

Best served immediately, but will keep for a couple of days in the fridge.

Yacón Power

YACÓN, A perennial plant grown in the Andes, is used as a concentrated sweetener among native Andes populations. The plant's sweet-tasting tuberous root has antiaging properties and is high in protein, fiber, and vitamins A and C; and is also a good source of calcium, iron, phosphorus, and potassium. A valuable health food and alternative sweetener, yacón contains inulin, a complex sugar that improves the health of our lower intestines by feeding healthy bifidobacteria, which are probiotics, in the intestine. Inulin is a probiotic that helps with mineral absorption, combats cancer, and keeps our skin clear and healthy. Inulin can't be broken down by digestive enzymes in the stomach. It passes through the upper digestive tract intact, has almost no usable calories, and almost no impact on blood sugar.

Yacón syrup is dark in color, tastes like a blend of caramel and molasses, and is a low-calorie, low-glycemic sweetener with only 40 calories per two-tablespoon serving. It has half the sugar and only a third of the calories of agave syrup. Use it as you would agave or maple syrup in any recipe. Although yacón syrup is flash-pasteurized to kill bacteria, it has been found to retain most of its enzymes and nutritional benefits. It is available at natural food stores, online, and my Web site, www.AniPhyo.com/store.

SUPER CACAO-COCONUT ENERGIZER

MAKES 4 SERVINGS

When you're craving a caffeine bump, this creamy, rich, dark chocolate drink is a healthy way to get a superjazzy buzz. Made with cacao for zing and sweetened with dates and banana for energy, it is also full of omegas and potassium to make you glow. I leave the blender going for a minute or more to heat up this delight.

1 banana

¼ cup cacao nibs

¼ cup almonds

2 tablespoons tan or brown flaxseed

2 tablespoons shredded coconut

2 tablespoons pitted Medjool dates

1 tablespoon liquid coconut oil

2 teaspoons maca powder (optional)

3 cups filtered water

Place all the ingredients in a high-speed blender and blend until smooth. If you don't have a high-speed blender, you may want to first grind the almonds, flaxseed, and coconut into a meal for a smoother consistency.

SERVING OPTION: Place in a pot and heat on the stove until warm.

MYLKS AND SHAKES

My dairy-free mylks are made by blending nuts or seeds with water. Agave or dates can be added as a sweetener. Just as with dairy milk, nut mylks are thin in consistency, and delicious with cereals and added to smoothies.

I don't bother straining the nut fiber from my mylks because fiber is good for me. You can strain your mylks through a strainer or nut mylk bag (available at most health food stores or online—search for "nut milk bag") if you prefer. You can use the pulp in place of nut meals in dehydration recipes such as those for cookies and crackers. Or you can feed it to your dog (avoid giving your dog macadamias, though, as they are poisonous to pets), or compost it.

 # BASIC NUT MYLK

MAKES 4 SERVINGS

Use your favorite nuts to make a basic mylk. If you're concerned about calories or sugar, sweeten with a pinch of stevia instead of the dates or agave syrup.

> ½ cup almonds, cashews, pecans, or your favorite nut
>
> ½ cup pitted dates, or ¼ cup agave syrup
>
> A pinch of sea salt
>
> 5 cups water

Place all the ingredients in a high-speed blender and blend until smooth.

Will keep for at least 4 days in the fridge.

VANILLA ALMOND MYLK

MAKES 4 SERVINGS

If you can treat yourself to whole vanilla bean, your taste buds will thank you for it. Plus the little black seeds will be visible in your mylk, and look pretty.

> 1 recipe Basic Nut Mylk (page 41)
>
> 1 vanilla bean, or 1 tablespoon alcohol-free vanilla extract

Follow the directions for Basic Nut Mylk, adding the vanilla.

Will keep for at least 4 days in the fridge.

CHOCOLATE MYLK

MAKES 4 SERVINGS

Cacao powder has less fat than the whole cacao nib and tastes more like traditional cooked cocoa powder. You can use the same amount of nibs instead of powder for a stronger dark chocolate flavor that's more bitter, or even carob powder for a caffeine-free version.

> 1 recipe Basic Nut Mylk (page 41)
>
> 3 tablespoons cacao powder

Follow the directions for Basic Nut Mylk, adding the cacao powder.

Will keep for at least 4 days in the fridge.

CHOCOLATE FLURRY SHAKE

MAKES 4 SERVINGS

> 1 recipe Basic Nut Mylk (page 41) made with almonds
> 2 tablespoons cacao powder
> 2 tablespoons cacao nibs
> 2 cups ice

Follow the directions for Basic Nut Mylk, adding the cacao powder and nibs. Add the ice last, and blend to mix. Serve immediately.

STRAWBERRY MYLK

MAKES 4 SERVINGS

Fresh fruit is always my preference, but you can also use frozen strawberries to make this deliciously sweet pink mylk.

> 1 recipe Basic Nut Mylk (page 41)
> 2 cups strawberries
> 1/2 vanilla bean pod, whole, or 1/2 tablespoon alcohol-free vanilla extract

Follow the directions for Basic Nut Mylk, adding the strawberries and vanilla.

Will keep for at least 4 days in the fridge.

MINERAL GREEN MYLK

MAKES 4 SERVINGS

Algae, such as spirulina, are considered a superfood because they are superrich in nutrients. Packed with more chlorophyll than is found in any other food source, they contain amino acids, vitamins, and trace minerals that tone and strengthen our immune system, and increase energy levels. Chlorophyll, gram for gram, contains more protein than any animal product, so it's great for building muscle. You can substitute the same amount of wheat grass powder, if you prefer.

> 1 recipe Basic Nut Mylk (page 41)
> 3 tablespoons spirulina powder
> 1/2 vanilla bean pod, whole, or 1/2 tablespoon alcohol-free vanilla extract

Follow the directions for Basic Nut Mylk, adding the spirulina and vanilla.

Will keep for at least 4 days in the fridge.

MATCHA SHAKE

MAKES 4 SERVINGS

Matcha is a powdered Japanese green tea. The tea leaves are picked and dried, the stems and veins are removed, and only the leaf is stone-ground. Traditionally, sweets are eaten before drinking *matcha* to complement its delicious flavor. Green tea does contain caffeine, so you may want to add a touch of maca powder to this smoothie to help rebuild your adrenals. *Matcha* teas can usually be found at local teahouses or coffee shops, in natural food stores, and, of course, online.

> $^3/_4$ cup almonds
>
> $^3/_4$ cup pitted dates
>
>   1 tablespoon *matcha*
>
>   3 cups filtered water
>
> $^1/_2$ teaspoon maca powder (optional)
>
>   1 cup ice

Combine the almonds, dates, *matcha*, water, maca (if using), and ice in your high-speed blender and blend until smooth. Add the ice and blend until mixed well.

Best served immediately, but will keep for several days in the fridge.

VARIATION: If you're avoiding caffeine, replace the *matcha* with the same amount of spirulina blue-green algae. Spirulina is a tiny aquatic plant with more protein than soy, more vitamin A than carrots, and more iron than beef. It's also a great source of phytochemicals that protect us from illness and aging.

You can also replace the *matcha* with 1 tablespoon of alcohol-free vanilla extract plus a teaspoon of mint extract.

The Power of Matcha Green Tea

WITH FINE *MATCHA* powder, you ingest whole tea leaves ground into a powder, resulting in a beverage that is ten times more potent—with 137 times more antioxidants—than regular brewed green tea.

Matcha boosts your metabolism by up to 40 percent, helps control body weight, and regulates healthy blood sugar levels. It's a strong blood detoxifier, is packed with antioxidants, helps control free-radical damage, prevents heart disease and cancer, reduces cholesterol, and increases circulation for beautiful, clear skin.

Green tea also has been found to help our brain produce more alpha waves, which decreases tension and stress, while increasing mental focus and concentration.

CHILLED CHAI FROSTY SHAKE

MAKES 4 SERVINGS

This is another drink that uses my Basic Nut Mylk recipe; I use a little less water here for a thicker, creamer consistency. This light, cool, frothy chai is made with rich maple-flavored pecans and hints of India-inspired spices. I like to leave the blender blending for 30 seconds or more on high speed to create a bubbly froth. I'll add the ice at the very last moment to chill, then serve right away just like a cappuccino with froth.

> 1 recipe Basic Nut Mylk (page 41) made with pecans and dates, and only 3 cups of water (instead of 5)
>
> ½ teaspoon alcohol-free vanilla extract
>
> ¼ teaspoon ground cardamom
>
> ¼ teaspoon ground cinnamon
>
> 1 cup ice

Follow the directions for Basic Nut Mylk, adding the vanilla, cardamom, and cinnamon. Blend until smooth. Add the ice and blend to mix.

Best served immediately, but will keep for several days in the fridge.

ELIXIRS

My elixirs are made by mixing together fruit and water, plus sometimes a bit of white wine, kombucha, or kefir for extra sparkle and taste (for recipes for making your own kombucha and kefir, see pages 52–59). Elixirs are clear and vibrantly colorful, and any pulp is strained out. Serve these beautiful elixirs in a martini glass when entertaining, or for a romantic dinner for two.

• • •

RASPBERRY LEMONADE

MAKES 4 SERVINGS

A classically tart lemonade mixed with beautiful red raspberries with added effervescence and probiotic goodness from kombucha or kefir. You can substitute kombucha or kefir with Thai baby coconut water to make an electrolyte-rich lemonade.

> 1/2 cup fresh or thawed frozen raspberries
> 2/3 cup freshly squeezed lemon juice (from about 4 lemons)
> 1/2 cup agave syrup
> 3 cups kombucha or kefir

Place all the ingredients in a high-speed blender and blend until smooth. Strain through a plastic sieve into a pitcher. Serve over ice.

Will keep for 2 days in the fridge.

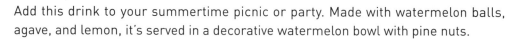

WATERMELON PUNCH

MAKES ABOUT 20 SERVINGS

Add this drink to your summertime picnic or party. Made with watermelon balls, agave, and lemon, it's served in a decorative watermelon bowl with pine nuts.

> 1 small seedless watermelon (about 10 pounds)
> 1/2 cup agave syrup
> 1 tablespoon lemon juice (from about 1 lemon)
> 2 cups ice cubes
> Pine nuts, for garnish

Cut the watermelon across one-third down from top, and cut a bit off the bottom so it sits flat.

Use a melon baller to scoop the flesh into a large bowl. Scrape out the remaining watermelon flesh and squeeze out the juice, using a sieve or cheesecloth, into the large bowl holding the scooped balls. Add the agave and lemon juice, and stir to mix well. Add 1 cup of the ice.

Transfer the punch to the watermelon bowl and add the remaining ice. Garnish with pine nuts and serve.

SERVING SUGGESTIONS: Add other fruits to the punch, such as cantaloupe or honeydew melon balls, strawberries, pineapple chunks, lychees, or mandarin orange slices.

GINGER-LEMON MARTINI

MAKES 2 COCKTAILS

A refreshing white wine martini made with tart lemon juice and ginger. Add jalapeño to kick up the heat in your elixir.

> 2 tablespoons agave syrup
>
> Palm sugar or shredded coconut, ground into a powder
>
> ½ lemon, sliced
>
> 1 (1-inch) piece fresh ginger, peeled and sliced
>
> 6 ounces white wine
>
> 1 cup ice
>
> Lemon zest, for garnish

Rim two glasses with the agave syrup and palm sugar. Set aside.

Place the lemon and ginger slices in an old-fashioned glass and muddle. Add the wine and swirl. Transfer the mixture to a cocktail shaker, with the ice. Shake.

Strain the elixir into the rimmed cocktail glasses. Garnish with the lemon peel. Enjoy immediately.

SERVING SUGGESTION: Add 1 to 2 tablespoons sliced fresh jalapeño to your muddle mixture. If you really like it hot, use your sliced jalapeño to rim your glasses.

PEAR SPRITZER

MAKES 4 COCKTAILS

A wonderful party drink. You can use apple if an Asian pear is unavailable. You can substitute white wine with kefir, kombucha, or skip it all together and just use sparkling water, if you prefer.

> 1 Asian pear, peeled, cored, and sliced thinly
> 1½ cups white wine
> 2 cups sparkling water, chilled
> 4 lime wedges, for garnish

Place the pear slices in a pitcher. Add the wine, and place in the fridge for 30 minutes to 2 hours.

Fill four glasses with ice. Strain the wine and place a few pear slices in each glass. Top off each glass with sparkling water. Garnish each glass with a lime wedge.

WATERMELON COOLER

MAKES 4 COCKTAILS

This recipe calls for frozen watermelon. If you're in a hurry, just add ice cubes when blending to chill.

> 2 cups watermelon cubes, seeded
> ½ cup white wine
> Juice of 1 lime
> 1 tablespoon agave syrup
> 4 slices of watermelon or wedges of lime, for garnish

Freeze the watermelon cubes for an hour or two.

Place the watermelon, wine, lime juice, and agave in a high-speed blender and blend until smooth.

Strain into four cocktail glasses. Garnish each glass with slice of watermelon or wedge of lime.

POMEGRANATE-MINT-CUCUMBER FIZZ

MAKES 2 SERVINGS

A bright red elixir packed with antioxidants from pomegranate, which fight free-radical damage and accelerated aging. Cucumber and mint add a cool flavor. Feel free to substitute sparkling water with kefir or kombucha.

- 1/4 cup chopped, peeled cucumber
- 1/4 cup fresh mint
- 1/2 cup pomegranate juice
- 1 cup ice
- 1 cup sparkling water
- 2 fresh mint stems, for garnish
- 2 cucumber slices, for garnish

Place the cucumber and mint in a bar glass and muddle. Add the juice and swirl to mix. Pour into a bar shaker, with the ice, and shake. Strain into two glasses. Top off with a splash of sparkling water and serve immediately. Garnish with a mint stem poked through a cucumber slice.

Will keep for a day or two in the fridge.

MUDDLED STRAWBERRIES IN COCONUT KEFIR

MAKES 4 SERVINGS

Naturally effervescent and probiotic rich coconut kefir is muddled with fresh strawberries to add a sweet red color and flavor. This recipe can be made with water kefir, too (for kefir recipes, see pages 54 to 56).

- 1 cup fresh strawberries
- 4 cups coconut kefir, chilled (page 54)

Divide the strawberries and kefir among four glasses. Use a fork to mash and muddle the strawberries in the kefir before serving.

SUN TEAS

Making sun tea is slow-cooking your tea with the heat of the sun. All you need is a large glass jar, such as a 1- or 2-quart mason jar or a gallon jug. Fill it with filtered water and tea bags, then place in the sun to brew. Usually four teabags per liter works great.

Extreme raw fooders don't even boil their water, hence the sun tea. If you don't mind boiled water, you can always make traditional tea to use in the following recipes. Never boil your water in a microwave. It will change the molecular structure of your water and emit dangerous radiation.

• • •

TEA LATTE

MAKES 4 SERVINGS

Tea is brewed in a glass jar in the sun. Once it is ready, your favorite nut mylk is added over ice to make a delicious cold latte drink.

>   1 liter filtered water
>   4 tea bags
>   1 cup of your favorite nut mylk (pages 41–42)

Fill a clean glass jar with the filtered water and tea bags. Cover and set in the sun for between 2 and 5 hours, depending on how dark you want your tea.

Once the tea has brewed to your liking, remove from the sun. Open the lid and remove the tea bags. Cover and place the jar in the fridge to chill, or pour the tea over ice into glasses. Add ¼ cup of nut mylk per glass, to serve.

POMEGRANATE-BERRY SUN TEA

MAKES 4 SERVINGS

Raspberry Lemonade ice cubes and frozen blueberries are added to brewed green tea just before serving, to create a festive presentation.

> 1/2 recipe Raspberry Lemonade (page 46)
> 4 tea bags pomegranate green tea
> 1 liter filtered water
> 3/4 cup blueberries, frozen

Fill two ice cube trays with Raspberry Lemonade, and freeze.

Fill a clean glass jar with the filtered water and tea bags. Cover and set in the sun for between 2 and 5 hours, depending on how dark you want your tea. Remove the tea bags and chill in the fridge for at least 1 hour.

To serve, place the frozen blueberries and ice cubes in the tea.

THAI ICED TEA

MAKES 4 SERVINGS

Thai tea leaves are sun brewed in water, then the tea is sweetened with agave. Nut mylk is added for creaminess.

If you don't have Thai tea leaves, you can use a black tea instead. Add a pinch of cinnamon and a couple of large slices of dried mango before brewing.

> 1 cup Thai tea leaves
> 4 cups filtered water
> 1/2 cup agave syrup
> 2 cups Vanilla Almond Mylk (page 41)

Place the tea leaves in a tea bag, and brew in the water for several hours in the sun.

Remove the tea leaves and stir in the agave syrup and mylk. Serve and enjoy.

CULTURED DRINKS

These drinks are a refreshing and delicious way to obtain more good-for-us probiotics, the beneficial bacteria we need to build a healthy inner body environment.

The friendly bacteria in cultured drinks create a healthy digestive system and colon, to help us break down and digest our food and absorb more nutrients. They also help remove toxins from our body, detoxing us from the inside out.

Kefir, my favorite and the simplest to make, and kombucha are made with the help of a living culture that ferments and "brews" the drink. Rejuvelac is another popular drink made by fermenting grains in water alone, without the help of a living culture.

KEFIR

Kefir is a probiotic drink with healing properties that slows down our aging process. It's made using kefir "grains," which originate in Mexico. These grains are not actually a cereal but are a mother culture that digests sugar in a fermentation process, resulting in a fizzy, carbonated beverage similar to champagne.

Although some varieties of kefir require dairy (and many people have likened kefir to yogurt), raw water kefir is available as well. Unlike dairy yogurt, kefir contains about thirty strains of bacteria and yeast. The culture comes in small translucent balls called "grains," which are made up of a polysaccharide called kefiran, organic acids, yeasts, and bacteria.

Kefiran has antitumor properties, is an anti-inflammatory, and boosts the immune system. Kefir is known to lower cholesterol levels; helps with heart and artery disease; regulates blood pressure; aids in digestion; and heals the liver, kidneys, spleen, pancreas, gall bladder, and stomach ulcers.

Water kefir is brewed using "water kefir grains," as opposed to "dairy kefir grains" used in dairy milk. The grains allow us to create a new recipe of water kefir every 24 to 48 hours. It's a great, healthy, soda replacement that's delicious.

Ideally, you want to use living grains, not grains that have been dehydrated or frozen. Try to avoid powder starters; the bacteria are not as active and will only make eight batches, if you're lucky, before you have to buy more starter powder. You'll only need to buy living grains once, and they'll grow and expand indefinitely when cared for properly. You can buy water kefir grains online. I list a couple of places in my resources section (see page 308). I got mine from Cheree at www.stichingtime.com.

COCONUT KEFIR

MAKES 1 QUART

This recipe calls for Thai young green coconuts, which can be found at most Asian markets and natural food stores. Whole green coconuts are large, and the ones at the stores are usually shaved down to the white, spongy, pith layer.

To open your coconut, see page 55. Make sure not to use any metal when making this recipe, as it will damage your living cultures. Use only plastic and glass.

Coconut kefir makes a healthy soda substitute. Kefir is said to decrease sugar cravings; clear our complexions; aid in digestion; and provide nutrients, minerals, and healthy bacteria that restore balance to our intestinal flora. It will be ready to drink in just a day or two.

NOTE: One coconut will usually yield around 1½ to almost 2 cups of water, and around ¾ to 1 cup of meat to use in Coconut Bacon (page 76) and Coconut Kefir Cheeze (page 106).

> 2 coconuts
>
> 1 to 2 tablespoons water kefir grains

Open your coconuts and pour the coconut water through a plastic strainer into a large measuring cup or bowl. Then, transfer the water to a large, glass canning or mason jar. Using a funnel will make it easier. Fill your glass jar only three-quarters to four-fifths full. NOTE: Make sure water is clear; if the water is pink, it's rancid.

Next, add your kefir grains to the jar with the coconut water. Close the lid and place the jar someplace that's 70° to 74°F. In colder climates, you can place your jar in your oven, with only the oven light on.

The longer your water ferments, the less sweet and more sour and vinegary it will taste. The water will turn milky in color. The brew time should not exceed 48 hours. There's really no minimum brew time; the shorter the time, the more sugar and sweeter your brew. Ideally, you want to brew the coconut water for somewhere between 24 and 48 hours. You can taste your water every 24 hours to check if it's slightly fizzy, like champagne, and to achieve the sugar level and flavor you desire.

Once your brew is done, pour it into a nonmetal bowl, catching the grains in a plastic sieve. Use these grains to start your next recipe right away.

Pour the strained kefir water into another glass jar, and enjoy immediately. Store in the fridge.

Will keep for several weeks in your fridge.

Opening and Scraping a Young Coconut

SINCE WRITING my first book, *Ani's Raw Food Kitchen*, I've found a quieter way to open a coconut without the need of a heavy cleaver. A sharp knife of any size, even a pocketknife, will work. So, now I can take a coconut hiking or camping without lugging my cleaver along.

1. To open a coconut, lay it on its side. Use a knife to shave the white pith, or coir, off the top of the coconut. Shave toward the top center point of the coconut. Rotate coconut, and repeat until you fully expose the hard center, which looks like smooth wood and contains the water.

2. Next, set the coconut upright and use the heel of your knife to gently tap the edge of the hard exposed center. The coconut has a natural stress line around the crown, in a circle that will give and crack open.

3. Place the heel of your knife in the opening and rock backward and forward to increase the opening. It should split to create a large, circular opening.

4. Pull back and remove the top from the coconut. Pour the coconut water into a container.

To scrape out your coconut's meat, use a strong, large spoon. I find it easier to hold the spoon's curve opposite of the coconut's curve, upside down compared with how we hold it to scoop soup. I like to see if I can get all the meat out in one piece. Place the meat in a bowl and clean it by running your fingers over it to remove any hard pieces.

1. 2. 3. 4.

WATER KEFIR

MAKE 2 CUPS

Whereas kombucha and rejuvelac, and even coconut kefir, can taste a bit vinegary, water kefir's taste is the most palatable. It's really delicious, like a soda.

This is an alternative way to make beneficial kefir when coconuts are not available, or when you want a faster, easier process. Just dissolve sugar or agave syrup in water, add raisins and lemon slices plus the grains, and brew for 24 to 48 hours. This recipe was inspired by Cheree from www.stichingtime.com, where I order my grains.

As with kombucha brewing, some people are concerned about the sugar used to feed the culture's fermentation process. I've done extensive research and have found that though the water may still taste sweet at 48 hours of brewing, the sugar content is very low.

Allowing for a secondary fermentation, by placing the water kefir, after the grains have been removed, in a glass jar at room temperature for another day or two, will decrease the sugar content even more, while substantially increasing B-group vitamins.

NOTE: Keep metal away from your kefir grains.

> 2 cups filtered water
> 1/3 cup organic Sucanat, turbinado sugar, or agave syrup
> 1 tablespoon raisins
> 1/4 cup lemon slices, with rind on (about 1/2 lemon)
> 1 to 2 tablespoons water kefir grains

Pour the water into a glass jar with a lid. Don't fill all the way to the top, and make sure to leave a couple of inches of air. Dissolve the sugar in the water by stirring or shaking with the lid on. Add the raisins and lemon slices, and the kefir grains. Close the lid.

Place the jar in a dark cabinet for 24 to 48 hours, to brew and ferment. You can stir the brew once a day, or just leave it alone for 2 days. When ready, use a plastic spoon or sieve (do not use metal) to scoop the lemon and raisins off the top. Then, stir slightly and pour the water through a plastic sieve to catch all of your water kefir grains.

Pour the water into a glass container, and either place in the fridge and enjoy immediately; or leave at room temperature for another day or two for secondary fermentation, then place the jar in the fridge to enjoy.

Will keep for a month or more in the fridge.

Use the kefir water grains to start another batch immediately.

Is Sugar Vegan? Turbinado vs. Sucanat vs. White Sugar

I'VE ALWAYS known that white sugar is refined and processed. But, I was really surprised to find out that white sugar is refined with bone char, so it's not vegan. According to PETA, Sucanat and turbinado are never filtered with bone char.

Turbinado sugar is similar to white refined sugar except for its color and contains only a tiny amount of molasses. It's made by evaporating and then crystallizing sugar cane juice. The crystals are spun in a turbine (hence the name) to remove any remaining water.

Sucanat ("SUgar CAne NATural") is pure dried cane juice. It's a nonrefined cane sugar and contains its full molasses content and flavor.

KOMBUCHA

A healing and detoxifying drink made from tea, sugar, and a culture called the "mother" or "mushroom," which is actually a symbiosis of acetic acid bacteria and yeast. This mother culture transforms the tea into enzymes; vitamins; organic acids; and substances with antibiotic, antiseptic, and detoxifying characteristics.

The earliest records of kombucha are from 414 BC in Korea, where it eventually migrated to China, Japan, Russia, and India. It's known for its antiaging properties, removes heavy metals and toxins from our bodies, and is a powerful detoxifier. It increases stamina, thins our blood, improves skin elasticity, tone, and color, helps our body flush acidic toxins, and even combats depression.

Kombucha is high in hyaluronic acid, which helps connective tissues and the collagen in skin stay moist and youthful. It can also be applied topically as a compress and is used in cultured food recipes as a starter to speed up the fermentation process.

The "mother mushroom" culture is a jellylike membrane that will constantly grow. You can grow your own mother from scratch, using unpasturized kombucha tea in place of the mother when brewing. This process takes longer to brew because of the small amount of bacteria and yeast. Whereas it takes about two weeks when you start from a mother, it will take about a month when starting from scratch.

Kombucha can be made with caffeinated or caffeine-free teas. Drink a maximum of two cups per day as a preventative. Kombucha is similar to vinegar in that it contains a high amount of acetic acid, so I'd recommend a maximum of two cups a day.

KOMBUCHA

MAKES 1 GALLON

Make your kombucha with black, oolong, or green tea. The culture prefers to have at least some black tea in the mix. Using caffeine-free tea can be more challenging because it lacks tannin, and you'll need to use about six times more than caffeinated tea. Avoid using herbs and aromatic teas such as Earl Grey, as the aromatic oils can kill your kombucha culture.

Use spring water; avoid distilled or reverse osmosis water, as the brew needs the trace minerals in the water. Use a wide-topped glass, china, or enamel bowl to brew; this will allow for good breathing of the culture, plus it'll be easier to remove the mother culture later. Or, use a wide-mouthe gallon jug. Avoid using metal bowls or spoons when making this recipe, as it will damage the culture.

The longer kombucha is left, the more sour and vinegary the taste, and the less sugar it will contain. Factors such as not using enough starter, poor hygiene, cigarette smoke, sunlight, contact with metal, and water without minerals can spoil a culture. A dead culture will darken and sink to the bottom.

Order kombucha mushrooms online at www.stichingtime.com. You can start with the stringy culture found in a bottle of kombucha drink, but it will take much longer to brew that way because of the small amount of bacteria and yeast. Remember, whereas it takes about two weeks when you start from a mother, it will take about a month when starting from scratch.

> 2½ quarts spring water
>
> ¼ cup loose tea leaves, or 6 regular tea bags
>
> 1 cup raw sugar, Sucanat, or turbinado sugar
>
> Kombucha mushroom culture from the previous brew, about the size of a saucer
>
> 1½ cups kombucha from the previous brew, or ½ cup white vinegar as a starter substitute

Boil your water for at least 5 minutes, then turn off the heat. Add the tea and sugar, and let steep until completely cool before removing the leaves or bags. Remember, the sugar is for the culture to eat and will help grow a new baby culture on top of the tea, creating enzymes and other beneficial properties. Although I've not had much success with these, you can try to use agave or honey, but their bacterial contaminants may degrade the culture over time.

Pour 2½ quarts of your room-temperature tea into a 1-gallon wide-mouthed glass jar, or a glass or ceramic bowl. Make sure to leave air on the surface, not filling your container completely.

Add the mushroom and the starter. Taste once with a clean spoon to make sure it tastes slightly tart. If not, add ¼ cup of white vinegar to prevent mold.

Cover the jar with a new coffee filter and secure it with a rubber band. A fine cloth won't keep fruit flies out, and towels are too thick. Place the brew away from sunlight in a stable environment where it will never be moved. Select a place with a temperature between 68° and 83°F.

A clear or translucent film will begin forming on top of the liquid within a few days and will smell fermented. After seven to twelve days, the new mushroom culture baby on top of the liquid will be about a ¼- to ⅜-inch thick, which tells you it's ready to drink. The culture may be gray, cream, or peach in color.

When ready to bottle your brew, first transfer the baby culture that's grown on the top and the original to a clean bowl, as the starter for your next batch.

Stir up the sediment that formed on the bottom of the bowl, and bottle your brew in glass bottles, tightly capped. The sediment contains the yeast that will make it fizzy, and it will need another day or two after bottling at room temperature to build up enough pressure to make a fizz.

Will keep for up to thirty days in the fridge.

Your kombucha should taste a bit tart, and a little sweet, with slight effervescence. Each recipe will be different. As your culture multiplies, you can place both into one jar, or give one to a friend with some starter tea to start his or her own brew.

The easiest way I like to flavor my kombucha is by mixing fruit juices with the kombucha before drinking. A good ratio to start at is about 5 to 10 percent juice to 90 to 95 percent kombucha. Adjust to your liking.

REJUVELAC

Rejuvelac is the fermented drink of choice for Dr. Ann Wigmore, an old-school natural health educator who founded the Ann Wigmore Institute in Puerto Rico in

1990. She taught that rejuvelac should be used as a replacement to water on the live foods program.

Rejuvelac contains friendly bacteria necessary for a healthy colon and for helping our body remove toxins and is a good source of B-complex vitamins and vitamins C and E. It's made using any cereal grain, such as barley, oats, rye, wheat, unhulled millet, or buckwheat, and any whole-grain rice. Each grain creates its own unique flavor. I personally prefer the taste of kefir, then kombucha, to rejuvelac. Rejuvelac has a tart lemonade flavor.

REJUVELAC
MAKES ABOUT 2 QUARTS

For best results, you want to use fresh, organic grains when making your rejuvelac. Use a 2-quart wide-mouthed glass mason jar to make your brew.

2 cups grains (any cereal grain or whole-grain rice will do)
Filtered or spring water

Place your grains into your 2-quart jar, and fill with water to rinse. Pour off any floating debris and cloudy water. Fill the jar again and rinse until the water is clear. Then, add new water to fill the jar to 1 to 2 inches from top. Let the grains soak for about 12 hours.

Pour the water out of the jar by tipping it carefully. Add fresh water, and rinse and drain the grains well. Try to leave as little water in the jar as possible between rinses. Set the jar someplace dark between 68° and 80°F and sprout the grains for 24 to 72 hours, until a tail grows out at the end of the seed. Rinse the grains a couple of times daily while sprouting, draining well.

Next, fill the jar almost to the top with fresh water, leaving a couple of inches of air. Cover with a coffee filter, and secure with a rubber band. Place the brew in a dark cabinet and let ferment for 24 to 72 hours at room temperature (between 68° and 80°F). You'll know it's ready when it smells fermented and has a tart lemonade flavor.

Pour the brew through a plastic strainer into a large bowl, to remove your grains from the rejuvelac. You could make another batch of brew with these grains. It won't take as long to ferment but won't be as strong, either. Use these sprouted grains to make a raw cracker or cereal (see pages 112 and 63).

Will keep for several days in the fridge.

4

BREAKFAST

BREAKFAST IS MY most important meal. It fuels me up and powers me through my day. Enjoying whole raw foods for breakfast will fill your body with vitamins, minerals, and powerful antioxidants to give you a powerful head start to your day.

I was inspired to create the following recipes because it's near impossible to go out to enjoy any breakfast or brunch that's free of wheat, gluten, soy, and dairy. And, as with every other recipe in this book, *raw* is not synonymous with giving up the delicious tastes of your favorite foods. This chapter includes breakfast goodies such as crepes filled with fruit, kream, and chocolate; savory scrambles; vegetable quiches; toast with jam and butter; biscuits and gravy; and cereals that are great to take with you on the road.

What a great way to start every day!

CEREALS

The simplest cereals are made by placing nuts, seeds, and/or dried or fresh fruit in a bowl, and enjoying with your favorite mylk. However, I also have recipes that are a bit more complex—and totally worth the effort. Buckwheat Crispies in a bowl with mylk is reminiscent of a crisped rice cereal. Oatmeal and porridge can be made in a food processor, and superfood chia seeds thicken into a gel when hydrated in your favorite mylk.

• • •

DRIED FRUIT, PECAN, AND COCONUT RAWNOLA
MAKES 4 SERVINGS

A simple mix of coconut, pecans, and your favorite dried fruits. A great travel food, this cereal can be enjoyed everywhere with a splash of your favorite mylk.

$\frac{1}{4}$ cup shredded, dried coconut

$\frac{1}{2}$ cup crushed pecans

$\frac{3}{4}$ cup mixed dried fruit, such as cranberries, raisins, cherries, and/or blueberries

Place all the ingredients in a mixing bowl. Toss to mix well, and serve with your favorite nut mylk.

I like to make a large recipe of dehydrated buckwheat and keep it stored in a big jar. I place these Buckwheat Crispies in a bowl with mylk to make a quick cereal, add them to cakes for a crispy texture, and grind them into a powder and coat vegetables before dehydrating to make a light tempura shell. I sprinkle them into wraps and on smoothies to add an extra texture of crunch.

BUCKWHEAT CRISPIES

MAKES 2 CUPS

This recipe's from *Ani's Raw Food Kitchen*. I'm including it here again because we'll be using these crisps to add a light crunch to cakes, cereals, and desserts.

1 pound buckwheat groats

Soak the groats in a large mixing bowl with three times the amount of water. Leave overnight. Rinse well the next morning, and drain.

Spread evenly on 14-inch-square Excalibur Dehydrator mesh trays, and dry at 104°F for 3 to 5 hours, or until completely dry.

Store the Buckwheat Crispies in an airtight glass jar. Will keep for several months.

CHOCOLATE CRISPIES

MAKES 4 SERVINGS

A simple cereal made by pouring Chocolate Mylk over a bowlful of Buckwheat Crispies. This makes a great midafternoon snack, too.

2 cups Buckwheat Crispies (page 63)
1/2 cups Chocolate Mylk (page 41)

Divide the Buckwheat Crispies among four serving bowls. Serve with the Chocolate Mylk.

SERVING SUGGESTION: Add 1 to 2 tablespoons of goji berries to each bowl of cereal.

STRAWBERRY CRISPIES

MAKES 4 SERVINGS

A superfast, fun, strawberry cereal made by pouring Strawberry Mylk over a bowlful of Buckwheat Crispies.

A bowl of these Strawberry Crispies makes me want to watch Saturday morning cartoons. Which, by the way, I was rarely allowed to watch when growing up, and always felt like I'd missed out. Perhaps that's what attracted me to my early career in animation and digital video.

> 2 cups Buckwheat Crispies (page 63)
> 1 cup sliced strawberries
> 1½ cups Strawberry Mylk (page 42)

Divide the Buckwheat Crispies among four serving bowls. Top with the strawberries. Serve with the Strawberry Mylk.

SERVING SUGGESTION: Enjoy your Buckwheat Crispies with whatever flavor mylk you have on hand. Add fresh and dried fruits, and even nuts or seeds, to create your own personal favorite.

APPLE-NUT PORRIDGE

MAKES 4 SERVINGS

A delicious creamed porridge packed with beautifying vitamins and omegas from nuts and flaxseeds and kissed with sweet red goji berries and figs.

> ½ cup of your favorite nuts
> 2 apples, cored and diced
> 1 tablespoon ground flaxseed
> 2 tablespoons agave syrup
> 1 tablespoon goji berries
> 6 dried figs, chopped

Place the nuts, apples, ground flaxseeds, and agave in a food processor. Process into a chunky porridge texture of your liking.

To serve, divide among four bowls. Top with the goji berries and figs, and serve.

SERVING SUGGESTION: Enjoy with your favorite mylk.

BASIC SPROUTED OATMEAL
MAKES 4 SERVINGS

Enjoy this basic oatmeal recipe on its own, or mix in your favorite flavors, fruits, nuts, and favorite mylk.

- 2 cups whole oat groats, soaked overnight in 4 cups of water, and rinsed well before using
- ½ cup pitted dates, or 1 cup sliced banana, or ¼ cup agave syrup
- 2 tablespoons filtered water, as needed
- 1½ tablespoons of your favorite flavoring, such as alcohol-free vanilla extract, cacao nibs or powder, or carob powder (optional)
- ½ cup of your favorite fruit or nuts, such as goji berries, raisins, or almonds (optional)

Place the oats and dates (or other sweetener) in a food processor with the water, and process into a creamy texture similar to cooked oatmeal. For a thinner consistency, add another ¼ cup of water and process.

Add the optional flavoring and fruits and nuts, if desired. Pulse to mix well.

SERVING SUGGESTION: Enjoy with your favorite mylk.

SUPER CHIA CEREAL

MAKES 4 SERVINGS

Chia is an Aztec superfood that builds strength and energy. Hydrated chia seeds absorb more than twelve times their weight in water, keeping us hydrated all day long. Chia gel gives this cereal its thick texture. A supersource of energy, this cereal travels great on camping trips and long treks.

> ½ cup chia seeds
> ½ cup pumpkin seeds
> ½ cup currant or raisins
> ½ cup chopped dehydrated apples
> 3 cups of your favorite mylk

Place all the ingredients in a mixing bowl and stir well. Wait for 5 to 10 minutes for the dry ingredients to become hydrated and the cereal to thicken. Serve and enjoy.

SERVING SUGGESTION: Top with fresh fruit before serving.

OPTIONS: Start with ½ cup of chia seeds and your favorite mylk, then add whatever nuts, seeds, fresh or dried fruit you have on hand to create your personalized flavor combos. One of my favorite combos is chia in mylk with dehydrated apples, raisins, and cinnamon. Another is chia in mylk with pecans, cranberries, and dried shredded coconut.

CREPES

Yes, there is such a thing as raw crepes! These are easy to make, and can be a base for a meal any time of the day—breakfast, lunch, or dinner. Banana or Apple Crepe wrappers, made by blending fruit with flax meal and then dehydrating, are filled with kream or sauce and fresh fruit. A savory crepe is made by filling crepe wrappers with your favorite scramble and a spicy jalapeño sauce.

• • •

BANANA-CHOCOLATE-HAZELNUT CREPES
MAKES 4 SERVINGS

This crepe is inspired by the delicious-smelling banana Nutella crepes made fresh on the streets of Paris. Here's my healthy and guilt-free version. Feel free to substitute your favorite nuts if you can't find hazelnuts, and carob powder for cacao if you don't want the caffeine.

CREPES
1 recipe Banana Flax Crepes (page 68) (four crepes)

FILLING
1 recipe Chocolate-Hazelnut Kream (page 68)

TOPPING
1 recipe Chocolate Fudge Sauce (page 282)

Lay one crepe onto each of four serving dishes. Scoop about ¼ cup of Chocolate Hazelnut Kream in a line down the center of each crepe. Fold the crepe in half or roll it up with the filling inside.

To serve, drizzle with the Chocolate Fudge Sauce.

SERVING SUGGESTION: Sprinkle with cacao powder for looks. Garnish with slices of banana, hazelnuts, or cacao nibs.

BANANA FLAX CREPES

MAKES 4 CREPES

Mild in flavor, these crepes can be enjoyed in a savory or sweet recipe. Use to wrap salads, make burritos, and form wontons. The flax in this recipe makes for a crepe-like consistency that's less leathery than a fruit leather.

> 1 cup mashed banana, packed (about 2 whole)
> ½ cup flax meal
> ½ cup water, or as needed

Place the banana in the bottom of a high-speed blender. Add the flax meal and water, and blend until smooth.

Spread the mixture evenly onto one lined 14-inch-square Excalibur Dehydrator tray.

Dehydrate for 4 to 6 hours at 104°F, or until completely dry.

CHOCOLATE-HAZELNUT KREAM

MAKES ABOUT 1 CUP

Inspired by Nutella, a chocolate hazelnut spread from Italy. My version is a creamy superfood that's packed with antioxidants to keep us healthy and strong.

> 1 cup hazelnuts (also known as filberts)
> 2 tablespoons cacao powder
> 2 tablespoons agave syrup
> ½ to ⅔ cup filtered water, as needed

To make your kream, place the hazelnuts, cacao powder, agave, and water in a high-speed blender. Blend until smooth, adding only as much water as needed to create a thick cream.

STRAWBERRY CREPES

MAKES 4 SERVINGS

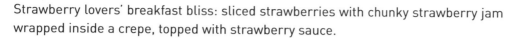

Strawberry lovers' breakfast bliss: sliced strawberries with chunky strawberry jam wrapped inside a crepe, topped with strawberry sauce.

> **1 recipe Apple Crepes (page 69) (four crepes)**
> **l recipe Strawberry Jam (page 96)**
> **1 cup sliced strawberries**
> **1 recipe Strawberry Sauce (page 280)**

Lay one crepe on each of four serving dishes. Spread ¼ cup of Strawberry Jam on each crepe. Top each with ¼ cup of sliced strawberries. Fold in half or roll up. Drizzle with Strawberry Sauce before serving.

SERVING SUGGESTION: Garnish with strawberries and mint.

APPLE CREPES

MAKES 4 WRAPPERS

Mild in flavor, these crepes make a great wrap for savory and sweet recipes. The flax in this mixture creates a crepelike consistency, rather than that of a rubbery fruit leather. Err on the side of less agave rather than more, or your crepes will stay mushy and won't dry fully.

> **1 cup cored and diced apple**
> **½ cup flax meal**
> **2 tablespoons agave syrup**
> **½ cup water, or as needed**

Place the apples in the bottom of a high-speed blender. Add the flax meal, agave, and water. Blend until smooth.

Spread the mixture evenly onto one lined 14-inch-square Excalibur Dehydrator tray.

Dehydrate for 4 to 6 hours at 104°F, or until completely dry. You can also flip the crepes, peel off the liner, and dehydrate for another couple of hours until dry.

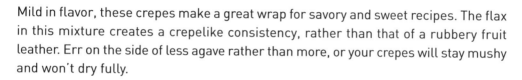

VANILLA KREAM CREPES

MAKES 4 SERVINGS

These crepes are filled with a cashew kream and topped with a pretty orange marmalade.

> 1 recipe Apple Crepes (page 69) (four crepes)
> 1 recipe Whipped Cashew Kream (page 266)
> 1 recipe Orange Marmalade (page 96)

Lay one crepe upon each of four serving dishes. Spread ⅓ cup of Cashew Kream down the center of each crepe. Roll up. Top with Orange Marmalade before serving.

SERVING SUGGESTION: Garnish with sliced oranges and mint.

LEMON KREAM-FILLED CREPES
WITH RASPBERRY SAUCE

MAKES 4 SERVINGS

Apple crepes are filled with a tangy Lemon Kream, then topped with bright red raspberry sauce and fresh raspberries.

> 1 recipe Fresh Fruit Jam (page 96) made with raspberries
>
> ¼ cup agave syrup
>
> 2 recipes Apple Crepes (page 69)
>
> 2 recipes Lemon Kream (page 71)
>
> ½ cup fresh raspberries

To make the sauce, follow the directions for Fresh Fruit Jam made with raspberries. Add the agave syrup and process.

Cut each Apple Crepe wrapper in half, so you have four pieces. Lay one crepe on each of four serving dishes. Spread ½ cup of Lemon Kream down the center of each crepe and sprinkle with 2 tablespoons of raspberries. Roll up.

Top with jam and fresh raspberries before serving.

SERVING SUGGESTION: Grind dried coconut into a powder, and sprinkle over your crepes through a sieve to give a powdered sugar look.

LEMON KREAM

MAKES 1 CUP

Cashews blended with fresh lemon juice and zest create a creamy, rich, and tangy sauce.

If you don't have a high-speed blender, use the grinder top with your Personal Blender or your coffee grinder to first grind the cashews into a powder before using, to help create a smooth, creamy consistency.

> 1 cup cashews
>
> ½ cup lemon juice (from about 2 lemons)
>
> 1 teaspoon grated lemon zest
>
> ¼ cup filtered water, or as needed

Place all the ingredients in a high-speed blender. Blend until smooth, adding only as much water as needed to create a thick, smooth kream.

SAVORY MORNING CREPES
WITH JALAPEÑO CHEEZE SAUCE

MAKES 4 SERVINGS

A savory crepe filled with your favorite scramble and topped with a spicy sauce. Delicious for both brunch and dinner.

> 1 recipe Apple Crepes (page 69)
> 1 recipe of your favorite scramble (pages 79 to 85)
> 1 recipe Jalapeño Cheeze Sauce (page 104)

Lay one crepe on each of four serving dishes. Scoop your favorite scramble onto half of each crepe. Fold over the other half, or roll up.

Top with Jalapeño Cheeze Sauce, and serve.

Will keep for one day in the fridge.

PANCAKES

My raw pancakes are truly moist and fluffy, with a consistency very similar to that of cooked wheat pancakes! You've got to try making them so you can see for yourself how amazing the texture and flavor are.

I make my pancake batter by blending together bananas and flax, which both bind and hold together rich Brazil nuts. Bananas add a light, airy, fluffy consistency when blended, the Brazil nuts add a smoothness, while the flax helps hold everything together.

Finally, sweet, soft, fluffy pancakes to enjoy syrups, butters, and sauces with!

• • •

BRAZIL NUT-BANANA PANCAKES
MAKES 6 PANCAKES

Deliciously light pancakes. Enjoy with agave syrup, maple syrup, or any of the Jams and Butters (pages 96 to 100), or Sauces (pages 280 to 282).

> 2 cups mashed bananas, packed (about 3 whole)
> 1 cup Brazil nuts, processed into a powder
> 1 cup flax meal
> 2 teaspoons ground cinnamon
> 1 cup filtered water, or as needed

Place the banana in the bottom of a high-speed blender. Add the processed Brazil nuts, flax meal, cinnamon, and water. Blend until smooth.

Ladle ½ cup of the mixture into six circles on two lined 14-inch-square Excalibur Dehydrator trays (four on one tray, the remaining two on the second tray). Spread into pancake shapes.

Dehydrate for 5 to 7 hours at 104°F. Flip, peel off the Paraflexx lining, and dehydrate for another 2 to 4 hours, to desired consistency.

Serve with your favorite jam, sauce, or syrup.

BRAZIL NUT–BANANA PANCAKES WITH BLUEBERRY SYRUP AND SLICED BANANAS

MAKES 4 SERVINGS

> 1 recipe Brazil Nut–Banana Pancakes (page 73) (four pancakes)
>
> 1 cup sliced banana and/or berries
>
> 1 recipe Basic Fruit Sauce (page 280) made with blueberries

Lay one pancake on each of four serving dishes and top with the fruit. Drizzle with the sauce and serve.

BACON

I like to make raw vegan bacon using the fatty meat from fresh Thai baby coconuts in the same way cooked jerky is made. You can buy these young coconuts at natural food stores and Asian markets. Young coconuts are different from the traditional brown furry ones we're used to seeing. The young ones typically have the shell trimmed off, exposing their white spongy pith. They look white on the outside.

You may be able to order coconuts online, but they are very heavy, and it will be expensive.

In case coconuts are not available, I'll show you how to make bacon from eggplant instead, by first wilting it with salt, then marinating and dehydrating it the same way as the coconut meat.

• • •

COCONUT BACON

MAKES 4 SERVINGS

Thai baby coconut is a favorite raw food for its electrolyte-rich living water. Plus, the inside of each coconut is lined with the coconut meat used to make this recipe.

The thickness of each coconut's meat varies from thinner, more translucent in color, and gelatinous in consistency to harder, whiter, and thicker—sometimes up to ¼-inch thick. The thicker meats make for better bacon, only because it shrinks a lot during dehydration.

Adding a few drops of liquid smoke will give your bacon a barbecue flavor.

    2 cups coconut meat (from 3 to 4 Thai baby coconuts)
    3 tablespoons Nama Shoyu or Bragg Liquid Aminos
    2 tablespoons olive oil
    A few drops of liquid smoke flavoring (optional)

When scraping the meat out of your coconuts, try to keep pieces as large as possible. Clean the meat by running your fingers over its surface, picking off any pieces of hard husk. Rinse with filtered water as a last step, and drain well.

Place the coconut meat in a mixing bowl and add the remaining ingredients. Toss to mix well. Lay the meat in a single layer on two 14-inch square Excalibur Dehydrator trays.

Dehydrate for 6 to 8 hours at 104°F. The length of time will depend on how thick your coconut meat is. Check it and dry it to your liking. Don't overdehydrate, because the more you dry it, the more it will shrink, and you'll be left with only a small amount of bacon.

OPTIONS: Replace the smoke flavor with herbs and spices to make different flavors. Try chipotle powder, garlic, dill, or oregano.

EGGPLANT BACON

MAKES 4 SERVINGS

Eggplant turns crispy hard when dehydrated, with a texture similar to that of cooked bacon. Here, it is sliced into bacon shapes and softened with salt, then marinated in olive oil and salty Nama Shoyu, for a healthier alternative to cooked bacon.

> 1 medium-size eggplant (about 2 cups, sliced)
>
> 1 tablespoon sea salt
>
> 2 tablespoons Nama Shoyu or Bragg Liquid Aminos
>
> 2 tablespoons olive oil
>
> 1 tablespoon agave syrup
>
> A few drops of liquid smoke flavoring (optional)

Slice your eggplant into thin rounds, using a mandoline slicer. Then, use a knife to slice the rounds into 1½ by 4-inch slices similar in shape and size to cooked bacon.

Place the eggplant strips in a mixing bowl and toss with the salt to coat. Set aside for 10 to 20 minutes to soften and until the eggplant releases water. Gently squeeze any excess moisture from the eggplant, and discard the liquid.

Place the eggplant in a mixing bowl. Add the Nama Shoyu, olive oil, agave, and smoke flavoring (if using), and toss to mix well.

Spread the marinated eggplant evenly on Excalibur Dehydrator mesh trays, and dry at 104°F for 1 to 2 hours, until dry and crisp or to your desired texture.

OPTIONS: Use spices and flavors to create variations. For example, try ½ teaspoon of chipotle powder, ½ teaspoon of ground cumin, or another 1 to 2 tablespoons of agave syrup.

SCRAMBLES

These scrambles are made by mixing together different vegetables with combinations of nuts and seeds to create a chunky mixture similar to a cooked vegetable scramble.

• • •

CORN TORTILLA AND MUSHROOM SCRAMBLE WITH HEIRLOOM TOMATO SALSA

MAKES 4 SERVINGS

My version of *chilaquiles*—a dish from Baja, Mexico, which is made by sautéing strips of tortillas with salsa. This recipe adds marinated mushrooms to the mixture.

The mushrooms are marinated, then tossed with sliced Soft Corn Tortillas and Heirloom Tomato Salsa.

> 2 cups sliced mushrooms, any type
>
> 2 tablespoons Nama Shoyu or Bragg Liquid Aminos
>
> 3 tablespoons extra-virgin olive oil
>
> 1 recipe Soft Corn Tortilla (page 173)
>
> 1 recipe Heirloom Tomato Salsa (page 81)

Begin by marinating your mushrooms: toss with Nama Shoyu and oil. Set aside to marinate for 5 to 10 minutes, or longer.

Slice two or three tortillas into 1-inch strips, and then cut in half lengthwise. Place in a mixing bowl. Add the salsa and mushrooms and toss lightly. Serve immediately.

SERVING SUGGESTION: Top with Chipotle Cheeze (page 104) and/or slices of avocado.

Marinating Mushrooms

IN RAW food, mushrooms are softened and marinated to create a cooked consistency by tossing in a salty substance, such as Nama Shoyu, Bragg, or sea salt, and some olive oil.

The salt helps the mushrooms release water, so they wilt and soften, while the oil adds a slippery consistency for a real "cooked" mouth feel.

I prefer the savory flavor of salt or Bragg to marinate and to speed up marinating time.

But when I want to avoid a salty flavor, I marinate my mushrooms in olive oil and a splash of lemon or lime juice, or even apple cider vinegar. The acids from citrus and vinegar also help to soften and release water. Use the same amounts of lemon or lime juice or apple cider vinegar to Nama Shoyu or Bragg.

When marinating, try adding herbs and spices, such as fresh garlic, basil, rosemary, or onion.

If you want to use your dehydrator, you can toss your mushrooms in just the olive oil, and then dry them on trays in a dehydrator at 104°F for 2 to 3 hours, to soften. This will help wilt your mushrooms, to create that cooked consistency.

HEIRLOOM TOMATO SALSA

MAKES 1 CUP

Salsas are traditionally raw. This simplified version uses gorgeous heirloom tomatoes with fresh cilantro, garlic, and the heat of jalapeño.

> 1 cup seeded and diced heirloom tomato
> ¼ cup chopped fresh cilantro
> ½ teaspoon minced garlic
> ½ to 1 teaspoon chopped jalapeño
> ¼ teaspoon sea salt

Place all the ingredients in a mixing bowl and mix well.

Will keep for 2 days in the fridge.

OPTION: For a sweeter, crispier salsa, add ½ cup of fresh corn kernels.

LOVE-THE-CHICKS PÂTÉ

MAKES 4 SERVINGS

This is the basic scramble recipe from *Ani's Raw Food Kitchen*. I'm using it here again as the base for two new, easy-to-make scrambles I'm sure you'll love.

> **2 cups almonds**
>
> **1 cup sunflower seeds**
>
> **½ teaspoon sea salt**
>
> **2 teaspoons ground turmeric, for color (optional)**
>
> **1 cup water, or as needed**

Place the almonds, sunflower seeds, sea salt, and turmeric (if using) in a food processor. Process into a powder. Add the water and process until well mixed. The texture should be chunky, rather than creamy smooth.

Use the following recipes or add your favorite ingredients to this base to make different "scrambles."

SPINACH, MUSHROOM, AND THYME SCRAMBLE

MAKES 4 SERVINGS

Marinated mushrooms are tossed with fresh spinach and thyme and my Love-the-Chicks Pâté for a delicious morning scramble. Top with Cashew Gravy before serving.

> **2 cups sliced mushrooms, any type,**
>
> **3 tablespoons Nama Shoyu or Bragg Liquid Aminos**
>
> **3 tablespoons extra-virgin olive oil**
>
> **2 cups spinach, well washed**
>
> **1 recipe Love-the-Chicks Pâté (page 82)**
>
> **1 tablespoon fresh thyme, or ½ tablespoon dried**

Begin by tossing the sliced mushrooms in the Nama Shoyu and olive oil. Set aside to marinate for 5 to 10 minutes. Next, add the spinach to the mushrooms, and marinate for 5 minutes, until slightly wilted.

Fully squeeze the marinade out of the mushroom mixture. Place the mushrooms and spinach in a bowl with the Love-the-Chicks Pâté and thyme. Toss to mix well.

SERVING SUGGESTION: Top with Cashew Gravy (page 94).

HUEVO-LESS RANCHEROS WITH RED ENCHI-LADA SAUCE AND PICO DE GALLO

MAKES 4 SERVINGS

Marinated onion is mixed with tomato and bell pepper, scooped onto a Soft Corn Tortilla, and topped with a delicious Red Enchilada Sauce and fresh Pico de Gallo.

   ½ cup diced yellow onion

   1 tablespoon Nama Shoyu or Bragg Liquid Aminos

   1 tablespoon extra-virgin olive oil

   1 cup seeded and diced tomato

   ½ cup seeded and diced bell pepper

   1 recipe Love-the-Chicks Pâté (page 82)

   1 recipe Soft Corn Tortilla (page 173)

   1 recipe Red Enchilada Sauce (page 84)

   1 recipe Pico de Gallo (page 85)

   1 ripe avocado, pitted and sliced

Start by tossing the onion in Nama Shoyu and olive oil. Set aside to marinate for at least 10 minutes. Squeeze the marinade out of your onion, and place the onion, tomato, and bell pepper in a mixing bowl with the Love-the-Chicks Pâté. Toss to mix.

Lay one tortilla on each of four serving dishes. Scoop the scramble onto the tortillas, and top with Red Enchilada Sauce and Pico de Gallo. Garnish with avocado slices and serve immediately.

RED ENCHILADA SAUCE

MAKES 2 CUPS

A versatile sauce to top your Huevo-less Rancheros and wet burritos. This sauce is also a delicious substitute for Italian marinara.

2 cups seeded and diced Roma tomatoes

2 tablespoons extra-virgin olive oil

1 tablespoon lime juice

1 teaspoon minced garlic

$\frac{1}{4}$ to $\frac{1}{2}$ serrano or jalapeño chile, seeded and diced, to taste

1 tablespoon chopped fresh oregano or cilantro, or $\frac{1}{2}$ tablespoon dried

2 tablespoons chopped onion

A few drops of liquid smoke flavor (optional)

Place the tomatoes, olive oil, lime juice, and garlic in a blender. Blend until smooth. Add the remaining ingredients and pulse gently to mix well.

Liquid Smoke

ONE WAY to add the taste of smoke without cooking is by using a liquid smoke flavoring made by condensing smoke from burning wood into water.

In case you're wondering whether liquid smoke is safe to eat, here's what the *San Diego Union-Tribune* said about it on July 29, 2009: "Carcinogenic compounds found in smoke can be filtered out as a part of the production process. Some of these flavorings, however, can contain mutagenic substances formed when wood is burned. . . . But if you use this seasoning periodically as part of a varied diet, any risk would be considered negligible."

I agree, and remember to keep everything in moderation. A few occasional drops of liquid smoke flavoring is okay by my book, but you should decide for yourself.

PICO DE GALLO

MAKES 2 CUPS

In traditional Mexican cuisine, this salsa is fresh and uncooked. My recipe is a mixture of tomato, onion, chiles, lime juice, and cilantro. Try adding other ingredients, such as cucumber, radish, or mango.

- **2 cups diced Roma tomatoes**
- **¼ cup white onion, chopped finely**
- **½ to 1 jalapeño pepper, seeded and chopped finely**
- **1 tablespoon fresh lime juice**
- **¼ cup chopped fresh cilantro**
- **½ teaspoon sea salt**

Place all the ingredients in a mixing bowl and toss to mix well.

Will keep for 2 days in the fridge.

SUN-DRIED TOMATOES AND COCONUT BACON SCRAMBLE

MAKES 4 SERVINGS

This scramble is made with young Thai baby coconut meat processed with almonds. Turmeric gives this scramble its yellow color, and it's peppered with red sun-dried tomatoes and Coconut Bacon bits.

- **1 cup almonds**
- **1½ cups coconut meat**
- **½ teaspoon salt**
- **2 teaspoons turmeric, for color (optional)**
- **½ cup water, or as needed**
- **½ cup chopped sun-dried tomatoes**
- **½ cup chopped Coconut Bacon (page 76) or Eggplant Bacon (page 78)**

First, place the almonds, coconut meat, salt, and turmeric (if using) in a food processor.

Process to mix well, adding only as much water as needed for everything to mix together.

Next, add the sun-dried tomatoes and Coconut Bacon. Pulse lightly to mix.

SERVING SUGGESTION: Serve drizzled with Cashew Gravy (see page 94).

QUICHE

Yes, even quiche has a place in my book! These quiches are made by dehydrating your crust first, then filling with vegetables and cheeze, and dehydrating for a couple of hours before serving warm.

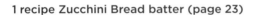

• • •

QUICHE CRUST

MAKES 4 SERVINGS, FILLED

My quiche crust is made using the same batter from my Zucchini Bread recipe, pressed into a pie dish. It's then dehydrated 12 to 14 hours to firm up.

> **1 recipe Zucchini Bread batter (page 23)**

Scoop your batter into a standard pie dish about 9 inches in diameter. Spread evenly along bottom and sides with your fingers or a wet spoon.

Place the pie dish in your Excalibur dehydrator and dry at 104°F for 12 to 14 hours. It will fit in the Excalibur if you leave out one of the trays to make more head room. Alternatively, directly on the dehydrator's liner, you can shape flat disks with raised edges, similar to the shape of pizza crust or tart. You want the edges to be dry, but it's okay if the center isn't 100 percent dry before using. Use this crust as a base for the following fillings.

SPINACH QUICHE

MAKES 4 SERVINGS

Onions are marinated and added to a sunflower cheeze with spinach, to make a creamy puree. The mixture is scooped into your Quiche Crust and then dehydrated for a couple of hours to warm before serving.

> **1 recipe Quiche Crust (page 86), dehydrated as directed**
> **1 cup sliced yellow onion**
> **1 teaspoon Nama Shoyu or Bragg Liquid Aminos**
> **2 teaspoons garlic (about 2 cloves)**
> **1 teaspoon sea salt**

2 cups sunflower seeds

¼ cup lemon juice (from about 2 lemons)

½ to ¾ cup filtered water, as needed

3 cups spinach, washed well and tightly packed

First, place the onion in a bowl with the Nama Shoyu, and marinate for at least 20 minutes to soften.

Place the garlic and salt in a food processor, and process the garlic into small pieces. Add the sunflower seeds; process into small pieces. Add lemon juice and water, as needed, to produce a thick consistency similar to that of cottage cheese.

Add the onions with its marinade and the spinach; pulse lightly to mix filling. Scoop into the Quiche Crust.

Dehydrate for 2 to 4 hours at 104°F and serve warm.

ASPARAGUS-MUSHROOM QUICHE

MAKES 4 SERVINGS

Chopped asparagus and mushrooms are mixed into a tangy cashew cream cheeze. The mixture is scooped into your Quiche Crust and dehydrated for a couple of hours before serving warm.

1 recipe Quiche Crust (page 86), dehydrated as directed

2 teaspoons garlic (about 2 cloves)

1 teaspoon sea salt

2 cups cashews

1/4 cup lemon juice (from about 2 lemons)

1/2 to 3/4 cup filtered water, as needed

1 cup sliced thinly and chopped asparagus

2 cups sliced mushrooms (any type)

Place the garlic and salt in a food processor, and process the garlic into small pieces. Add the cashews; process into small pieces. Add the lemon juice and water, as needed, to produce a thick consistency similar to that of cottage cheese.

Add the asparagus and mushrooms; pulse lightly to mix the filling. Scoop into your Quiche Crust.

Dehydrate for 2 to 4 hours at 104°F and serve warm.

BROCCOLI-CHEDDAR QUICHE WITH COCONUT BACON

MAKES 4 SERVINGS

Broccoli bits mixed with a cheezy orange–colored sunflower seed sauce and scooped into a Quiche Crust. It's then topped with Coconut Bacon bits. The quiche is dried in a dehydrator for a couple of hours before serving warm. Use Eggplant Bacon if you don't have coconuts available.

1 recipe Quiche Crust (page 86), dehydrated as directed

2 teaspoons garlic (about 2 cloves)

1 teaspoon sea salt

2 teaspoons turmeric, for color (optional)

2 cups sunflower seeds

1/4 cup lemon juice (from about 2 lemons)

½ to ¾ cup filtered water, as needed

1 cup broccoli florets, broken into small pieces

2 cups chopped Coconut Bacon (page 76) or Eggplant Bacon (page 78)

Place the garlic, salt, and turmeric (if using) in a food processor, and process the garlic into small pieces. Add the sunflower seeds; process into small pieces. Add the lemon juice and water, as needed, to produce a thick consistency similar to that of cottage cheese.

Add the broccoli and pulse lightly to mix the filling. Scoop into your Quiche Crust. Sprinkle with the Coconut Bacon bits.

Dehydrate for 2 to 4 hours at 104°F and serve warm.

TOAST AND BISCUITS

Raw toast is made by using your favorite crispy dehydrated breads, such as Basic Flax Cracker, Tomato Flax Cracker, or Rye Flatbread, as you would slices of toasted baked breads, but without the wheat and gluten.

Top with your favorite ingredients, such as jam and butter, tomato and fresh basil, or slices of creamy avocado and spicy chipotle powder.

The Biscuits and Gravy recipe is one of my favorites for a Sunday brunch. Buckwheat Biscuits with jam, butter, and kream are great for high tea in the late afternoon. That's the inspiration for the Scones with Clotted Kream and Jam recipe—a real treat—at the end of this section.

• • •

TOAST WITH JAM AND BUTTER

MAKES 4 SERVINGS

Enjoy this recipe with any of your favorite bread or pizza crust recipes, such as Rye Flatbread (page 23), Kalamata Olive Crostini (page 114), or Buckwheat Pizza Crust (page 213). Top with your favorite fruit jam and butter. Simple and delicious.

> 1 recipe of your favorite bread
> 1 recipe Fresh Fruit Jam (page 96)
> 1 recipe of your favorite butter (pages 98 to 100)

Divide the toast slices among four serving dishes. Serve with jam and butter.

TOAST WITH AVOCADO AND CHIPOTLE
MAKES 4 SERVINGS

This savory toast is topped with avocado slices and a pinch of spicy powdered chipotle, then drizzled with olive oil.

Enjoy this recipe with any of your favorite bread or pizza crust recipes, such as Rye Flatbread (page 23), Kalamata Olive Crostini (page 114), or Buckwheat Pizza Crust (page 213).

> **1 recipe of your favorite bread**
> **1 ripe avocado, pitted and sliced**
> **½ teaspoon powdered chipotle**
> **1 tablespoon extra-virgin olive oil**

Divide the toast slices among four serving dishes. Top with slices of avocado and pinches of powdered chipotle. Drizzle with olive oil and serve immediately.

TOAST WITH HEIRLOOM TOMATO AND BASIL
MAKES 4 SERVINGS

Toast is topped with slices of beautiful heirloom tomatoes and fresh basil, then drizzled with olive oil.

Enjoy this recipe with any of your favorite bread or pizza crust recipes, such as Rye Flatbread (page 23), Kalamata Olive Crostini (page 114), or Buckwheat Pizza Crust (page 213).

> **1 recipe of your favorite bread**
> **1 heirloom tomato, seeded and sliced**
> **¼ cup torn basil leaves**
> **¼ teaspoon ground black pepper**
> **1 tablespoon extra-virgin olive oil**

Divide the toast slices among four serving dishes. Top with slices of tomato, the basil, and pinches of black pepper. Drizzle with olive oil and serve immediately.

BISCUITS AND GRAVY

MAKES 4 SERVINGS

I love biscuits and gravy. But it can be hard to find wheat-free or even vegan biscuits or gravy out in the cooked world. So, I was inspired to come up with this recipe. Moist Buckwheat Biscuits are smothered in rich Cashew Gravy. You're going to love these, I promise; they are delicious!

> 1 recipe Buckwheat Biscuits (page 93), dehydrated as directed
>
> 1 recipe Cashew Gravy (page 94)
>
> 2 tablespoons chopped green onions, for garnish

Divide the biscuits among four serving dishes. Top with the gravy and garnish with the green onions. Serve immediately.

BUCKWHEAT BISCUITS

MAKES 4 SERVINGS

This recipe was created as I was trying to make a new bread texture. My friend Carol C. said the texture reminded her of biscuits, and I agreed.

These biscuits are light and stay moist and are very mild in flavor. Crispy on the outside, they taste great, and are savory when smothered with gravy. Serve them as scones for high tea, with jam and butter, and your favorite sun teas or smoothies.

If you don't have Buckwheat Crispies on hand, just substitute 2 cups of buckwheat groats instead.

> 2 cups Buckwheat Crispies (page 63)
>
> ¼ cup golden flaxseed
>
> ¼ cup olive oil
>
> 1 teaspoon sea salt
>
> 1½ cups filtered water

Grind the Buckwheat Crispies to a powder, then place in a food processor. Then grind flaxseeds to a powder and add to the food processor. Add the oil and salt; process to mix well. Add the water and process into a thick, doughy batter.

Scoop the batter into ⅓-cup biscuit shapes (you should be able to make about ten), on a lined 14-inch-square Excalibur Dehydrator tray. Dehydrate for 8 to 10 hours at 104°F.

Flip and dehydrate for another 2 to 4 hours, or until desired consistency. You want the biscuits to have a crust around the outside and be soft but not mushy on the inside.

Will keep 1 day at room temperature in a brown bag. You can refrigerate for several days or freeze, but the biscuits will loose their crispy crust.

OPTIONS: Mix dried fruits such as cranberries or raisins, or chopped nuts into your batter before forming your biscuits, to create new flavors.

CASHEW GRAVY

MAKES 1 CUP

Cashews are blended with nutritional yeast for a cheeselike gravy that's great with scrambles, on nachos, and over biscuits.

½ cup cashews

¼ cup nutritional yeast

1 tablespoon olive oil

1 tablespoon unpasturized yellow miso

2 teaspoons lemon juice

½ cup water

Blend all the ingredients together in a high-speed blender until smooth.

Will keep for 4 to 5 days in the fridge.

SCONES WITH CLOTTED KREAM AND JAM

MAKES 4 SERVINGS

A classic English afternoon tea is served with scones that are split and spread with strawberry jam and topped with clotted cream. For this recipe, you'll use Whipped Cashew Kream as a healthy alternative to traditional, fat-laden clotted cream, and homemade strawberry jam, with butter of your choice, on top of my moist Buckwheat Biscuits, served with your favorite sun tea with mylk.

1 recipe Buckwheat Biscuits (page 93), dehydrated as directed

1 recipe of your favorite sweet butter (pages 98 to 100)

1 recipe Whipped Cashew Kream (page 266)

1 recipe Fresh Fruit Jam (page 96), made with strawberries

Split the biscuits in half horizontally, and place a top and bottom on each of four serving dishes, the soft insides facing upward.

Spread each half with butter, top with kream and jam.

JAMS AND BUTTERS

My raw jams are healthier than store-bought jams, which are often preserved using processed white sugar. These simple recipes are made by pulsing together fresh fruits, with semisoft dates as a sweetener. The consistency is chunky and thicker than a sauce for a full-fruit experience.

Butter is made by beating soft coconut oil for a whipped butter consistency. For a savory flavor, I add salty miso paste. For a sweet butter, I use flavorings with low-glycemic agave syrup.

• • •

ORANGE MARMALADE
MAKES 1 CUP

Orange is processed with zest and sweet dates to make a chunky, fresh jam.

> 1 cup seeded orange segments (remove all peel and pith)
> 2 tablespoons fresh orange zest
> ¼ cup pitted Medjool dates, packed

Place all the ingredients in a food processor and pulse lightly to mix into a chunky marmalade.

FRESH FRUIT JAM
MAKES 1 CUP

Make your own healthy fruit preserve. Choose your favorite in-season fruit, such as persimmon, raspberry, strawberry, pineapple, or blueberry, and mix in a food processor with dates.

For a smoother consistency, you can blend in a smaller-scaled blender rather than in food processor.

> 1 cup of your favorite fruit
> ¼ cup pitted Medjool dates, packed

Place all the ingredients in a food processor and pulse lightly to mix into a chunky jam consistency.

Will keep in the fridge for 2 to 3 days.

Coconut Oil Is a Saturated Fat

THERE'S A debate in the raw food community over coconut oil and its saturated fat. On the plus side, eating it is said to raise your HDL, which is the "good" cholesterol in your body, and this helps the ratio of good-to-bad improve for the better.

I love coconut oil for its flavor, but use it in moderation.

MISO BUTTER

MAKES ½ CUP

This butter is slightly salted with unpasturized miso and is so delicious you'll forget there's no dairy in it. It has the consistency of a whipped butter and melts like butter, too! Use on your pancakes, scones, and toast, just as you would dairy butter.

1 to 2 tablespoons unpasturized white miso
½ cup coconut butter, softened but not liquid

Place the miso, to taste, and coconut butter in a bowl and mix together with a spoon.

Will keep for a week or more at room temperature.

VANILLA BUTTER

MAKES ½ CUP

I found vanilla butter at a French patisserie, and it sounded delicious, so that inspired me to create this guilt-free version. This is a sweet butter without salt.

½ cup coconut butter, softened but not liquid
1 tablespoon alcohol-free vanilla extract, or 1 vanilla bean, seeded
1 to 2 teaspoons agave syrup

Place the ingredients in a bowl, adding the agave syrup to taste, and mix together with a spoon.

Will keep for a week or more at room temperature.

LAVENDER BUTTER

MAKES ½ CUP

A sweet butter with aromatic lavender from fresh or dry lavender flowers or extract.
   Pick fresh, unsprayed lavender flowers, discarding the green parts. Wash well, then chop into the tiniest pieces possible. Alternatively, seek out culinary lavender in the spice section of gourmet stores (never consume lavender sold as a potpourri ingredient). Add to softened coconut butter and let sit overnight to allow for the flavor to absorb into the butter. Adjust to use as much or as little as you wish of the lavender buds for a stronger or lighter scent and flavor.

½ cup coconut butter, softened but not liquid

1 teaspoon dried culinary lavender, pulverized in food grinder, or 1 table-spoon fresh flowers, finely chopped, or ½ teaspoon culinary lavender extract

1 teaspoon agave syrup

Place the ingredients in a bowl and mix together with a spoon.

Will keep for a week or more at room temperature.

Make Your Own Extracts

AN EASY WAY to make your own extract is by mixing culinary lavender buds or vanilla bean with vodka in a small glass jar with a tight-fitting lid. Vodka is a distilled alcohol, so it's not raw. I only tend to use at most a tablespoon at a time, so enjoy using my homemade extracts. But, if you're sensitive to alcohol or vodka, you may want to just buy organic alcohol-free extract, and skip these homemade recipes.

Your extracts will last for years, and you can keep topping off the vanilla extract with more vodka as you use it. Make sure to shake well to mix.

LAVENDER EXTRACT

To make lavender extract, place ¼ cup of crushed culinary lavender buds in a glass jar with 1 cup of vodka (ideally organic vodka). Close the lid and let the jar stand in a cool, dark place for at least 1 week, up to 6 weeks if you can. (The longer an extract sits, the stronger it will be.) Shake the jar daily to help infuse the lavender in the vodka.

When ready, strain out the lavender. Now you have your own homemade lavender extract to use in cookies, sauces, and butter.

VANILLA EXTRACT

To make vanilla extract, you'll need three vanilla beans. Slice each lengthwise with a sharp knife. Place the beans in a glass jar and cover completely with 1 cup of vodka (ideally organic vodka). Shake the jar every day or two, and store in a dark, cool place for at least 2 months.

CHOCOLATE BUTTER

MAKES ½ CUP

Coconut butter is mixed with cacao powder and agave syrup to make a smooth, decadent chocolate butter. Use this to spread onto your pancakes, toasts, biscuits, and even cookies.

½ cup coconut butter, softened but not liquid

2 teaspoons cacao powder

1 teaspoon agave syrup

Place the ingredients in a bowl and mix together with a spoon.

Will keep for a couple of weeks or more at room temperature.

5

SNACKS AND ACCOMPANIMENTS

IN THIS CHAPTER, I'll show you how to make recipes that can be used to dress up any dish. Recipes include easy cheezes made by blending or processing nuts or seeds; chips and crackers made with vegetables and flax, then dehydrated until crispy; and even dehydrated crunchy vegetables such as Kale Chips, made by coating kale with a sweet red bell pepper sauce, and "Fried" Onion Rings made with a crispy buckwheat coating. Seasoned nuts are easy to make by marinating and then dehydrating to intensify the flavors of the seasonings.

I will also show you how easy it is to make your own sauerkraut and cucumber pickles by soaking vegetables in a salt bath, then setting them aside to pickle. I'll introduce you to Korean-inspired, probiotic-rich pickled vegetables called kimchi, made with garlic, ginger, and chili pepper. All are simple to make, but require waiting time for the fermentation to take place.

CHEEZES

A lot of people list dairy cheese as one of the more challenging items to replace in a vegan or raw lifestyle. The good news is that it's easy to create tangy, creamy, delicious cheezes without worrying about dairy.

Raw vegan cheeze is made by blending or processing nuts and seeds into a cream- or pâtélike consistency. I add lemon juice to achieve a tartness like that of a fermented dairy cheese, and bit of garlic to add a savory flavor. Since all cheeze is salty, I add a pinch of sea salt, too. You can use these cheezes in the same way you would any dairy cheeze: on pizza; in sandwiches, burgers, wraps; and on salads.

I'll start by showing you how to make Basic Cheeze. The consistency is similar to that of ricotta or whipped cream cheese. Unlike dairy cheeze, Basic Cheeze won't become stringy when melted. Adding more water will create a smoother, melted sauce consistency that works great on nachos and as a dip.

A second style of cheeze is dry and crumbly, just like Parmesan. It's my Rawmesan Cheeze made of ground nuts with a bit of garlic and salt. It's easy to make and can be used as you would a dairy Parmesan, sprinkled onto soups and pizzas.

All my cheezes are full of protein and calcium and don't cause inflammation nor raise cholesterol levels the way dairy does. If you're transitioning to raw foods, you can use these dairy-free cheezes in your cooked food recipes, such as macaroni and cheese or enchiladas; you can also just sprinkle them onto your salad or use as a dip for vegetables, for some tasty, animal-free protein.

These cruelty-free versions of cheese are made with nuts and seeds full of minerals that will keep your skin clear and radiant, and your body lean and strong.

Clean Karma Is Eco Green

THE UNITED NATIONS REPORT "Livestock's Long Shadow" says that the production of live-stock creates more greenhouse gases than does all of our planet's transportation industry.

Per person per year, the average carbon emissions from an animal product–based diet are eleven tons, whereas the emissions on a plant-based diet are only six tons. That's almost half.

To make food for an animal-based diet, it takes three acres of land and 2,500 gallons of water a day. A plant-based diet needs only a sixth of an acre of land and 300 gallons of water a day. That's $\frac{1}{18}$ of the land, and eight to nine times less water.

According to the USDA, one acre of land can produce 20,000 pounds of vegetables, but only 165 pounds of meat.

In addition to being better for our health, you can see how enjoying more plant-based, whole, raw foods helps our planet.

BASIC CHEEZE
MAKES ABOUT 2 CUPS

This is the base recipe for raw vegan cheeze. Try using your favorite nuts and seeds—such as almonds, cashews, Brazil nuts, pumpkin seeds, sunflower seeds, and macadamia nuts—to add variety to your flavors and textures.

> 1 teaspoon coarsely chopped fresh garlic
> $\frac{1}{2}$ teaspoon sea salt
> 2 cups of your favorite nut or seed
> $\frac{1}{4}$ cup fresh lemon juice (from about 2 lemons)
> $\frac{1}{4}$ cup water, as needed

Place the garlic and salt in a food processor and process into small pieces. Add the nuts or seeds, and process into small pieces. Add the lemon juice and water; process to mix well. Add more or less water to reach your desired consistency.

Will keep for 4 to 5 days in the fridge.

OPTIONS: Add fresh or dried herbs such as basil or rosemary, or pitted olives and sun-dried tomatoes, to create new flavors of cheezes.

CHIPOTLE CHEEZE

MAKES 2 CUPS

An example of how to add spice and a new flavor to the Basic Cheeze recipe, this is a deliciously smoky and slightly spicy cheeze.

1 recipe Basic Cheeze (page 103), made with cashews or pine nuts

$\frac{1}{2}$ to 1 teaspoon powdered chipotle

Follow the directions for making Basic Cheeze, adding chipotle powder to taste.

Will keep up to 1 week in the fridge.

SERVING SUGGESTION: Enjoy in South of the Border Wraps (page 180), as a dip, tossed with spiralized zucchini noodles, and in nachos made with Salted Flax Chips (page 108).

COOKED VARIATIONS: Toss with brown rice macaroni for a Chipotle Mac and Cheeze, and enjoy with organic blue corn chips.

JALAPEÑO CHEEZE SAUCE

MAKES 2 CUPS

A delicious sauce mixed with fresh jalapeño for an added kick. Adjust the amount of jalapeño per your spice preference. Removing the seeds will make the pepper less spicy, too.

To make a sauce consistency, which is runnier than a cheeze, just add a bit more water to your favorite Basic Cheeze recipe.

1 recipe Basic Cheeze (page 103), made with your favorite nut or seed

1 tablespoon jalapeño pepper, to taste

$\frac{1}{2}$ to $\frac{3}{4}$ cup water, as needed

Follow the directions for Basic Cheeze, adding the jalapeño and additional water.

Will keep for 4 to 5 days in the fridge.

CHEDDAR CHEEZE SAUCE

MAKES 2 CUPS

This sauce is colored orange with turmeric to look like Cheddar. Drizzle over fresh vegetables, asparagus spears, or dehydrated Battered Zucchini Sticks (page 116) or "Roasted" Bell Peppers (page 118).

Turmeric works to decrease inflammation in the body. The less inflammation we have, the better we feel, and the tighter and leaner we look.

> 1 recipe Basic Cheeze (page 103), made with sunflower seeds
> 1 tablespoon turmeric, for color (optional)
> ½ to ¾ cup water, as needed

Follow the directions for Basic Cheeze, adding the turmeric and additional water.

Will keep for 4 to 5 days in the fridge.

OPTION: Spread your Cheddar Cheeze Sauce on a lined dehydrator tray and dry at 104°F for 6 to 8 hours, until dried. Crumble and use like Parmesan.

RAWMESAN CHEEZE

MAKES ½ CUP

Sprinkle an extra layer of savory goodness on soups, salads, wraps, and pizzas. I use cashews for their color, although pine nuts work just as well. If you don't mind a darker-colored Rawmesan, feel free to use your favorite nut or seed instead.

> ½ cup cashews, ground into a powder
> ½ teaspoon minced garlic
> ¼ teaspoon sea salt

Mix the ingredients together in a small bowl.

Will keep for 5 days in the fridge.

GENERAL TIP:
Get Experimental

CASHEWS AND ALMONDS have the mildest flavors and work great in cheeze recipes. But it's fun to experiment with other nuts and seeds, such as walnuts, sunflower, hemp nut, and pumpkin seeds, which can yield a whole new flavor profile.

CHEEZY SPRINKLE
MAKES ABOUT ¾ CUP

Nutritional yeast has a cheeselike flavor all on its own, with 8 grams of protein and 320 milligrams of potassium, and only 1 gram of fat per two-tablespoon serving. Here, it's combined with cashews and a pinch of salt, for a rich, tangy mixture. Use as you would any cheese: sprinkle on soups, salads, or in wraps, and to garnish.

> ½ cup cashews, ground into a powder
> ¼ cup nutritional yeast
> ¼ teaspoon sea salt

Mix together all the ingredients in a food processor.

Will keep for at least a week in the fridge.

COCONUT KEFIR CHEEZE
MAKES ABOUT 1 TO 1½ CUPS

The young Thai coconut meat left over after making Coconut Kefir (page 54) makes a great probiotic cheeze similar to cottage cheese. Friendly bacteria, probiotics eat up the sugar in the coconut meat during the fermentation process and create a deliciously light, pungent cheeze that's creamy, white, and delicious as a sauce, cheeze, and dip.

> 2 cups coconut meat (from 2 to 3 young coconuts)
> ¼ cup coconut kefir
> Coconut water (optional)

Clean your coconut meat by running your fingers over its surface to ensure all hard bits are removed. Place in a blender with the coconut kefir and blend until smooth. If you need more liquid, add a small amount of coconut water to the blender, as needed, to produce a chunky consistency similar to that of cottage cheese.

Transfer the mixture to a close-fitting bowl or jar with an airtight lid. Set out at room temperature for 24 hours. Then, store in the refrigerator.

CHIPS

Chips are great for scooping up delicious dips, sauces, guacamole, and salsa. Made by blending vegetables with flax and then dehydrating, Salted Flax Chips are used to make delicious Nachos. Kale is marinated with oil and spices to make Chipotle Kale Chips or tossed with a red bell pepper sauce and dehydrated to make cheeselike Cheddar-Kale Chips that can be enjoyed on their own as a snack, or rolled up inside nori or a wrap, or serve with a sandwich or burger for added crispness.

• • •

SALTED FLAX CHIPS

MAKES 32 CHIPS

These chips are light and crisp, just like tortilla chips, and are fun to use for finger food such as nachos, and for dipping guacamole and fresh salsa.

> 1 cup chopped celery
> 1³/₄ cups flax meal
> 2 tablespoons dried oregano
> 1¹/₂ cups filtered water
> 1 teaspoon coarse sea salt

Place the celery, flax, oregano, and water in a high-speed blender. Blend until smooth.

Spread evenly onto one lined 14-inch-square Excalibur Dehydrator tray. Sprinkle with the sea salt.

Dehydrate for 5 to 6 hours at 104°F. Flip and score into four horizontal and vertical rows. Then score each square diagonally in half into two triangle chips. Dehydrate for another 6 to 8 hours, until dried and crisp.

NACHOS

Just like traditional baked nachos, my raw version is topped with salsa, cheeze, avocado, and delicious vegan "meat."

As a fresh, crunchy alternative to dehydrated flax chips, slice jicama or sun chokes and use as your "chips" topped with cheeze, salsa, and taco meat.

> 1 recipe Salted Flax Chips (page 108)
> 1 recipe Taco Nut Meat (page 146)
> 1 recipe Chipotle Cheeze (page 104)
> 1 recipe Heirloom Tomato Salsa (page 81)
> 1 ripe avocado, pitted and diced

Assemble your nachos by placing the Salted Flax Chips on a serving platter. Top with the taco meat, cheeze, salsa, and avocado. Enjoy immediately.

CHIPOTLE-KALE CHIPS

I decided to try dehydrating kale because I had many bunches on hand, and I flipped when I first discovered kale chips: light, crispy, and delicious, just like potato chips, but super green and healthy. You won't be able to eat just one. Simply toss kale in olive oil and spices, and dehydrate into chips.

If you don't have a dehydrator, you can use an oven set to a low temperature with the door propped open, or even bake these at 300°F for 15 minutes, which is definitely not raw, but still better for you than traditional potato chips. Hopefully, you'll be convinced to buy a dehydrator so your next batch will be made in a more eco manner that doesn't use as much energy.

> 6 cups bite-size pieces of kale, tightly packed (about 1 bunch)
> 3 tablespoons agave syrup
> 2 tablespoons extra-virgin olive oil
> 1/2 teaspoon sea salt
> 1/2 to 1 teaspoon powdered chipotle

Place all the ingredients in a large mixing bowl, adding the chipotle to taste, and toss to mix well.

Spread on two 14-inch-square Excalibur Dehydrator trays and dry at 104°F for 4 to 6 hours, until dried.

CHEDDAR-KALE CHIPS

Nutritional yeast is mixed with red bell pepper and cashews to make a cheeze that is then used to coat the kale before dehydrating it. The cheeze mixture is orange and tastes like Cheddar. These chips are hearty and crispy-chewy, and my absolute favorite.

1 cup red bell pepper, seeded and chopped

1 cup cashews

2 tablespoons nutritional yeast

2 to 4 tablespoons water, as needed

2 tablespoons agave syrup

1 tablespoon olive oil

½ teaspoon sea salt

6 cups bite-size pieces of kale, tightly packed (about 1 bunch)

Place the red bell peppers in a blender, then the remaining ingredients, except for the kale. Blend, using only enough water to process into a thick cream.

In a large mixing bowl, toss the pepper mixture with the kale, coating it evenly.

Spread the kale onto two 14-inch-square Excalibur Dehydrator trays, and dry at 104°F for 8 to 10 hours.

OPTIONS: Use Cheddar-Kale Chips in Caterpillar Nori Roll (page 253) to add a chewy, sweet crunchiness.

CRACKERS

I'll start you off with a Basic Flax Cracker recipe, to which you can add flavorings, spices, and other ingredients to customize your own personal cracker flavors.

BASIC FLAX CRACKER

MAKES 9 CRACKERS

This crispy basic cracker recipe will show you how simple it is to make flax crackers. When flax is wet, it becomes gelatinous in consistency and binds together to make a dough that can be spread across your dehydrator tray on its liners or parchment paper. In general, you want to use about 2 to 3 cups of batter per 14-inch-square Excalibur Dehydrator tray.

When you do your first flip of the crackers in the dehydrator, score the dough with a dull butter knife to create lines along which to break up the crackers when they have dried. You can make nine slices of crispy "toast," or score the dough more finely to create square croutons to top salads and soups.

> **2 cups flaxseeds**
>
> **2 cups filtered water**
>
> **1 teaspoon sea salt, or to taste (optional)**

In a bowl, mix the flaxseeds with the water and salt. You'll notice the batter becoming gooey and the seeds begin to bind together to make a dough. Add a little bit more water if the batter becomes too thick to spread, but you don't want the batter dough to be watery.

Spread the batter evenly on a lined 14-inch-square Excalibur Dehydrator tray (line the tray with parchment paper). The batter should be about ⅛-inch thick.

Dehydrate for 5 to 6 hours at 104°F. Flip your crackers directly onto the mesh tray, then peel away the lining or paper. Using a butter knife, score lines in your batter to portion your cracker dough into nine squares. Dehydrate for another 3 to 4 hours, or until completely dried and crispy, then remove from the tray and bend along the score lines to break into slices.

OPTIONS: Add flavors and spices such as 1 tablespoon dried herbs (or 2 tablespoons fresh), 1 teaspoon of minced garlic, and ¼ cup sun-dried tomato or pitted, chopped olives.

To make your crackers less crispy, dehydrate less or add a tablespoon of olive oil.

And, as you'll see in the next recipe, adding vegetables increases the amount of cellulose fiber in your batter for a softer, lighter, breadlike texture.

TOMATO FLAX CRACKER

MAKES 9 CRACKERS

Once you've mastered the Basic Flax Cracker recipe (page 112), you can then experiment by replacing the filtered water with a watery vegetable instead, such as tomato, as in this recipe, or onion, celery, and carrot. The vegetable fiber will add a lighter texture to your cracker and more flavor and color.

> 2 cups flaxseeds
>
> 2 cups tomatoes
>
> 1 teaspoon minced garlic
>
> 1 cup water, or as needed

Place all the ingredients in a food processor and mix well, adding just enough water to create a spreadable batter consistency.

Spread the batter evenly on a lined 14-inch-square Excalibur Dehydrator tray. The batter should be about ⅛-inch thick.

Dehydrate for 5 to 6 hours at 104°F. Flip your crackers directly onto the mesh tray, and peel away the liner. Using a butter knife, score lines in your batter to portion your cracker into nine squares. Dehydrate for another 3 to 4 hours, or until completely dried and crispy, then remove from the tray and bend along the score lines to break into slices.

OPTIONS: Replace the tomato with another watery vegetable, such as red bell pepper, celery, onion, and even carrot. Add more filtered water as needed to create the right spreadable consistency.

KALAMATA OLIVE CROSTINI

MAKES 9 SERVINGS

Crostini means "little toasts" in Italian and are made by slicing bread thinly, then toasting and grilling it so it's crispy. Drizzle with olive oil or salt or serve with your favorite toppings; use as a garnish for soups; or use like croutons, broken up, on salad. The buckwheat gives this recipe a lighter, crispier texture.

½ cup dried buckwheat groats

1 cup chopped celery

1 cup flax meal

1½ cups filtered water

½ cup pitted and chopped kalamata olives

Grind the buckwheat into a powder, then place in a high-speed blender. Add the celery, flax meal, and water. Blend until smooth. Add the olives last; pulse lightly to mix into the batter.

Spread the batter evenly on a lined 14-inch-square Excalibur Dehydrator tray. Dehydrate for 6 to 8 hours at 104°F. Flip onto tray, peel away the liner, and score into nine squares. Score each slice diagonally so you have a total of eighteen little triangular toasts. Dehydrate for another 4 to 6 hours, until dried.

VEGETABLES

The act of cooking food steams away much of the food's water content. In the same way, dehydration is one way to "cook" vegetables in raw food.

Light dehydration will help to soften tough vegetables, such as asparagus, and wilts red bell peppers and onions to take their crunch away.

Dehydrating for longer periods of time, on the other hand, removes all moisture to create a light, crisp texture. Coating your vegetables in olive oil will help to soften them while also slowing down how quickly and fully their water is lost in your dehydrator.

• • •

BASIC BUCKWHEAT BATTER

MAKES 4 SERVINGS

Coat any vegetable with this basic batter and dehydrate, to add a light and crispy crunch to the outside—similar to a tempura or panko (Japanese bread crumb) batter, but lighter and healthier for you.

If you don't have Buckwheat Crispies on hand, just use buckwheat groats instead.

> 2 cups Buckwheat Crispies (page 63), ground into a powder
> 1 teaspoon sea salt
> ½ teaspoon cayenne

Place the buckwheat powder, salt, and cayenne in a bowl and mix well.

OPTIONS: Dip slices, sticks, or spears of your favorite vegetables and even fruit into this batter, and dehydrate to add a crunchy outer layer. To help the powder stick better, you may want to toss your veggies with a couple of tablespoons of olive oil first.

BUCKWHEAT-BATTERED "FRIED" ONION RINGS
MAKES 4 SERVINGS

Thinly sliced onion is dipped into buckwheat batter and dehydrated to create a battered and fried, delicious onion ring. The texture is similar to that of a lightly fried tempura batter, and the flavor is delicious!

The longer the onions are dehydrated, the milder the onion flavor will become. Using a sweet onion gives a milder onion flavor.

> **4 cups thinly sliced sweet onion**
>
> **3 tablespoons extra-virgin olive oil**
>
> **2 tablespoons filtered water**
>
> **1 recipe Basic Buckwheat Batter (page 115)**

Prep the onions by tossing in the oil and water. Then, dip the onions into the Basic Buckwheat Batter to coat well.

Gently place the onions in a single layer on two lined 14-inch-square Excalibur Dehydrator trays, and dehydrate at 104°F for 4 to 6 hours, or until completely dried and crisp.

BATTERED ZUCCHINI STICKS
MAKES 4 SERVINGS

Zucchini sticks are tossed in buckwheat batter, then dehydrated to soften the inside while adding a light crispy crunch to the outside.

> **3 zucchini, cut like French fries**
>
> **3 tablespoons extra-virgin olive oil**
>
> **2 tablespoons filtered water**
>
> **1 recipe Basic Buckwheat Batter (page 115)**

Prep the zucchini by tossing in the oil and water. Then, dip into the Basic Buckwheat Batter to coat well.

Gently place the zucchini sticks in a single layer on two lined 14-inch-square Excalibur Dehydrator trays, and dehydrate at 104°F for 5 to 7 hours, or until the outside is dried and crisp.

"ROASTED" BELL PEPPERS

MAKES 4 SERVINGS

Bell peppers are tossed in olive oil, then dehydrated to soften and remove the fresh crispiness of this vegetable. The result is a soft consistency like that of roasted peppers.

> **4 cups seeded and sliced red bell pepper**
> **½ cup extra-virgin olive oil**
> **1 teaspoon minced garlic**

Toss the bell pepper with the olive oil and garlic to mix well.

Gently place the bell pepper in a single layer on two lined 14-inch-square Excalibur Dehydrator trays, and dehydrate at 104°F for 3 to 5 hours, or until soft. Be careful not to overdry, you just want to soften the peppers.

If you leave them too long to dry, they will shrink and become crispy. If this happens, they will work great as a colorful sprinkle to add to soup and salads.

SEASONED NUTS

Marinated and dehydrated nuts are nice to keep on hand, to add an extra layer of crunch and flavor to any dish, savory or sweet. Use them to top salads, ice cream sundaes, and crepes.

Just marinate the nuts and spread on dehydrator trays. Dehydrate and enjoy.

• • •

TAMARI ALMONDS

MAKES 2 CUPS

These almonds make a great topping for Asian-inspired noodle dishes, such as Pad Thai with Kelp Noodles (page 227) and Sesame Noodles (page 228).

¼ cup Nama Shoyu or Bragg Liquid Aminos

1 tablespoon onion powder

½ teaspoon sea salt

2 cups almonds

Place Nama Shoyu, onion powder, and salt in a mixing bowl and mix well. Add the almonds and mix to coat well.

Spread the almonds on a lined 14-inch-square Excalibur Dehydrator tray, and dehydrate for 2 to 3 hours at 104°F, or until dried.

STICKY MAPLE-PEPPER PECANS

MAKES 2 CUPS

This recipe calls on maple syrup for its flavor. Maple syrup is not raw, though, so if you're concerned, use agave instead.

> 1/4 cup maple or agave syrup
>
> 1 teaspoon sea salt
>
> 1/2 teaspoon cayenne
>
> 2 cups pecan halves

Place the syrup, salt, and cayenne in a mixing bowl and mix well. Add the pecans and mix to coat well.

Spread the pecans on a lined 14-inch-square Excalibur Dehydrator tray and dehydrate for 2 to 4 hours at 104°F, until dried.

GINGER CANDIED WALNUTS

MAKES 2 CUPS

Sweet walnuts candied with agave syrup, flavored with a hint of fresh ginger. These nuts spruce up both savory and sweet dishes.

> 1/4 cup agave syrup
>
> 1 teaspoon sea salt
>
> 1 tablespoon grated fresh ginger, or 1 teaspoon ground
>
> 2 cups walnut halves

Place the syrup, salt, and ginger in a mixing bowl and mix well. Add the pecans and mix to coat well.

Spread the pecans on a lined 14-inch-square Excalibur Dehydrator tray, and dehydrate for 2 to 4 hours at 104°F, until dried.

PICKLED VEGETABLES

Raw sauerkraut, kimchi, and pickles are examples of live-culture probiotic foods that contain lactobacilli, a beneficial bacteria that improves our digestion and over-all health. Pickled vegetables are a good source of fiber and such essential nutri-ents as iron, vitamins K and C and are a great way to preserve cabbage and other vegetables.

Live-culture foods help restore beneficial bacteria we've damaged by taking antibi-otics, which kill both good and harmful bacteria in our body. Damage caused to our flora by poor diet, stress, and pharmaceuticals can lead to life-threatening diseases.

Probiotics support healthy elimination of waste from our body. When elimination is poor, toxic waste sits in our intestines and is reabsorbed into our body. A healthy gut contributes to our overall well-being.

Enjoy the pickled vegetables in this chapter as an accompaniment to most savory dishes, cooked or raw. They'll improve digestion so you can absorb more nutrients from the food you eat, plus you'll feel more energized.

SAUERKRAUT

Sauerkraut is an easy pickled vegetable to make. All you need to do is slice your cabbage, place it in a saltwater brine, then leave it to ferment.

Cabbage ferments quickly at room temperature and is ready to eat in 2 to 3 weeks. When temperatures are cooler, fermentation takes longer, but the sauerkraut will be crunchier and have more flavor. Once it's ready to eat, store your kraut in the re-frigerator to keep it from spoiling. If it turns dark brown, it's gone bad.

Here is a basic recipe:

BASIC GREEN CABBAGE SAUERKRAUT

MAKES ABOUT 6 CUPS
PICKLING TIME: 2 WEEKS

Cabbage is softened in saltwater, then left at room temperature to ferment and pickle. Using a mandoline slicer will make it easier to shred your cabbage.

1 tablespoon sea salt

1 cup filtered water

1½ pounds green cabbage (about 1 medium head), cored and grated into ⅛-inch strips.

Place the salt and water in a large bowl; mix to dissolve the salt. Add the cabbage and mix well. Place a plate on top of the cabbage in the bowl. Next, add a weight on top of the plate. Stacks of more plates work well, or if you're camping, use large, clean rocks. Cover and set aside the container at room temperature for 2 days.

Check your sauerkraut, and skim off any thin layer (a skin) you may see on top. Then, repack it down again. Check every 3 days. After 2 weeks, taste to see if it tastes ready for eating. Once it's to your liking, transfer it to a glass quart jar, and store in the fridge.

Will keep for many weeks in the fridge. The flavor will mature for the next few weeks.

GARLIC SAUERKRAUT

MAKES ABOUT 6 CUPS

PICKLING TIME: 2 WEEKS

It's easy to make new sauerkraut flavors by adding spices and herbs such as fresh dill, thyme, rosemary, or chiles. Here, I add garlic and onion to give it a more savory flavor.

1 recipe Basic Green Cabbage Sauerkraut (page 121)

2 cloves garlic, chopped

1 sliced yellow onion

Follow the recipe for Basic Green Cabbage Sauerkraut, adding the garlic and onion before setting the sauerkraut to ferment.

CUCUMBER PICKLES

Pickles are faster and even easier to make than sauerkraut. And I've included a couple of recipes here so you can make some to enjoy with your sun burgers and in your Thousand Island Dressing (see page 188).

I include two types of recipes. The first is vinegar free, made using a salt brine, and is ready in one day. The second uses vinegar as a way to speed up the pickling process, which happens overnight.

SLICED CUCUMBER PICKLES (VINEGAR-FREE)

MAKES ABOUT 1 CUP
PICKLING TIME: 1 DAY

Cucumber is softened in salt and lemon juice, then set aside for a day to pickle. Add 2 tablespoons of fresh dill, or other dried or fresh herbs and spices, to this basic recipe to make additional flavors.

> 1 cup peeled cucumber, cut into 1/4-inch-thick rounds
>
> 1 teaspoon sea salt
>
> 2 tablespoons lemon juice

In a mixing bowl, toss the ingredients together. Place in a pickle press, under pressure. Or, place a plate over the mixture in the bowl, and stack heavy plates on top of it. Set aside at room temperature for a day.

Will keep in the fridge for several days.

SLICED PICKLES IN VINEGAR

MAKES 1 QUART
PICKLING TIME: OVERNIGHT

Sliced cucumber, carrot, and onion are softened in vinegar and salt. They're flavored with pickling spice, which is usually made up of allspice, bay leaves, cardamom, cinnamon, cloves, coriander, ginger, mustard seeds, and peppercorns.
  This recipe will be ready to enjoy after pickling overnight.

> 3/4 cup apple cider vinegar
>
> 1 teaspoon sea salt
>
> 2 teaspoons ground pickling spice
>
> 1 cup filtered water
>
> 1 cup cucumber (use one 6 to 8 inches in length), peeled and cut into 1/4-inch-thick rounds
>
> 1/2 cup carrot peeled and cut into 1/4-inch pieces
>
> 1/4 cup sweet yellow onion, sliced into 1/4-inch pieces

Place the vinegar, salt, pickling spice, and water into a 1-quart mason jar with a lid. Mix well. Add the remaining ingredients and close the lid tightly. Shake to mix well.

Set aside at room temperature for 3 to 4 hours. Then place in the fridge overnight.

Will keep for a week or more in the fridge.

KIMCHI

The Korean style of pickling and culturing vegetables is my favorite, perhaps because of my Korean heritage, or because I love spices and the kick of garlic and ginger.

Traditionally, kimchi was made to last through long, cold winter months when fresh vegetables weren't available, and recipes vary by region and family taste. Kimchi can be made with different vegetables, cabbages, cucumbers, and daikon radishes, to name a few variations.

As I developed the kimchi recipes in this chapter, I'd pass them to my mother to make sure they still taste authentically Korean. Sometimes, she'd call one of her two sisters (one's in New York City; and the other, in Seoul, Korea) for another opinion. So be assured these recipes are pretty close to the traditional flavors and textures. Mom and my friend So Young, both of whom are from Korea, helped me change Korean ingredients to those found here in the States.

I start you off in this section with simple recipes such as Napa Cabbage Kimchi, made by softening cabbage in salt water, then adding spices and setting aside for a few days to pickle.

For the recipes in the later part of this section, I recommend making a jar of Kimchi Sauce, a spicy red pepper paste, to keep on hand. When you find your favorite kimchi vegetables on sale, you can bring them home and make a jar of kimchi quickly and easily with this premade sauce.

Enjoy my simplified vegan versions of Korean-inspired kimchi as an accompaniment to any dish, on salads, even in sandwiches when you want to kick up the flavor from just everyday lettuce.

NAPA CABBAGE KIMCHI

MAKES ABOUT 8 CUPS (1/2 GALLON)
PICKLING TIME: 2 TO 3 DAYS

This is the simplest recipe for making spicy Korean-style kimchi and will be ready to eat in about 3 days. Cabbage is softened in salt water, then spices are added. Cabbage is set aside for 2 to 3 days to marinate, ferment, and ripen.

If you don't have Korean chili powder, just use the kind of red pepper flakes sprinkled on pizza. Grind it into a powder before using.

> 1 napa cabbage, cut crosswise into 2-inch chunks
>
> 1/2 medium-size daikon radish, peeled and cut into quarters lengthwise, then into 1/2-inch-thick chunks
>
> 2 tablespoons sea salt
>
> 1/2 cup water
>
> 2 green onions, sliced into 2-inch lengths
>
> 3 cloves garlic, minced
>
> 1 tablespoons grated fresh ginger
>
> 1 tablespoons Korean chili powder

Place the cabbage and daikon pieces in a large mixing bowl.

Place the salt and water in a separate small bowl; mix to dissolve. Pour over the vegetables. Set aside at room temperature overnight to soften.

The next day, drain, reserving the saltwater the vegetables were soaked in. Add the green onions, garlic, ginger, and chili powder to the cabbage mixture, and mix well.

Tightly pack the mixture into a 1/2-gallon glass jar with a lid. Pour the saved saltwater into the jar, leaving 1 inch of space at the top. Tightly close the lid.

Leave the jar in a cool, dark place for 2 to 3 days (depending on the temperature and how pickled and fermented you want your kimchi). Refrigerate after opening.

Will keep for a couple of weeks in the fridge.

PICKLED GREEN PEPPERS

MAKES ABOUT 8 CUPS (½ GALLON)
PICKLING TIME: 2 WEEKS

Instead of softening in saltwater, peppers are preserved in soy sauce and vinegar. Enjoy these savory peppers whole or sliced and served as a side dish or accompaniment. Pickles will be ready to eat in 2 weeks.

1 pound Korean green peppers or Anaheim chiles, washed

¾ cup Nama Shoyu

¾ cup apple cider vinegar

¾ cup filtered water

2 tablespoons agave syrup

Place the peppers in a ½-gallon glass jar with a lid. Add the Nama Shoyu and vinegar.

In a small bowl, mix the water and agave syrup well. Pour over the peppers.

Tightly close the jar and store in a cool, dark, dry place for 2 weeks. Refrigerate after opening.

Will keep in the fridge for at least a couple of months.

SPICY KOREAN CUCUMBER SLICES

MAKES ABOUT 2 CUPS
PICKLING TIME: 10 MINUTES

Sliced cucumbers are softened in salt, then spiced with red pepper, tart vinegar, sweet agave, and sesame oil. I prefer using toasted sesame oil for the flavor. If you want to keep this raw, just substitute with raw sesame oil and some sesame seeds. If you don't have Korean chili powder, just use red pepper flakes ground into a powder instead.

This pickle requires no pickling time and is ready to eat after about 10 minutes of softening time.

2 cups cucumbers, unpeeled, sliced ¼-inch thick

1 tablespoon sea salt

1 teaspoon Korean chili powder, or to taste

2 teaspoons apple cider vinegar

1 teaspoon agave syrup

3 tablespoons julienned carrots

1 tablespoon toasted sesame oil

Place the cucumbers in a mixing bowl and toss to coat with the salt. Set aside for 5 to 10 minutes to soften and release liquid. Gently squeeze the excess liquid from the cucumbers, and discard the liquid.

Return the cucumbers to the mixing bowl. Add the chili powder, vinegar, agave syrup, carrots, and sesame oil, and toss to mix well.

Will keep for 3 days in the fridge.

OPTION: Add 1 teaspoon of sesame seeds when tossing.

PICKLED GINGER

MAKES 2 CUPS

PICKLING TIME: 1 WEEK

This recipe is ready to eat in a week's time. A great side dish, accompaniment, and relish. Ginger's great for decreasing inflammation and increasing circulation.

Enjoy this with the Japanese-style *nori maki* recipes (pages 253 to 259).

> **2 pounds fresh ginger, peeled, washed, and sliced paper-thin**
>
> **1 cup apple cider vinegar**
>
> **¼ cup agave syrup**

Into a 2-quart glass jar with a lid, place spiral layers of the ginger. Stack one layer on top of another.

In a mixing bowl, combine the vinegar and agave syrup. Stir to mix well. Pour into the jar with the ginger.

Close the jar lid tightly and leave to marinate and ferment at room temperature for 1 week. The vinegar and ginger will change color to pale pink.

Store the jar in the fridge, where it'll keep for several months.

KIMCHI SAUCE

MAKES ABOUT 2½ CUPS

If you're into investing a bit of time up-front, make up a jar of this sauce to keep in your fridge. It'll make it easy to make kimchi later.

You'll be salting and wilting your vegetables, draining, then rubbing on a few spoonfuls of this sauce before setting them aside to pickle.

You ideally want to use Korean chili flakes to make this sauce, for their unique flavor. But, if they aren't available, just use red pepper flakes, making sure to grind them into a powder before using them.

> **1 cup Korean chili flakes**
>
> **½ cup water**
>
> **4 tablespoons Garlic Paste (page 130)**
>
> **2 teaspoons minced fresh ginger**
>
> **1 tablespoon fine sea salt**
>
> **2 tablespoons agave syrup**

Place all the ingredients in a mixing bowl. Using a rubber spatula, mix into a smooth paste. Transfer the paste to a glass jar with a lid.

Will keep for 2 months in the fridge, if sealed in an airtight jar.

Garlic Paste

GARLIC PASTE IS more flavorful than minced garlic, with a smoother consistency. To make your paste, process peeled cloves until smooth in a food processor.

Garlic paste can be kept in a closed glass jar in the fridge for 2 to 3 months, and in your freezer for up to 6 months. The paste will darken over time, and the flavor will deepen.

CUBED DAIKON RADISH KIMCHI

MAKES ABOUT 4 CUPS

PICKLING TIME: 1 DAY

This is the easiest of the kimchis to make. Simply cut daikon radish into cubes and sprinkle with sea salt. Add Kimchi Sauce, and set aside to marinate. It'll be ready to eat in just a day.

It's very important to always protect your skin from the spicy Kimchi Sauce when mixing with your hands, by wearing rubber or disposable latex or plastic gloves.

Cubes are a traditional shape for this kimchi, but I like to cut my daikon into strips rather than cubes because I think they look prettier and have a texture that I like even more.

> 2 pounds daikon radishes (about 2 large), sliced into 1-inch cubes (wash and chop the leaves also if you desire)
>
> 2 tablespoons coarse sea salt
>
> ½ cup Kimchi Sauce (page 129)
>
> 4 green onions, sliced into 1-inch lengths
>
> 1 small apple, peeled, cored, and grated

Place the daikon cubes and optional leaves in a large bowl. Sprinkle with the sea salt and set aside at room temperature for 2 hours to wilt.

Drain any liquid from the daikon and place the cubes and leaves in a dry bowl. Add the Kimchi Sauce. Put on a pair of gloves, then rub to coat the daikon with the Kimchi Sauce. Add the green onion and apple, and mix well.

Place the mixture in a glass 1-quart jar and close the lid tightly. Leave for one day at room temperature to pickle. Refrigerate after opening.

Will keep for 2 weeks in the fridge.

GREEN CABBAGE KIMCHI

MAKES ABOUT 6 CUPS

PICKLING TIME: 1 DAY

This is my Korean version of Basic Green Cabbage Sauerkraut. Rather than being shredded, the cabbage is sliced into 2-inch squares. It is soaked in salt water, then drained and rubbed with Kimchi Sauce before setting aside to pickle, and is ready to eat after one day.

> **1 recipe Basic Green Cabbage Sauerkraut (page 121),
>   sliced into 2-inch squares**
>
> **5 tablespoons Kimchi Sauce (page 129)**

In large bowl, combine the salt and water; mix to dissolve the salt. Add the cabbage and soak for 2 hours.

Drain and discard the water from the cabbage. Put on gloves to protect your hands, add the Kimchi Sauce, and rub into the cabbage.

Place the mixture in a ½-gallon glass jar and close the lid tightly. Leave for one day at room temperature. Store in the fridge after opening.

Will keep for 2 weeks in the fridge.

STUFFED MINI CUCUMBER KIMCHI

MAKES 8 CUCUMBERS

PICKLING TIME: 1 DAY

Mini cucumbers are stuffed with daikon, onion, and green onions to make a pretty Korean-style spicy pickle. Only one day of pickling time is needed before you can enjoy them.

> **8 mini cucumbers**
>
> **1 tablespoon sea salt**
>
> STUFFING
>
> **1 cup julienned daikon radish**
>
> **¼ cup julienned yellow onion**
>
> **2 julienned green onions**
>
> **2 tablespoons Kimchi Sauce (page 129)**

Slice each cucumber lengthwise, leaving 1 inch at the bottom uncut. Rotate and cut lengthwise again, again leaving 1 inch at the bottom uncut. (The 1-inch base holds together the four sliced quarters of each cucumber.)

Place the cucumbers in the bottom of a small tray or bowl, and sprinkle salt inside the flesh and on the outside of the cucumbers. Set aside for 2 hours at room temperature.

Drain and discard the liquid from the cucumbers.

In a separate bowl, combine the stuffing ingredients and mix well. Use one-eighth of the stuffing mixture per cucumber, fill open spaces of each cucumber, fitting the cucumber quarters tightly against the stuffing.

Pack the stuffed cucumbers into glass jars to fit them tightly (don't choose jars that will leave extra air around the cukes). Close the lids tightly and enjoy the following day.

Will keep for 3 days in the fridge.

6
SOUPS

RAW SOUPS ARE made using pretty much the same ingredients as in cooked soup, with the ingredients simply blended together rather than cooked on the stove. Raw soups are faster to make, and cleanup is much easier, as all you have to do is rinse out the blender container.

Nuts are blended in to create a creamy soup consistency; then, toppings will add another layer of texture, flavor, and color.

I'm frequently asked about hot soups and raw food in cold winter months. I've personally found raw food best enjoyed in hotter climates. If you want a warm soup, you can just keep the blender going longer to create a low heat. Keep checking the heat level with your finger if you want to keep it raw. Once it gets warm to your touch, stop blending.

If you're craving a hot soup and aren't as concerned with keeping it 100 percent raw, you can heat these soups in a saucepan to your desired temperature. They are still superhealthy and free of chemical preservatives, flavorings, and colorings and have been made from scratch, using whole, fresh, organic ingredients. But do keep in mind that beneficial enzymes are damaged at higher temperatures. For me, raw is below 104°F, and any hotter damages nutrients and enzymes.

TORTILLA SOUP WITH JALAPEÑO-LIME KREAM

MAKES 4 SERVINGS

Tomatoes are blended with cumin, oregano, and garlic to make the base for this soup. It's then topped with chips, fresh cilantro, and a dollop of Jalapeño-Lime Kream.

SOUP BASE

3 cups chopped tomatoes

1 cup olive oil

2 teaspoons sea salt

1 teaspoon garlic

1 teaspoon jalapeño pepper, to taste

$^1/_2$ teaspoon ground cumin

$^1/_2$ teaspoon dried oregano

2 cups water

TOPPINGS

1 recipe Salted Flax Chips (page 108), sliced, for garnish

$^1/_4$ cup fresh cilantro, chopped finely

1 recipe Jalapeño-Lime Kream (page 134)

Place all the soup ingredients in a high-speed blender and blend until smooth. Divide among four serving bowls. Top each portion with sliced Salted Flax Chips, cilantro, and a dollop of Jalapeño-Lime Kream, and serve immediately.

JALAPEÑO-LIME KREAM

MAKES 1 CUP

A fresh green jalapeño pepper and tart lime are blended in a cashew kream. This savory kream can top soups, pastas, or can add spice to sandwiches and wraps. For a spicier kick, leave the seeds in the jalapeño.

I use a smaller Personal Blender to make just one cup of this kream. If you're using a larger blender, you'll need to double this recipe to make sure the mixture covers the blades to blend properly. You can also use a food processor, but you won't get the same smooth texture as you would by blending.

1 cup cashews

$^1/_4$ cup seeded, chopped jalapeño pepper (about 2 whole)

1 teaspoon lime zest

¼ cup lime juice (from about 2 limes)

1 tablespoon extra-virgin olive oil

½ teaspoon sea salt

¼ cup filtered water, or as needed

Begin by grinding half of your cashews at a time into a powder. Place this powder in a 1-cup blender. Add the remaining ingredients and blend until smooth. Add only enough water as needed to produce a smooth, creamy consistency.

Will keep for 3 days in the fridge.

CORN CHOWDER

MAKES 4 SERVINGS

This is a chunky soup made in your food processor. Corn is mixed with thyme and garlic to make a delicious chowder that's topped with Coconut Bacon bits and a dollop of Jalapeño-Lime Kream.

1 teaspoon garlic

½ teaspoon dried thyme

½ teaspoon sea salt

4 cups corn kernels (from about 4 ears of corn)

¼ cup extra-virgin olive oil

2 cups water

1 recipe Coconut Bacon (page 76), diced

1 recipe Jalapeño-Lime Kream (page 134)

Place the garlic, thyme, and salt in a food processor, and process into small pieces. Add the corn, oil, and water and process into a chunky chowder.

Divide among four serving bowls. Top each portion with diced Coconut Bacon and a dollop of Jalapeño-Lime Kream, and serve immediately.

TOMATO AND TARRAGON BISQUE

MAKES 4 SERVINGS

Tomatoes are blended with tarragon, parsley, and a hint of nutmeg to create a uniquely spiced tomato soup. Garnish with fresh sprigs of tarragon.

SOUP BASE

3 cups seeded and chopped tomatoes

$3/4$ cup extra-virgin olive oil

1 teaspoon chopped garlic

$1/8$ teaspoon grated nutmeg

1 tablespoon fresh tarragon, packed

1 teaspoon fresh parsley, packed

2 teaspoons sea salt

2 cups water

TOPPING

Tarragon sprigs, for garnish

Place all the soup ingredients in a high-speed blender and blend until smooth. Divide among four serving bowls.

Garnish each portion with tarragon sprigs and serve immediately.

SERVING SUGGESTION: Thinly slice greens, such as mild spinach, sweet romaine, or heartier kale or chard, and use them to top the soup, for added texture and color.

KREAM OF BROCCOLI WITH RED BELL PEPPER KREAM

MAKES 4 SERVINGS

Broccoli is blended with sweet cashews to make the soup base. Because raw food is all about simulating the look, flavors, and textures of the cooked version, I've added spinach for a greener color while also helping to mellow out the strong taste of raw broccoli.

SOUP BASE

1 cup chopped broccoli

1 cup spinach, washed well and packed

1 cup cashews

½ cup extra-virgin olive oil

2 teaspoons sea salt

2 cups water

TOPPING

1 recipe Red Pepper Kream (page 138)

Place all the soup ingredients in a high-speed blender and blend until smooth. Divide among four serving bowls.

Top each portion with a dollop of Red Pepper Kream and serve immediately.

RED PEPPER KREAM

MAKES 1 CUP

Creamy cashews are blended with red bell peppers for color and flavor. Tart lemon juice and a pinch of salt are added for a full flavor profile.

I like to use my smaller blender to make this kream. If you're using a larger blender, double the recipe so your blender blades are covered. You can also use a food processor; your kream will just not be as smooth as when blended.

½ cup cashews

1 cup seeded and chopped red bell pepper

1 tablespoon lemon juice

½ teaspoon sea salt

2 tablespoons filtered water, or as needed

Begin by grinding your cashews into a powder. Then, place all the ingredients in a Personal Blender and blend until smooth.

Will keep for 3 days in the fridge. Stir before using.

MANGO GAZPACHO

MAKES 4 SERVINGS

A refreshingly cool, sweet, and tart fruit soup that's perfect for summertime. Fruit is mixed with fresh mint, tart lime, spicy ginger, and cayenne.

   Have fun substituting your favorite fruits for the diced pineapple and melon. Apples and pears work great, too. The spice of the cayenne is a great complement to the sweet fruits.

- 2 cups cubed mango
- 1 cup orange juice
- 1 cup pineapple, diced into $1/2$-inch pieces
- 1 cup of your favorite melon, diced into $1/2$-inch pieces
- $1/2$ cup mango, diced into $1/2$-inch pieces
- 2 tablespoons chopped mint leaves
- 1 tablespoon lime juice (from about 1 large lime)
- 1 tablespoon minced fresh ginger
- $1/8$ teaspoon cayenne, or to taste

Place the cubed mango and orange juice in a blender and blend until smooth. Transfer to a mixing bowl. Add the remaining ingredients and toss to mix well. Chill for 30 minutes before serving.

Will keep for 2 days in the fridge.

GAZPACHO ANDALUZ

MAKES 4 SERVINGS

A Spanish-inspired chunky version of gazpacho made with diced tomatoes and chopped bell pepper, cucumber, and Spanish onion.

2 cups seeded and diced ripe tomato

1/4 cup finely chopped Spanish onion

1 cup chopped bell pepper (any color)

1 cup peeled and chopped cucumber

1/3 cup extra-virgin olive oil

1 teaspoon minced garlic

1 tablespoon lemon juice (from about 1/2 lemon)

1/4 teaspoon sea salt

2 cups filtered water

Place all the ingredients in a mixing bowl and mix well. Chill for at least 30 minutes before serving.

TOM YAM GOONG

MAKES 4 SERVINGS

A Thai-inspired hot and sour soup with the flavor of kaffir lime leaves and peppery galangal.

Galangal is a pale yellow root related to the ginger root. Feel free to use the same amount of ginger if you can't find galangal. You can also use your favorite mushrooms instead of straw mushrooms.

TOPPINGS

1/4 cup thinly sliced shallot

1/2 cup sliced straw mushrooms

3 tablespoons chopped green chile peppers (about 3 Thai or 1 serrano pepper)

1/4 cup lime juice

1 tablespoon Nama Shoyu or Bragg Liquid Aminos

1/4 cup extra-virgin olive oil

2 tablespoons chopped cilantro leaves, for garnish

SOUP BASE

1 teaspoon garlic

5 medium kaffir lime leaves

1 tablespoon galangal or ginger root

2 tablespoons chopped lemongrass, lower stalks only

1/8 teaspoon cayenne

3 cups filtered water

Prepare the topping first: Marinate the shallot, mushrooms, and peppers in the lime juice, Nama Shoyu, and olive oil for at least 15 minutes. Set aside.

Place all the soup ingredients in a high speed blender. Blend to mix well. If you're not using a high-speed blender, you'll want to grate and chop your ingredients before blending. Pour the soup base through a mesh strainer into a large serving bowl.

Top the soup with the marinated mixture and chopped cilantro before serving.

WONTONS IN A LIGHT SESAME-SOY BROTH WITH PEAS

MAKES 4 SERVINGS

Marinated napa cabbage is packed inside Apple Crepe squares to make wontons. The marinade and peas are added to water, for a light broth in which to serve the wontons.

Another option is to thinly slice daikon radish to use as your wrapper. Slice as thinly as possible, then fill the circles with the filling and fold into semicircular wontons.

WONTONS

2 cups finely chopped napa cabbage

2 tablespoons finely sliced yellow onion

1/4 cup finely chopped green onions

1 tablespoon Nama Shoyu or Bragg Liquid Aminos

1 tablespoon toasted sesame oil

1 recipe Apple Crepes (page 69), dehydrated as directed

SOUP BASE

1/2 cup peas, fresh or frozen

4 cups water

To make the wonton filling, place the cabbage, green onions, Nama Shoyu, and sesame oil in a bowl and toss to mix well. Set aside for at least 15 minutes to marinate and soften.

To make the wonton wrappers, cut the Apple Crepes into sixteen 3½-inch squares.

To fill the wontons, first squeeze all excess liquid from the marinated filling, saving the marinade to use in the soup base. Then, place about a teaspoon of filling in the center of each wonton wrapper. Hold the wrapper shiny side up; that's the side that was against the lining. Fold in half diagonally to make a triangle shape, making sure the ends meet. Press down firmly on the ends to seal. Wet the corners of your triangle by dipping your fingertip in a small bowl of water, and bring the two ends together so they overlap. Press to seal. (See Mandu Making, page 238.)

To make the soup base, pour the marinade into a large bowl, along with peas and water. Mix well. Ladle into four serving bowls. Add the wontons and serve immediately.

OPTION: Instead of using Apple Crepes, you can slice daikon radish circles paper thin. Fill, and fold in half to form a semicircle.

MEXICAN LIME SOUP

The inspiration for this dish comes from a *sopa de Lima* recipe from the Yucatán, which is a tart soup. If you can find them, use Mexican or key limes in this recipe. You can even use lemon with the lime, to up the tartness.

½ cup sliced yellow onion

½ cup seeded and chopped mild green chiles (about 2 large)

¼ cup lime juice

1 teaspoon sea salt

1 teaspoon minced garlic

1 teaspoon fresh thyme, or ½ teaspoon dried

1 tablespoon extra-virgin olive oil

2 cups filtered water

2 cups seeded and chopped tomatoes

¼ cup chopped cilantro

2 large ripe avocados, pitted and sliced

Begin by placing the onion, chiles, lime juice, salt, garlic, thyme, and olive oil in a mixing bowl. Set aside to marinate and soften for at least 20 minutes.

Place the water and tomatoes in a high-speed blender. Blend until smooth. Add the marinated vegetables with their marinade. Pulse gently to mix.

To serve, divide among four serving bowls. Top with the cilantro and avocado slices. Serve immediately.

SERVING SUGGESTION: Serve with 1 recipe of Soft Corn Tortilla (page 173).

CURRIED COCONUT SOUP

MAKES 4 SERVINGS

Cool cucumber and tomato is blended with creamy avocado. Tart lemon juice, coconut oil, and curry powder give this soup a rich consistency and flavor.

> 1 cup diced ripe avocado (about 1 large avocado)
>
> 1½ cups peeled and diced cucumber
>
> 1 cup seeded and diced tomato
>
> 2 tablespoons lemon juice (from about 1 lemon)

⅓ cup coconut oil, set at room temperature until liquid

¼ cup fresh cilantro

1 tablespoon curry powder

1 teaspoon minced garlic

1 teaspoon sea salt

1 cup coconut milk from a young Thai baby coconut, or filtered water

Place all the ingredients in a blender and blend until smooth.

To serve, divide among serving bowls. Top each portion with fresh cilantro leaves. Enjoy immediately.

Will keep for 1 day in the fridge.

TOMATO CHILI WITH TACO NUT MEAT (BEAN-FREE)

MAKES 4 SERVINGS

A vegetable chili made with chopped tomatoes, bell peppers, celery, mushrooms, and corn kernels. Spiced with cumin and oregano, for a real chili flavor similar to the cooked bean version. Top with Taco Nut Meat for an added layer of texture and Southwest flavor.

3 cups seeded and chopped tomatoes

1 cup seeded and chopped, mixed red and green bell pepper

¼ cup chopped celery

¼ cup chopped yellow onion

⅓ cup chopped mushroom (any type)

⅓ cup corn kernels

1 teaspoon minced garlic

2 teaspoons chile powder

1 teaspoon ground cumin

¾ teaspoon dried oregano

¼ teaspoon sea salt

1 recipe Taco Nut Meat (page 146)

Place all the ingredients in a mixing bowl and mix well. Transfer about one-third of the mixture to a high-speed blender and puree. Place the puree back in the mixing bowl.

To serve, divide among four serving bowls. Top each portion with Taco Nut Meat (recipe follows), and enjoy.

SERVING SUGGESTION: Serve topped with a dollop of Jalapeño-Lime Kream (page 134).

TACO NUT MEAT
MAKES ABOUT 1 CUP

Walnuts are ground and spiced with cumin and coriander to make this taco-flavored nut meat crumble. Use it to top salads and soups, and inside wraps to add taco flavor and texture.

> 1 cup walnuts
> 1 tablespoon extra-virgin olive oil
> 1 tablespoon ground cumin
> 2 teaspoons ground coriander
> 1 teaspoon Bragg Liquid Aminos or Nama Shoyu
> ¼ teaspoon sea salt, or to taste

Place the walnuts in a food processor and process into small pieces. Add the remaining ingredients; pulse to mix well.

Will keep for 1 week in the fridge.

7

SALADS AND DRESSINGS

SALADS MAY SOUND basic and dull—after all, it's what a lot of people think of immediately when they hear "raw food." But there's a world of delicious salads waiting to be discovered. By mixing up different vegetables, textures, colors, and flavors, along with the change in our seasons, no two salads ever need to be alike.

I start this chapter by introducing you to three Basic Dressing recipes to show you how easy they are to make. From here, you can add flavors, herbs, and spices to make as many new varieties of dressings as your heart desires.

There's also an endless variety of salad mixes to explore. My recipes use everyday greens such as romaine and cabbage, watercress, seaweed, and Asian greens. You can always add dried or fresh fruits, too, such as papaya and cranberries.

I remember growing up in upstate New York, where the salads were mostly just iceberg lettuce with bottled dressings. Iceberg is refreshing in summer months with a Japanese-style light ginger dressing. But there are so many options with all sorts of leaves, vegetables, and even seaweed, that we can all be more creative. The possibilities are endless.

BASIC WHISKED DRESSING
MAKES 4 SERVINGS

This is the fastest dressing to make and requires only a bowl and spoon, or a whisk. Just mix together vinegar and your favorite oil with a pinch of salt and pepper. You can replace the 2 teaspoons of vinegar with 1 tablespoon lemon or lime juice, and add fresh or dried herbs and spices to mix it up.

On days when I don't even care to make any dressing at all, I'll just drizzle these ingredients directly onto my bowl of greens and toss. You can change the flavors by using different types of oil, such as hemp or flax, or oils infused with herbs.

2 teaspoons apple cider vinegar

3 tablespoons extra-virgin olive oil

½ teaspoon sea salt

A pinch of pepper

Place all the dressing ingredients into a small bowl and whisk together. Toss with about 6 cups of greens (about 1 pound).

OPTIONS: Try adding 1 tablespoon of chopped shallots or green onions, 2 tablespoons of chives, ½ teaspoon of grated garlic or ginger, or 1 tablespoon of agave syrup.

Beyond Olive Oil

TO MIX up your dressing flavors, try using other oils such as hemp, almond, sesame, flax, or coconut oil instead of olive oil. For this dressing, you'll want to lighten your oil with a bit of tartness from vinegar or citrus, such lemon, lime, or even orange for a sweeter taste.

Here's the basic ratio for mixing a tart liquid with oil to make a dressing:

3 tablespoons oil
1 tablespoon citrus juice, or 2 teaspoons apple cider vinegar
Black pepper and sea salt

Adjust the ratios to suit your taste buds. When I use a stronger oil such as hemp, for example, I may decrease the oil quantity and use only 2 tablespoons of it to 1 tablespoon of citrus juice. Or I may even use 1 tablespoon of hemp oil and 1 tablespoon of olive oil. Season to taste.

BASIC BLENDED DRESSING

MAKES 1 CUP

Dressings can be made with pretty much any vegetable or fruit. Just blend with a bit of olive oil.

To mix it up, add your favorite flavorings, such as garlic, fresh or dried herbs, or curry. And, if you like your dressing tarter, add 1 tablespoon of lemon or lime juice, or 1 to 2 teaspoons of apple cider vinegar.

If using a larger blender, you may want to double this recipe. I recommend doubling anyway so you'll have extra on hand in the fridge to use as a sauce for noodles or dressing on your next salad.

> 1 cup chopped fruit or vegetable, such as apple, orange,
>   red bell pepper, or tomato
>
> 1/3 cup extra-virgin olive oil
>
> 1/2 teaspoon sea salt, or to taste

Place all the ingredients in a Personal Blender and blend until smooth. If using a dry vegetable such as carrot, you may need to add a couple of tablespoons of water to achieve your desired consistency.

OPTIONS: Add 1 teaspoon of minced garlic, 1/2 teaspoon of fresh herbs such as oregano or basil, or 1/4 teaspoon of dried herbs. Try using other oils such as sesame or hemp.

CROUTONS

As in cooked food, croutons are squares of bread or crackers. You can use any of my cracker, bread, or pizza crust recipes cut into smaller squares as croutons. I particularly like my Nori Croutons for salads. The nori gives a salty flavor that brings out the flavor of most vegetables and dressings and adds more minerals from the ocean when sprinkled over any dish.

NORI CROUTONS

MAKES ABOUT 9 SERVINGS

Light, crispy croutons made with buckwheat, flax, and nori. Nori is a sea vegetable that's high in minerals and makes a great nutritional, as well as delicious, addition to any salad or soup.

> ⅓ cup dried buckwheat groats
>
> 1 cup flax meal
>
> 2 cups filtered water
>
> ¼ cup chopped nori, or laver flakes
>
> ½ cup brown flaxseeds

Grind the buckwheat into a powder; set aside.

Place the flax and water in a high-speed blender and blend to mix well. Add the buckwheat powder; blend to mix well. Add the nori and whole flaxseeds. Pulse gently to mix, being careful not to blend. You want to keep the nori and flaxseeds whole.

Spread evenly on a lined 14-inch-square Excalibur Dehydrator tray.

Dehydrate for 7 hours at 104°F. Flip, peel away lining, and score into ½-inch squares. Dehydrate for 6 to 8 more hours, until your desired consistency.

OPTIONS: Any of your breads can be made into croutons. Spread your batter double the usual thickness, so only half the dehydrator tray is covered, rather than the entire tray. Score into crouton-size squares and dehydrate.

TENDER GREENS WITH PINE NUTS
AND SWEET MUSTARD DRESSING

MAKES 4 SERVINGS

This is a simple salad of soft greens tossed with dressing ingredients, topped with pine nuts. If you don't have Homemade Mustard Sauce handy, just use an organic jarred mustard from the grocery.

You can substitute apple cider vinegar for the balsamic vinegar if you want to keep this as raw as possible.

SALAD

2 cups spinach, well washed

2 cups romaine lettuce

2 cups Boston lettuce

1 cup watercress

DRESSING

2 teaspoons Homemade Mustard Sauce (page 201)

1 tablespoon balsamic vinegar

2 tablespoons agave syrup

1 tablespoon pine nuts

Place all the salad ingredients in a large mixing bowl. Add the dressing ingredients and toss to mix well. Serve immediately.

SEAWEED AND CUCUMBER SALAD

MAKES 4 SERVINGS

This Korean-inspired recipe is refreshing and cooling, great for summertime picnics in the park. The sea vegetable *wakame* is tossed with cucumbers in tart apple cider vinegar with a splash of sesame oil. Sea vegetables are full of minerals and iodine from the ocean and help regulate our thyroid and improve overall health.

1 cup dried *wakame*

2 cups sliced cucumber

2 tablespoons apple cider vinegar

3 tablespoons toasted sesame or cold-pressed extra-virgin olive oil

1/2 teaspoon minced garlic

First, soak the *wakame* in about 1 cup of filtered water. Set aside to hydrate for at least 5 minutes. Squeeze the excess water from the *wakame* and place the seaweed in a mixing bowl with the remaining ingredients. Toss to mix well.

Will keep for 1 day in the fridge.

ASIAN GREENS WITH LEMON-TAHINI DRESSING

MAKES 4 SERVINGS

A creamy smooth dressing, packed with calcium from the tahini, is tossed with beautiful spicy greens and sliced radishes. Lemon, sesame, and oregano add another layer of wonderful flavor.

DRESSING

¼ cup tahini

¼ cup lemon juice

2 tablespoons Bragg Liquid Aminos

¼ cup water, or as needed

SALAD

2 cups chopped *matsuma* (Japanese mustard greens)

2 cups chopped mustard greens

10 radishes, sliced

½ cup corn kernels

1 tablespoon fresh basil leaves

Place the dressing ingredients in a bowl and mix with a spoon. Pour over the salad and toss to mix well.

Will keep for 2 days in the fridge.

GENERAL TIP:
Traveling Salads

IF YOU'RE GOING to save some salad to enjoy for lunch the next day, or will be traveling with salad out of your fridge, or whenever you want to extend your salad's shelf life, store the dressing and veggies separately and mix just before eating.

Use this same tip for any of your dishes that are served with a sauce, such as noodles, pizza, and burgers.

VIETNAMESE CABBAGE SALAD WITH FRESH
MINT MAKES 4 SERVINGS

Napa cabbage, carrots, and cucumber are mixed with fresh mint, cilantro, and basil, and then tossed in a whisked shallot and lime vinaigrette for a bright and flavorful salad.

DRESSING

¼ cup thinly sliced shallot (about 1 large)

¼ cup lime juice

3 tablespoons agave syrup

1 teaspoon sea salt

1 teaspoon apple cider vinegar

SALAD

4 cups shredded napa cabbage

1 cup shredded carrots

½ cup cucumber, halved vertically and sliced thinly into half-moons

¼ cup torn fresh mint leaves

¼ cup fresh cilantro leaves

2 tablespoons torn basil leaves

GARNISH

3 tablespoons chopped almonds

Place all the dressing ingredients in a mixing bowl. Mix well.

Add the salad ingredients to the bowl and toss. Set aside to marinate and soften the cabbage, or serve right away for a crunchier salad.

Top with the almonds and serve.

Will keep for 2 days in the fridge.

GREEN PAPAYA SALAD

MAKES 4 SERVINGS

This is my version of the traditional Thai recipe. A light whisked dressing of lime and agave is tossed into papaya and carrots with red chiles and garnished with cilantro, basil, and almonds.

If you don't have green papaya, try using green mango instead.

DRESSING

2 tablespoons lime juice

2 tablespoons agave syrup

SALAD

4 cups julienned papayas

2 cups shredded carrots

2 red chilies, sliced thinly, or to taste

GARNISH

½ cup chopped fresh cilantro

½ cup chopped fresh basil

⅓ cup chopped almonds

Whisk together the lime juice and agave syrup in a large mixing bowl. Add the salad ingredients and toss well. Set aside and leave to marinate for 15 to 20 minutes.

To serve, top with the herbs and almonds.

Will keep for 2 days in the fridge.

WATERCRESS WITH CRANBERRIES AND AL-MONDS

MAKES 4 SERVINGS

This is a watercress lover's salad. If you're not a fan of watercress, this might just make you into one: spicy watercress is tossed in a light whisked dressing and garnished with almonds and cranberries.

DRESSING

1 recipe Basic Whisked Dressing (page 149)

SALAD

4 cups watercress

GARNISH

½ cup slivered almonds

¼ cup cranberries

1 recipe Rawmesan Cheeze (page 105) or Cheezy Sprinkle (page 106)

Several pinches of cracked black pepper

In a large mixing bowl, whisk the Basic Whisked Dressing to blend and add the watercress, tossing to coat.

To serve, top with the almonds and cranberries. Sprinkle with cheeze and black pepper.

Will keep for 1 day in the fridge.

SPRING GREENS IN CURRY DRESSING

MAKES 4 SERVINGS

Delicate spring greens are tossed in a creamy curry dressing. This dressing is so tasty and versatile, I recommend making a double or triple batch so you can keep extra on hand in a jar in your fridge to dress up plain greens any time.

DRESSING

1 recipe Basic Blended Dressing (page 151)

2 teaspoons curry powder

SALAD

8 cups mixed greens, such as mesclun, mâche, arugula,
   or spinach (about 1 pound)

1 cup snap peas

To make the dressing, blend curry powder with the Basic Blended Dressing.

To serve, toss the salad with the dressing and serve immediately.

SERVING SUGGESTION: Use a spiralizer to slice a beet into long strands. Use the beet "noodles" to garnish each salad.

CHINESE CHICKENLESS SALAD

MAKES 4 SERVINGS

A sweet sesame-ginger dressing is whisked together and tossed with napa and red cabbage, carrots, and green onions.

DRESSING

2 tablespoons Nama Shoyu or Bragg Liquid Aminos

2 teaspoons apple cider vinegar

1 teaspoon minced garlic

1 teaspoon minced ginger

1 tablespoon toasted sesame oil

2 tablespoons agave syrup

SALAD

6 cups thinly shredded napa cabbage

2 cups shredded red cabbage

2 cups shredded carrot

½ cup thinly sliced green onion (about 3 whole)

GARNISH

¼ cup sliced almonds

Whisk all the dressing ingredients together in a small bowl.

Place the salad ingredients in a large mixing bowl. Pour the dressing over the vegetables and toss to mix.

To serve, divide the salad among four serving dishes. Garnish each portion with the almonds and serve immediately.

YIN AND YANG SALAD WITH JALAPEÑO-TAHINI DRESSING

MAKES 4 SERVINGS

Cabbage, romaine lettuce, carrots, cucumbers, peas, and fresh cilantro are tossed in a lemon-tahini dressing with the added heat of a green jalapeño. Jalapeño-Tahini is one of my favorite dressings.

JALAPEÑO-TAHINI DRESSING

⅓ cup tahini

⅓ cup lemon juice (from about 2 lemons)

2 tablespoons Bragg Liquid Aminos or Nama Shoyu

1 tablespoon jalapeño (about ¼ whole), or to taste

1 teaspoon minced garlic

3 to 4 tablespoons filtered water, as needed

SALAD

4 cups thinly shredded cabbage,

2 cups torn romaine lettuce

½ cup julienned carrots

½ cup sliced cucumbers

½ cup peas

¼ cup fresh cilantro leaves

GARNISH

3 tablespoons sesame seeds

Place all the dressing ingredients in a blender. Blend until smooth.

Place all the salad ingredients in a large mixing bowl. Toss with the dressing.

To serve, top the salad with the sesame seeds.

Will keep for 2 days in the fridge.

RED CABBAGE AND GRAPEFRUIT

MAKES 4 SERVINGS

A very simple, easy-to-make salad that's beautiful in color. Segments of fresh grapefruit and red cabbage are mixed with tart red cranberries and pumpkin seeds, and tossed with lemon juice.

SALAD

4 cups thinly sliced red cabbage

2 cups segmented grapefruit, pits, peel, and pith removed

3 tablespoons dried cranberries

2 tablespoons pumpkin seeds

DRESSING

2 to 3 tablespoons lemon juice

A pinch of salt

A pinch of pepper

Place the salad ingredients in a large mixing bowl. Add the dressing ingredients and toss to mix.

Will keep for 2 to 3 days in the fridge.

SAUERKRAUT-AVOCADO SALAD

MAKES 4 SERVINGS

This is a quick salad I enjoy on superbusy days. Just toss your favorite greens with an avocado and sauerkraut. The avocado adds a creaminess, while the sauerkraut gives the salad a salty, tart flavor that's delicious. If you don't have hemp nuts, use your favorite seed or nut, such as sesame or chopped almonds, to add that extra layer of texture.

6 cups lightly packed greens

2 cups cubed ripe avocado (from about 2 medium-size avocados)

½ cup Basic Green Cabbage Sauerkraut (page 121), packed, excess liquid squeezed out

2 tablespoons hemp nuts

Place all the ingredients into a large mixing bowl. Toss to mix well. Serve immediately.

Will keep for 1 day in the fridge.

Brazil Nut–Banana Pancakes with Blueberry Syrup and Sliced Bananas, page 75

Lemon Kream–Filled Crepes with Raspberry Sauce, page 70

Scones with Clotted Kream and Jam, pages 94 to 95

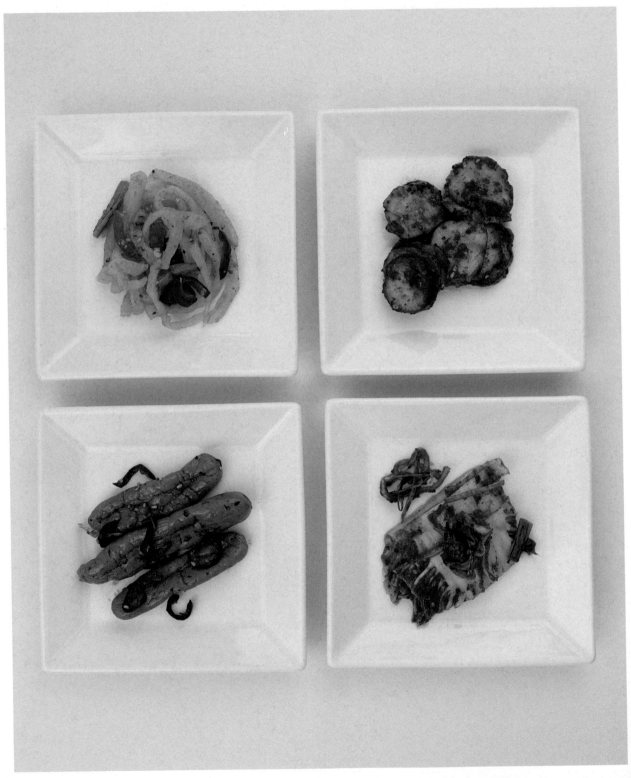

Pickled Vegetables, pages 121 to 132

Corn Chowder, page 135

Mediterranean Wrap with Red Pepper Hummus (Bean-Free), page 181

BLT Club, page 190

Lox, Tomato, Red Onion, and Capers, page 189

Fried Onion and Mushroom Pizza, pages 216 to 217

Pad Thai with Kelp Noodles, page 227

Korean Dumplings, pages 237 to 238

Cranberry-Cashew Wild Rice Pilaf, page 248

Maki with Marinated Spinach and "Peanut" Sauce, page 257

Custard Tartlets, page 267

Basic Flourless Cake, page 268

Goji Berry–Chocolate Chip Cookies, page 286

TACO SALAD

A bed of romaine and iceberg lettuce is topped with layers of Chipotle Cheeze Sauce, Heirloom Tomato Salsa, and Taco Nut Meat and garnished with Salted Flax Chips, for a delicious and nutritious variation.

> 4 cups shredded romaine lettuce
>
> 2 cups shredded iceberg lettuce
>
> 1 large ripe avocado, pitted and sliced
>
> 1 recipe Chipotle Cheeze (page 104)
>
> 1 recipe Heirloom Tomato Salsa (page 81)
>
> 1 recipe Taco Nut Meat (page 146)
>
> 1 recipe Salted Flax Chips (page 108)

To serve, divide the lettuce among four serving bowls. Top each portion with Chipotle Cheeze and Heirloom Tomato Salsa, sprinkle with Taco Meat, and garnish with Salted Flax Chips.

CAESAR SALAD BOATS WITH COCONUT BACON AND RAWMESAN CHEEZE

MAKES 4 SERVINGS

A beautiful salad served as stacked whole romaine leaves tossed in Caesar dressing, topped with bits of Coconut Bacon and sprinkled with Rawmesan. A faster substitute for Rawmesan is to sprinkle a tablespoon or two of nutritional yeast instead.

I love garlic and garlicky Caesar, so I use two teaspoons, about two cloves, of garlic in this recipe. For milder flavor, use just one teaspoon of garlic, and give it a taste. Gradually add more to your liking.

DRESSING
1 cup chopped celery or zucchini

1 to 2 teaspoons garlic

½ cup olive oil

1 tablespoon white miso

SALAD
12 large romaine lettuce leaves

GARNISH
1 recipe Coconut Bacon (page 76) or Eggplant Bacon (page 78), diced

1 recipe Rawmesan (page 105)

Place all the dressing ingredients in a high-speed blender. Blend until smooth.

Toss the romaine leaves in the dressing, coating well.

To serve, place three leaves onto each of four serving dishes. Top each portion with the Coconut Bacon bits, and sprinkle with 1 tablespoon of Rawmesan.

SERVING SUGGESTION: Serve with your favorite croutons.

8

WRAPS, SANDWICHES, AND BURGERS

THIS IS THE ultimate chapter for healthy, delicious, and versatile handheld recipes. Wraps are made by filling dehydrated Corn Tortillas or Tomato Wrappers, or your favorite leaves such as iceberg lettuce or romaine, with cheeze, pâté, hummus, sauce, and even salad. Sandwiches are made with flax flatbread filled with Coconut Bacon, cheeze, tomato, mock tuna salad, and even my raw version of lox with capers and onions. Vegetables and flax are mixed together to make my Sun Burgers, which are served with BBQ Sauce, Sun-Dried Tomato Ketchup, Aioli Mayonnaise, or Homemade Mustard Sauce for delicious, nutritious, soy-free, and gluten-free goodness.

Soy Story

BEING OF Korean descent, I was surprised to find that my mom and I are both allergic to soy. This allergy had been appearing in my skin as inflammation that I mistook as acne. A friend recommended I try eliminating soy, and my skin cleared up in a matter of weeks. I had thought soy was part of a healthy Asian diet. To my surprise, I discovered soy is actually toxic.

In Asia, soy is fermented to eliminate the antinutrients and soy toxins in raw soybeans. It's eaten only in small amounts in the form of tempeh, miso, and soy sauce. Nama Shoyu is a raw, unpasteurized, and safely fermented soy sauce used in raw foods to add a salty, rich flavor to recipes. It's full of enzymes that make it a living food.

The soy in America, on the other hand, is processed and not fermented. Dr. Kaayla Daniel, author of *The Whole Soy Story*, says, "Today's high-tech processing methods not only fail to remove the anti-nutrients and toxins that are naturally present in soybeans but leave toxic and carcinogenic residues created by the high temperatures, high pressure, alkali and acid baths and petroleum solvents." In an attempt to eat more protein, Westerners eat ten to twenty times more unfermented, highly processed soy than is eaten in Asia. Ironically, this unfermented soy contains enzyme inhibitors, which block protein absorption.

What's even scarier is that almost 90 percent of American soy is genetically modified, and the soy crop grown in the USA contains the highest levels of poisonous pesticide contaminants. No wonder soy is among the eight most common food allergens and has been linked to thyroid problems, including weight gain, fatigue, hair loss, loss of libido, kidney stones, a weakened immune system, infections, and digestive problems, to name a few. And, since soy doesn't taste so good, manufacturers flavor it with sugar, MSG, and other artificial chemicals to make it palatable.

Dr. Mercola points out, "Dow Chemical and DuPont, the same corporations that brought misery and death to millions around the world through Agent Orange, are now the driving forces behind the promotion of soy as a food for humans. They are financing anti-meat and anti-milk campaigns aimed largely at those concerned about animal welfare and the environment, trying to convince them that imitations such as 'soymilk' are not only healthier than the real thing, but better for the earth too.

"There is no evidence that consuming soy products can improve health, reduce environmental degradation or slow global warming. In fact, the evidence suggests quite the opposite."

Soy, like all food, is best in its natural, whole, raw food form. The bulk of the soy consumed in the USA is highly processed, and not so good for your health.

WRAPS

Unlike most traditional wraps, raw wraps are typically made using a large leaf—a collard green, green lettuce, cabbage, iceberg, or a romaine leaf. The leaf is then stuffed with such fillings as cheeze, avocado, tomato, sauce, vegetables, and/or salsa.

There are many different raw wraps to choose from. When choosing a leaf to use as a wrapper, consider its texture, flavor, and color. A burrito shell made from a cabbage leaf gives it a light, crisp crunch when bitten into. And surprisingly, collard's flavor is mild, and this leaf makes for a great wrapper because it is large and flat; plus, its dark green color give a strong contrast to lighter colors. Romaine and green leaves are softer, not as crisp, and work well when you want the fillings to claim the spotlight.

In addition to lettuce wraps, I'll be introducing you to wraps made using my Tomato Wrapper or Apple Crepe. These wrappers have a texture similar to that of the rice paper used for Vietnamese spring rolls. I've also included Mexican-inspired recipes that use Soft Corn Tortilla (see pages 171 and 179 for those wrapper recipes).

IF YOU'RE FEELING the need for something more than just a green lettuce wrap, you can always add on a whole wheat or spelt tortilla as the final outer wrapper layer. You'll still be eating up all the whole, fresh, raw food fillings, including the green wrapper full of minerals and chlorophyll. You're still nourishing your body.

CORN TOSTADA

MAKES 4 SERVINGS

A traditional tostada is made with a fried or toasted corn tortilla layered with lettuce, salsa, avocado, and olives, all of which are raw. In my recipe, I swap out the dairy cheese, cooked taco meat, and tortilla in favor of a spicy melted Chipotle Cheeze, my famous Taco Nut Meat, and delicious handmade Soft Corn Tortilla.

> 1 recipe Soft Corn Tortilla (page 172)
>
> 1 recipe Chipotle Cheeze (page 104)
>
> 4 cups shredded iceberg lettuce
>
> 1 recipe Heirloom Tomato Salsa (page 81)
>
> 1 recipe Taco Nut Meat (page 146)
>
> 1 ripe avocado, pitted and sliced
>
> ¼ cup pitted, chopped black olives

Place one Soft Corn Tortilla onto each of four serving dishes. Spread with a layer of cheeze. Top each with 1 cup of lettuce, then Heirloom Tomato Salsa, Taco Meat, avocado, and olives.

Serve and enjoy immediately.

Will keep for 1 day in the fridge.

SERVING SUGGESTION: For a crispier tostada substitute, use your favorite cracker or flatbread instead of the Soft Corn Tortilla.

SOFT CORN TORTILLA

MAKES 5 TORTILLAS

Inspired by handmade corn tortillas, but easier to make, these tortillas stay flexible from the corn kernels and olive oil. Simply blend or process your ingredients and scoop ¼-cup rounds onto your dehydrator tray to dry.

Although fresh is always preferred, you can use frozen organic corn kernels for ease and availability. To make corn bread slices instead of tortilla rounds, spread the batter evenly across one lined 14-inch-square Excalibur Dehydrator tray.

> 1½ cups corn kernels (from 3 to 4 ears of corn)
> ½ cup flax meal
> 3 tablespoons olive oil
> ¾ cup filtered water

Place all the ingredients in a high-speed blender and blend to mix.

Form four ¼-cup circles on one lined 14-inch-square Excalibur Dehydrator tray. Spread the batter evenly with the back of a spoon. Place the remaining ¼ cup of batter on a second lined dehydrator tray, and spread evenly. Dehydrate for 5 to 6 hours at 104°F. Flip over and peel away the liner. Dehydrate for 5 to 6 more hours, to your desired consistency.

Not just for lunch or dinner! Enjoy with a breakfast scramble (see pages 79 to 85).

WRAPPERS

My raw wrappers are similar in concept and texture to fruit leather, but less rubbery and sticky. Fruit is blended, sometimes with flax meal, then spread in a thin layer onto lined Excalibur Dehydrator trays and dried.

Wrappers can be used to make crepes when filled with kream, fruit, and sauce; as the "tortilla" to make a burrito or wrap; and to make Korean pockets called *mandu*, filled with marinated vegetables. Wrappers even make fettuccine noodles when sliced into long strips.

If you don't have a dehydrator, spread the batter onto a cookie sheet. Place the cookie sheet in a 140°F oven, with the oven door open about an inch or two. Dry for 3 to 5 hours, or until leathery but still pliable. This is hardly an eco-friendly way to dry, but hopefully the results will inspire you to invest in a dehydrator.

• • •

TOMATO WRAPPER

MAKES 4 WRAPPERS

A delicious red wrapper that has a fruit leather texture, but thinner and less sticky. Great to use to make vegetable hors d'oeuvre "pockets," wraps, and rolls.

Make sure not to put in more than a tablespoon of agave syrup, or your wrapper will never dry solid but will stay sticky, because agave doesn't dehydrate fully.

> 3½ cups seeded and chopped ripe tomato
> 1 tablespoon agave syrup

Place the tomato and agave in a high-speed blender and puree until smooth. The mixture will be a liquid. Carefully and evenly spread the mixture onto one lined 14-inch-square Excalibur Dehydrator tray. Dehydrate for 4 to 6 hours at 104°F, until completely dried. No need to flip the wrapper; just peel away the liner and use.

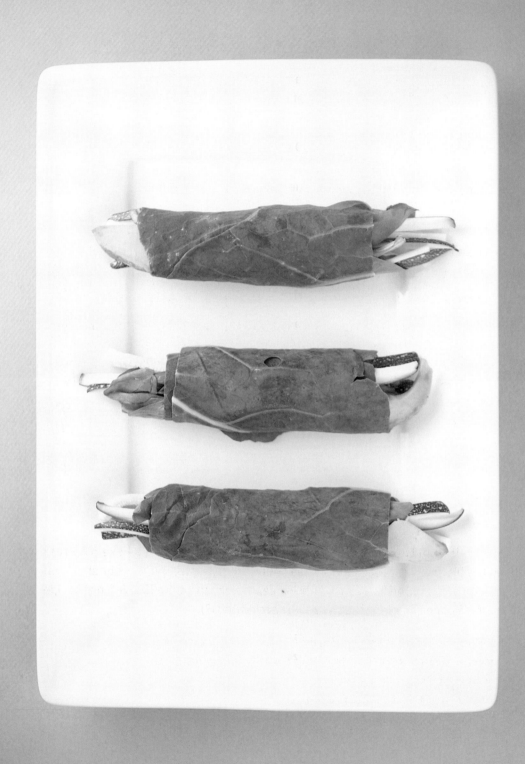

TAHINI ZUCCHINI ROLLS

MAKES 4 SERVINGS

Julienned zucchini strips are tossed in a creamy, delicious Lemon-Tahini Dressing and then rolled inside a wrapper made of either tomato or apple with fresh basil for bright flavor and color.

> 1 recipe Tomato Wrapper (page 173) or Apple Crepes (page 69)
>
> 1 cup julienned zucchini
>
> 1 recipe Lemon-Tahini Dressing (page 155), made with half the amount of water
>
> ¼ cup fresh basil leaves

Cut the wrapper into four strips. Cut each strip in half so each strip is about 3½ by 7 inches. Set aside.

Toss the zucchini with the thick Lemon-Tahini Dressing. Set aside.

To make your rolls, place a wrapper on a flat surface, such as a cutting board, positioned so it is taller than wide. Place a couple of basil leaves near the bottom of your wrapper (the side nearest you), and then arrange about 2 tablespoons of zucchini horizontally on top of the basil. The leaves will help keep your wrappers from becoming moist from the wet filling. Roll upward to enclose the filling. Repeat to make a total of eight rolls.

Serve immediately.

WET BURRITO

MAKES 4 SERVINGS

This burrito is made using a crunchy cabbage leaf, which is shaped like a bowl to hold all the fillings. An iceberg lettuce leaf will work well, too. For a softer shell that will soak up some of the Red Enchilada Sauce, replace the cabbage with one recipe of Tomato Wrapper (page 173) or Apple Crepes (page 69).

> 4 large green or red cabbage leaves
>
> 1 recipe of your favorite Basic Cheeze (page 103)
>
> 1 recipe Pico de Gallo (page 85)
>
> 1 recipe Taco Nut Meat (page 146)
>
> 1 recipe Red Enchilada Sauce (page 84)

Place one cabbage leaf on each of four serving dishes. Fill with Basic Cheeze, and top with Pico de Gallo and Taco Nut Meat.

To serve, drizzle with a generous amount of Red Enchilada Sauce. Enjoy.

Will keep for 1 day in the fridge.

CHEEZE ENCHILADA WITH RANCHERO AND MOLE SAUCE

MAKES 4 SERVINGS

Enchiladas are traditionally made with corn tortillas that are rolled up with cheese inside, then topped with a red sauce and more cheese. In my recipe, a savory cheeze is wrapped inside a Tomato Wrapper or Apple Crepe, and topped with Red Enchilada Sauce and delicious, spicy Chocolate Mole Sauce.

> 2 recipes Tomato Wrapper (page 173) or Apple Crepes (page 69)
> 2 recipes Coconut Kefir Cheeze (page 106) or your favorite Basic Cheeze (page 103)
> 1 recipe Red Enchilada Sauce (page 84)
> 1 recipe Chocolate Mole Sauce (page 177)
> 2 cups shredded iceberg lettuce

Take one wrapper and cover half of it with about ⅓ cup of cheeze. Then roll up and place the enchilada in a casserole pan. Continue until all eight wrappers are filled and rolled. Scoop the Red Enchilada Sauce on top of the enchiladas, and drizzle with Chocolate Mole Sauce.

Serve with shredded iceberg lettuce.

Will keep for 2 days in the fridge.

SERVING SUGGESTION: A quick wrapper substitute are sheets of nori. Just use instead of a dehydrated wrapper or crepe, in the same way. The crisp nori will get soft from the enchilada sauce and mole.

CHOCOLATE MOLE SAUCE

MAKES 1 CUP

This savory chocolate sauce will add a rich Mexican flavor to any dish. Top your enchiladas and nachos with this antioxidant-packed cacao sauce sweetened with low-calorie, low-glycemic agave syrup.

½ cup seeded and diced tomato

¼ cup olive oil

2 tablespoon cacao or cocoa powder

1 tablespoon agave syrup

1 teaspoon ground cinnamon

¼ teaspoon powdered dried chipotle

¼ teaspoon sea salt

2 tablespoons water, or as needed

Place all the ingredients in a high-speed blender and blend until smooth.

Will keep for 3 days in the fridge.

SERVING SUGGESTION: Enjoy in South-of-the-Border Wraps (page 180), drizzle over your enchiladas, and serve as a dip for vegetables and chips.

TOMATO AND OLIVE QUESADILLAS WITH MANGO-CUCUMBER SALSA AND SOUR KREAM

MAKES 4 SERVINGS

Soft tortillas sandwich tomatoes and black olives in creamy Cheddar Cheeze Sauce, served with a tomato and also Mango-Cucumber Salsa and Sour Kream.

2 recipes Soft Corn Tortilla (page 172)

1 recipe Cheddar Cheeze Sauce (page 105)

1 large tomato, sliced

¼ cup pitted, sliced black olives

1 recipe Heirloom Tomato Salsa (page 81)

1 recipe Mango Cucumber Salsa (page 178)

1 recipe Sour Kream (page 178)

Place one tortilla on each of four serving dishes. Top each with cheeze, then tomatoes and olives, and then more cheeze. Place another tortilla on top. Slice into two or four wedges, and serve with the salsas and sour kream.

Will keep for 1 day in the fridge.

MANGO-CUCUMBER SALSA
MAKES ABOUT 2 CUPS

A cool change from traditional tomato salsa. Try this in the summertime when beautiful orange mangoes and crispy, cool cucumbers are in season.

> 1 cup diced mango
> ½ cup chopped cucumber
> ½ cup seeded and diced tomato
> 2 tablespoons chopped red onion
> 2 tablespoons chopped fresh cilantro
> 1 tablespoon fresh lime juice
> A pinch of sea salt

Place all the ingredients in a mixing bowl. Toss to mix well.

Will keep for 1 day in the fridge.

SOUR KREAM
MAKES 1 CUP

Cashews are blended with lemon juice and water to make a white, tart kream that tastes and looks like dairy sour cream, but without the guilt or karma load.
  If you don't have a high-speed blender, grind your cashews into a powder first with the grinding attachment on a Personal Blender, or in a food processor. This will help you get a smoother texture when you blend.

> 1 cup cashews
> ¼ cup fresh lemon juice
> ⅓ cup filtered water, or as needed

Place all the ingredients in a high-speed blender and blend until smooth, adding enough water to produce your desired consistency.

SOUTH-OF-THE-BORDER WRAPS

MAKES 4 SERVINGS

Fresh tomatoes, onion, cilantro, and avocado top a spicy Chipotle Cheeze. Drizzle with delicious, rich Chocolate Mole Sauce. Enjoy in a romaine leaf boat for a low-carb delight.

> 4 large romaine lettuce leaves
>
> 1 recipe Chipotle Cheeze (page 104)
>
> 1 cup seeded and chopped tomato
>
> 2 tablespoons chopped red onion
>
> 2 tablespoons chopped fresh cilantro
>
> 1 cup diced ripe avocado (about 1 avocado)
>
> ½ recipe Chocolate Mole Sauce (page 177)

Begin by spooning about 2 tablespoons of your Chipotle Cheeze along the inside spine of your lettuce leaf. Next, sprinkle with your tomato, onion, cilantro, and avocado.

To serve, drizzle on about 1 tablespoon of Chocolate Mole Sauce.

Will keep for 1 day in the fridge.

For a cooked add-on, wrap everything up inside your favorite whole-grain or wheat-free tortilla.

GARDEN WRAP

MAKES 4 WRAPS

Your favorite vegetables are wrapped up inside a collard green leaf, with Avocado-Pistachio Pesto. These wraps travel and keep well and make for a great on the go handheld snack.

> 2 large collard leaves
>
> 1 recipe Avocado-Pistachio Pesto (page 216)
>
> ½ cup peeled, chopped cucumber
>
> ½ cup seeded and chopped red bell pepper
>
> ½ cup sliced mushrooms
>
> ½ cup sprouts

Cut the leaves away from the thick center stem of each collard leaf to make a total of four flat pieces. Spoon the Avocado-Pistachio Pesto across the bottom edge of the shorter width of each leaf. Top with cucumbers, bell peppers, mushrooms, and sprouts. Roll up into a wrap, and serve.

Will keep for up to 1 day at room temperature, or store for a day or two in the fridge.

I love the taste of fresh raw collards. To soften, sometimes I'll prepare the leaves, then leave out at room temperature to wilt for about 30 minutes. But if you prefer using a softer leaf or even a cooked tortilla, you can either substitute it for the collard, or add it. Do what suits your fancy. Either way, you'll still be eating super healthy and living eco green.

MEDITERRANEAN WRAP WITH RED PEPPER HUMMUS (BEAN-FREE)

MAKES 4 WRAPS

This recipe uses collard leaves for wrapping up vegetables, such as spinach, zucchini, black olives, and avocado, with a delicious Red Pepper Hummus.

> 2 large collard leaves
>
> 2 cups spinach, washed well
>
> ½ recipe Red Pepper Hummus (page 184)
>
> 1 ripe avocado, pitted and sliced
>
> ½ cup zucchini, cut into long, thin spears
>
> ¼ cup pitted, chopped black olives

Cut the leaves away from the thick center stem of each collard leaf to make a total of four flat pieces.

Top each collard section with spinach leaves. Then, spoon Red Pepper Hummus across the bottom edge of the shorter width of each leaf. Top with avocado, zucchini, and black olives. Roll up into a wrap and serve.

Will keep for up to a day at room temperature, or store for a day or two in the fridge.

RED PEPPER HUMMUS (BEAN-FREE)

MAKES 2 CUPS

This hummus is made using tahini, as in traditional recipes, but instead of chickpeas, I use red bell pepper and a pinch of cumin for a richer flavor. Sesame powder helps absorb some of the excess liquid from the juicy bell pepper.

> ½ cup sesame seeds, ground into a powder
>
> 2 teaspoons chopped garlic
>
> 1 teaspoon sea salt
>
> 2 cups seeded and diced red bell pepper
>
> ⅓ cup tahini
>
> ¼ cup lemon juice
>
> ½ teaspoon ground cumin

In a food processor, process the sesame seeds, garlic, and salt into small pieces. Add the remaining ingredients and process until smooth.

Will keep for 2 days in the fridge.

GENERAL TIP:
Hummus Flavors

HUMMUS CAN COME in as many flavors as your imagination will allow. Try replacing the red bell peppers with zucchini, using other herbs such as oregano or dill, and adding olives or sun-dried tomatoes.

CAESAR SALAD WRAP

MAKES 4 WRAPS

Add a twist to everyday salad by wrapping it up in a crepe or wrapper. Delicious Caesar Salad with Coconut Bacon and Rawmesan is rolled up inside a Tomato Wrapper or an Apple Crepe to make a beautiful handheld treat.

> **2 recipes Tomato Wrapper (page 173) or Apple Crepes (page 69),**
> **halved rather than quartered, for total of four wrappers**

> **TOSSED SALAD**

> **1 recipe Caesar Salad with Coconut Bacon and Rawmesan (page 166)**

Place one wrapper on each of four serving dishes. Fill with tossed salad and roll up into a wrap. Serve immediately.

OPTIONS: Try replacing the wrapper or crepe with a sheet of nori for light crispiness, or add a final layer of cooked tortilla or baked flatbread, if you prefer.

SANDWICHES

As the chapter on dehydrating showed, it's pretty easy to make raw bread. In a raw sandwich, bread is replaced with a flax flatbread. The texture is similar to that of a cooked Lebanese flatbread or pita bread. Most of the fillings in a raw sandwich are the same as in a cooked sandwich, such as lettuce and tomato and Thousand Island Dressing.

These recipes are my versions of classic comfort sandwiches you'd find in any diner.

The BLT club is made with my egg-free Mayonnaise, iceberg lettuce, tomato slices, avocado, and Coconut Bacon—yes, raw bacon! My Grilled Cheeze and Tomato sandwich uses a cheeze sauce similar to melted Velveeta, and my Cinnamon-Apple Open-Face Sandwich is a healthy sweet treat.

Not to be outdone, you'll also find recipes for mock lox (coconut is the secret here, too, and creates a look and feel like pickled herring). When it's layered on flatbread with tomatoes, onions, and arugula, and topped with capers, your Sunday breakfast will never be the same.

As with the other recipes in this book, feel free to use these recipes as a springboard to creating your own delicious combinations.

RECIPES ARE ABOUT putting together the right textures and flavors, whether cooked or raw. If you're missing cooked bread, enjoy any of these sandwiches on slices of your favorite organic, preferably handmade, and gluten-free bread instead.

COCONUT BACON REUBEN SANDWICH WITH THOUSAND ISLAND DRESSING

MAKES 4 SANDWICHES

Inspired by the classic Reuben, my version uses hearty Coconut Bacon as the meat. It's topped with a layer of cheeze, then Thousand Island Dressing and sauerkraut, and sandwiched between slices of Rye Flatbread.

 1 recipe Rye Flatbread (page 23)

 1 recipe of your favorite cheeze

 1 recipe Coconut Bacon (page 76) or Eggplant Bacon (page 78)

 1 recipe Thousand Island Dressing (page 188)

 1 cup of your favorite sauerkraut (pages 121 to 122)

Place a slice of Rye Flatbread on each of four serving dishes. Spread with a layer of cheeze. Top with slices of Coconut Bacon and drizzle with Thousand Island Dressing. Top with sauerkraut and a second piece of flatbread, and serve immediately.

THOUSAND ISLAND DRESSING

MAKES 1 CUP

I learned how easy it is to make Thousand Island Dressing in Seoul, Korea, of all places. They just mix up mayo with ketchup and pickles. I add some chopped onions, too. Use as a dressing or sauce on salads, in sandwiches, and in wraps.

 ³⁄₄ cup Aioli Mayonnaise (page 198)

 ¹⁄₄ cup Sun-Dried Tomato Ketchup (page 205)

 ¹⁄₄ cup chopped Sliced Cucumber Pickles (page 123) or Sliced Pickles in Vinegar

 1 tablespoon chopped onion

Mix all the ingredients well.

Will keep for 3 to 4 days in the fridge.

GRILLED CHEEZE AND TOMATO

MAKES 4 SERVINGS

A quick and simple sandwich to make. The cheeze sauce has the consistency of a melted cheese, and it's drizzled over thick slices of tomato between slices of flatbread.

8 slices of Zucchini Bread (page 23) or Sunflower Bread (page 24)
1 recipe of your favorite Cheeze Sauce (pages 103 to 106)
1 tomato, seeded and sliced thickly

Place a slice of bread on each of four serving dishes. Spread each with about ¼ cup of cheeze. Top with a slice of tomato and a second slice of bread. Serve immediately.

LOX, TOMATO, RED ONION, AND CAPERS

MAKES 4 SANDWICHES

Thai baby coconut meat is used as the "lox" in this sandwich, layered with creamy Aioli Mayonnaise, red onion and tomato slices, and capers. A good substitute for coconut meat is mango, sliced thinly. It has the same slippery consistency as coconut meat and lox.

8 slices of your favorite bread
¼ cup Aioli Mayonnaise (page 198)
1 tomato, seeded and sliced
1 cup sliced mango or Thai young coconut meat
½ cup arugula
¼ cup sliced red onion
¼ cup drained capers

Place a slice of bread on each of four serving dishes. Spread each portion with 2 tablespoons of Aioli Mayonnaise. Top with the tomato slices, then the mango, arugula, onion, and capers, and finally the remaining bread.

Will keep for several hours.

SERVING SUGGESTION: Serve with Cheddar Kale Chips (page 110), or plain arugula.

BLT CLUB

MAKES 4 SERVINGS

Iceberg lettuce, tomato, avocado, and Coconut Bacon are slathered with mayonnaise and sandwiched between three slices of flax flatbread.

This sandwich keeps for several hours, making it a great sandwich for the road when traveling or on a hike or picnic.

> 12 slices of Zucchini Bread (page 23) or Sunflower Bread (page 24) (about 1½ recipes)
>
> 1 recipe Aioli Mayonnaise (page 198)
>
> 8 leaves iceberg lettuce
>
> 1 tomato, seeded and sliced
>
> 1 ripe avocado, pitted and sliced
>
> 1 recipe Coconut Bacon (page 76)

Place a slice of bread on each of four serving dishes and spread with a couple of tablespoons of Mayonnaise. Top each portion with a lettuce leaf, then a slice of tomato, some avocado, and then another slice of bread. Spread that slice with additional Mayonnaise, and top with slices of Coconut Bacon, lettuce, and tomato. Spread a couple of tablespoons of Mayonnaise on one side of the remaining slices of bread, and place Mayonnaise side down atop your sandwiches.

The assembled sandwich will keep for a few hours.

OPTION: Use Eggplant Bacon if you don't have any Thai Baby Coconuts for Coconut Bacon.

MOCK TUNA SALAD

MAKES 4 SERVINGS

A good karma mock tuna salad made by mixing together creamy Mayonnaise with onion and celery. Carrot pulp is added to give this salad a flaked fish–like texture that's to live for.

In case you don't have a vegetable juicer, just visit your local smoothie bar. Order a carrot juice, and ask them for the pulp.

> 1 recipe Aioli Mayonnaise (page 198)
> 3 cups carrot pulp (from about 1 pound washed, peeled, juiced carrots)
> 1 cup chopped celery
> 1/4 cup chopped yellow onion
> 1 recipe of your favorite bread

Place the Aioli Mayonnaise, carrot pulp, celery, and onion in a mixing bowl. Mix well.

Assemble your sandwiches by spreading one-quarter of the mixture between two slices of bread. Top with sliced tomato and iceberg lettuce. Repeat to make the remaining sandwiches.

The assembled sandwiches will keep for a couple of hours. Mock Tuna Salad will keep for 2 days when stored separately in the fridge.

AB&B

MAKES 4 SERVINGS

A gooey sandwich filled with banana and almond butter, drizzled with agave syrup, and left to marinate and soak up the sweetness. Enjoy with a fork.

> 8 slices of Zucchini Bread (page 23) or Sunflower Bread (page 24)
> 1/2 cup almond butter
> 1/3 cup agave syrup
> 2 bananas, sliced

Place a slice of bread on each of four serving plates. Spread each portion with 2 tablespoons of almond butter and drizzle with some agave syrup. Top with half a sliced banana. Spread 2 tablespoons of almond butter onto one side of the remaining slices of bread, and complete each sandwich.

Drizzle 2 to 3 tablespoons of agave syrup over each sandwich. Set aside for 15 minutes or more to marinate. Eat with a fork.

Will keep for 1 day in the fridge.

CINNAMON-APPLE OPEN-FACED SANDWICH

MAKES 4 SERVINGS

Enjoy this sweet sandwich open-faced. Just combine your favorite butter with your favorite bread, stack with sliced apple, drizzle with agave syrup, and sprinkle with cinnamon.

> **4 slices of your favorite bread**
>
> **1 recipe Miso Butter (page 98), Vanilla Butter (page 98), Lavender Butter (page 98), or Chocolate Butter (page 100)**
>
> **1 apple, cored and sliced**
>
> **¼ cup agave syrup**
>
> **1 teaspoon ground cinnamon**

Place a slice of bread on each of four serving dishes. Spread each slice with your choice of butter. Top with sliced apples, drizzle with agave syrup, and sprinkle cinnamon on top.

Will keep for a day.

SUN BURGERS

My sun burgers are made with nuts, seeds, and vegetables . . . many of the same ingredients used when making a cooked veggie burger, minus the wheat, soy, and legumes. The texture of this sun burger when dehydrated is very familiar and similar to that of a falafel, as Andrew Zimmern described it in a recent episode of his *Bizarre Foods* show.

These recipes are versatile and can be enjoyed in different shapes, such as smaller slider-size burgers as hors d'oeuvres for parties. You can even enjoy undehydrated as a fresh pâté, as a filling in nori rolls and wraps, used as you would tuna salad on bread to make a sandwich, and even spooned on top of salads or used as a thick dip for vegetables.

IF YOU'RE NOT as concerned about being on a strict 100 percent raw food diet, all my burgers can also be pan-fried or baked. These burgers are still organic, fresh, super healthy, and clear of all chemicals such as preservatives, pesticides, and artificial colors and flavors, and soy. If you don't like raw flatbreads, enjoy your sun burger on a wheat-free spelt or whole-grain bun with organic ketchup and mustard. Although it won't be fully raw, you'll still be doing your part to live healthy, green, and happy.

SAVE-THE-SALMON BURGER WITH MANGO CHUTNEY

MAKES 4 SERVINGS

When I first served these burgers, people were curious as to the type of fish I used. I repeatedly told them it wasn't real fish, but mock salmon. And when I explained the ingredients and that it was not cooked, they were amazed.

The Mock Tuna Salad is made with carrot pulp, to simulate the fibrous texture of tuna fish, and is mixed together in a creamy Mayonnaise with chopped celery and onion. Patties are formed with this salad, and dehydrated for 2 to 4 hours to firm up. If you're short on time, you can eat this as is, it will be more like a save-the-salmon pâté than burger, but just as delicious.

1 recipe Mock Tuna Salad (page 192)

Form the Mock Tuna Salad into four burger-size patties (not too thick, to help them dry). Place on one 14-inch-square Excalibur Dehydrator Tray, and dehydrate for 2 to 4 hours at 104°F, until your desired consistency.

Serve on your favorite bread (see pages 23 to 24) with Mango Chutney (see page 197) and lettuce.

GENERAL TIP:
Dehydrating in Your Oven

THIS ADVICE ISN'T eco savvy, since conventional ovens are the Humvees of the kitchen. But, if you don't have a dehydrator yet, burgers can be placed in your oven at 140°F with the oven door propped open an inch or two with a chopstick or butter knife. This method of drying will take a very long time, but may be a good starting point to try sun burgers. And, if you decide you love them, like I do, then you'll probably want to invest in an Excalibur Dehydrator at some point.

MANGO CHUTNEY

MAKES 1 CUP

This chutney is inspired by my love for Indian food. My California version is made with fresh mango seasoned with cilantro and red chile. A delicious accompaniment to any burger, wrap, or rice dish.

> 1 cup diced mango
>
> 2 tablespoons lemon juice (from about 1 lemon)
>
> 1 teaspoon minced garlic
>
> 1 small red chile, chopped finely, or to taste
>
> 1/4 cup chopped cilantro
>
> 1/4 cup chopped yellow onion
>
> 1/2 teaspoon sea salt
>
> 1 teaspoon agave syrup (optional)

Place about 2 tablespoons of the mango in a Personal Blender with the lemon juice. Blend to mix and transfer to a small mixing bowl.

Add the remaining ingredients to mixing bowl and toss well to mix.

CHICKENLESS BURGER WITH AIOLI MAYONNAISE

MAKES 4 SERVINGS

Coconut meat is placed on top of this burger before dehydrating and becomes the unchicken "skin" for extra texture. The burger is made with sunflower seeds seasoned with sage and black pepper.

If you don't have Thai baby coconuts, don't fret. This burger's just as delicious without the coconut meat; just leave it off.

> 2 cups sunflower seeds
>
> 1 tablespoon minced garlic
>
> 2 cups chopped celery
>
> 1/4 cup olive oil
>
> 3/4 teaspoon salt
>
> 1 1/2 tablespoons dried sage or poultry seasoning
>
> 1/2 teaspoon ground black pepper
>
> 1 cup coconut meat

Place the sunflower seeds and garlic in a food processor. Process into small pieces. Add the celery, oil, salt, sage, and pepper, and process to mix well. Set aside.

Place the coconut meat in four flat bunches on a 14-inch-square Excalibur Dehydrator tray, so you can then place your patties on top. Form the sunflower mixture into four patties, about ¾-inch thick. Place on top of the coconut meat. Dehydrate for 2 to 3 hours at 104°F. Flip with the coconut meat attached, and dehydrate for another 2 or 3 hours.

 SERVING SUGGESTION: Serve with your favorite bread, such as Zucchini Bread (page 23), iceberg lettuce, tomato, and Aioli Mayonnaise (page 198). Or, make smaller croquette or slider-size burgers and serve with salad.

Serve the burgers on whole-grain buns with Vegenaise.

 ## AIOLI MAYONNAISE
MAKES 1 CUP

This creamy, rich, smooth mayonnaise with a garlic kick can be used in sandwiches, burgers, and wraps—you won't even miss the version full of animal products!

> 1 cup macadamia, cashew, and/or pine nuts
> ³/₄ cup filtered water, or as needed
> 1 teaspoon minced garlic, or to taste
> ¹/₂ teaspoon sea salt

Blend all the ingredients into a smooth mayonnaise, adding more water as needed to produce your desired consistency.

Store for 4 to 5 days in a tightly lidded glass jar in the fridge.

HEMP SUN BURGER WITH MUSTARD

MAKES 4 BURGERS

I made this burger for Andrew Zimmern on his L.A. episode of *Bizarre Foods* on the Travel Channel. Andrew said he would have preferred this burger on a regular bun instead of flax flatbread. If you're from the same camp, feel free to enjoy my burger on your favorite bun with all your favorite fixings.

Garden veggies such as celery, bell peppers, and onion are held together by flax, hemp, and sunflower seeds and spiced with oregano. Some may consider my burger bizarre, but it's just plain delicious.

> 1 cup chopped celery
>
> ½ cup chopped yellow onion
>
> 1 cup seeded and chopped red bell peppers
>
> ½ teaspoon sea salt
>
> 2 teaspoon dried oregano
>
> 1 cup ground sunflower seeds
>
> ½ cup ground flaxseeds
>
> ¼ cup hemp seeds
>
> ½ cup filtered water

Place all the ingredients in a mixing bowl, adding the water last. Mix well. Form into four balls, then flatten into patties.

Place on one 14-inch-square Excalibur Dehydrator tray, and dehydrate for 3 to 4 hours at 104°F.

Serve warm with your favorite Flax Flatbread (or on your favorite whole-grain bun). Garnish with Homemade Mustard Sauce (page 201), tomato, lettuce, and ketchup, as you would any burger.

The burgers will keep for 4 to 5 days in the fridge.

HOMEMADE MUSTARD SAUCE

MAKES ABOUT 1 CUP

Beware, black mustard seeds are the spiciest, so use them only if you like it hot. Otherwise, stick with the yellow seeds.

The seeds are soaked for two days, then pureed with agave syrup and salt to make a delicious homemade mustard sauce.

> ⅓ cup yellow or black mustard seeds
>
> ½ cup apple cider vinegar
>
> 2 to 3 tablespoons water, as needed
>
> 1 teaspoon agave syrup
>
> 1 teaspoon sea salt, or to taste

Begin by soaking your mustard seeds in the vinegar and water at room temperature for 2 days. Add more water as needed to ensure the seeds are submerged in the water.

Gently puree the soaked seeds in a food processor with the agave syrup and salt. Add water as needed to produce your desired consistency.

Store in a tightly lidded glass container in the fridge; this mustard will keep for at least 5 to 6 days.

BBQ BURGER

MAKES 4 SERVINGS

This burger's all about the Hickory BBQ Sauce. Choose your favorite burger and bread, and top with sauce and your favorite toppings. I like my burger sloppy, which means I top it with a generous amount of sauce! Beware: the chile powder in this sauce packs a punch in color as well as flavor, so be sure to use darker-colored cloth napkins or bandanas as napkins to avoid stains.

> 1 recipe of your favorite burger
>
> 1 recipe Hickory BBQ Sauce (page 202)
>
> 1 recipe of your favorite bread

Serve your favorite burger on the bread of your choice, topped with BBQ Sauce, sliced onions, and lettuce.

HICKORY BBQ SAUCE
MAKES ABOUT 1 CUP

Tomato is blended with sweet mango, tart apple cider vinegar, and chile powder to make a delicious sauce you'll want to use on your burgers, as a dip for your vegetables, and in your wraps.

I like to add a smoky flavor by using a drop or two of smoke flavor. I use flavorings sparingly and find this one adds a layer of taste and smell that is easy to miss with raw foods. Decide for yourself if you'd like to use it by reading Liquid Smoke, page 84.

> 1 cup seeded and chopped tomato
>
> 3 tablespoons apple cider vinegar
>
> 2 tablespoons agave nectar
>
> 2 tablespoons chopped yellow onion
>
> 1 teaspoon garlic
>
> 1 tablespoon chile powder
>
> ⅓ cup dried mango
>
> 1 or 2 drops liquid smoke (optional)

Place all the ingredients, except the dried mango, in a high-speed blender. Blend until smooth. Add the mango gradually and blend, to thicken your sauce. Add more or less mango to produce your desired consistency. Note that the sauce will thicken as time passes and the dried mango absorbs even more of the liquid.

SLOPPY JOE
MAKES 4 SERVINGS

Chickenless Burger is crumbled into a marinara sauce with chile powder, to create a sloppy, saucy burger.

I used to love how marinara would soak into bread. If you're not concerned with keeping to a strict 100 percent raw diet, feel free to make your Sloppy Joe on a wheat-free or whole-grain bun. Whatever suits your fancy. The sauce and burger are still superclean, green, and healthy for you!

> 1 recipe Chickenless Burger (page 197), dehydrated as directed and crumbled
>
> ½ recipe Cherry Tomato Marinara (page 240)
>
> 1 tablespoon chile powder

Place the ingredients in a mixing bowl, and toss well to mix.

Serve on your favorite bread with romaine lettuce. Enjoy immediately.

PORTOBELLO BURGER

MAKES 4 SERVINGS

Marinated portobello mushroom slices are topped with Avocado-Pistachio Pesto, Buckwheat-Battered "Fried" Onion Rings, and "Roasted" Bell Peppers, to make a mushroom lovers' dream burger.

   2 portobello mushrooms, stems removed, sliced into $\frac{1}{4}$-inch slices

   2 tablespoons Nama Shoyu or Bragg Liquid Aminos

   1 tablespoon lime juice

   3 tablespoons extra-virgin olive oil

   1 recipe Avocado-Pistachio Pesto (page 216)

   1 recipe Buckwheat-Battered "Fried" Onion Rings (page 116)

   1 recipe "Roasted" Bell Peppers (page 118)

   4 tomato slices

   4 romaine leaves

   1 recipe of your favorite bread

Place the mushrooms in a bowl with the Nama Shoyu, lime juice, and olive oil. Set aside to marinate for at least 20 minutes.

Squeeze the excess marinade from the marinated mushrooms, and discard the marinade. Arrange the mushroom slices on your favorite bread. Top with the remaining ingredients and serve immediately.

INSIDE-OUT BURGER

MAKES 4 BURGERS

These burger patties are assembled on the outside as your "bun," then filled with such fillings as lettuce, tomato, onions, and Aioli Mayonnaise (page 198).

> 4 cups peeled, chopped carrots and/or beets
>
> 1 teaspoon minced garlic
>
> 1 teaspoon sea salt
>
> 2 tablespoons extra-virgin olive oil
>
> ³/₄ cup almond meal
>
> ¹/₂ cup flax meal
>
> 1 recipe Sun-Dried Tomato Ketchup (page 205)

Place the carrots, garlic, salt, and olive oil in a food processor and pulse into small pieces. Add the almond and flax meal, and mix well.

Form into ½-cup patties, and flatten to about ½- to ¾-inch thick. Place on one 14-inch-square Excalibur Dehydrator tray. Dehydrate for 3 to 4 hours at 104°F.

To serve, use two patties as your "bun," and fill with your favorite burger fillings, such as lettuce, tomato, onion, and mayonnaise, ketchup, or mustard.

SUN-DRIED TOMATO KETCHUP

MAKES ABOUT 1 CUP

Sun-dried tomatoes give this ketchup its beautiful red color and thick consistency. The dried tomatoes absorb excess juice and liquid from blending fresh tomatoes and tart apple cider vinegar.

> 1 cup seeded and diced tomato
>
> 2 teaspoons apple cider vinegar
>
> 1 teaspoon agave syrup
>
> ¹/₂ teaspoon sea salt
>
> ¹/₄ cup sun-dried tomatoes

Place the fresh tomato, vinegar, agave syrup, and salt in a high-speed blender, and blend until smooth. Add the sun-dried tomatoes and blend to mix well.

Will keep for 4 days in the fridge.

9

PIZZA AND NOODLES

A **RAW PIZZA** or raw noodles may not sound very appetizing. But raw pizza is actually my favorite of all raw food entrées. Pizzas are made by layering sauces such as a marinara that's been blended with fresh tomatoes and herbs, or a pesto made with pistachios and basil, with fresh pizza toppings such as olives, tomatoes, battered and "fried" onions, and my dairy-free cheeze. Noodles are made from sliced or spiralized fresh vegetables, dehydrated and sliced vegetable wrapper "fettuccine," or a package of low-calorie, mineral-rich, kelp noodles. Noodles are tossed in sauces and broths to make such pasta dishes as Korean-style Jap Chae, Teriyaki Noodles, and Vietnamese Pho.

Give these pizzas and pastas a try and you'll quickly agree that raw pizzas and noodles are delicious—and they are good for you!

PIZZA

As with any recipe, raw pizza is about simulating flavors and textures. In my raw pizzas, the marinara is already similar to a cooked marinara, which is made by blending tomatoes with Italian herbs. My cheeze is much like a melted dairy cheese in consistency and flavor, and the toppings are the same as those on a baked pizza, such as tomatoes, olives, onions, peppers, basil, and pineapple. You can start to see that raw pizzas are really not very different from a cooked pizza. I like to drizzle them with olive oil as a finishing touch. The oil gives my raw pizza that oil-on-your-lips taste similar to dairy cheese.

One thing that is different in raw pizza is the crust: it's wheat and gluten free and made from flax and vegetables, so it's superhealthy. I like to use a dehydrated crust, which has a texture similar to baked crust once all the toppings and sauce are on it. But dehydrated crust isn't a must-have; in this chapter I'll introduce you to a delicious no-dehydration-required instant crust that works great for times when you want a pizza quickly and don't have a premade crust ready.

I'll start you off with some of the basics to show you how easy it is to begin with your favorite crust, then layer on all of your favorite toppings. Just as baked pizza always tastes better the next day, my raw pizzas also taste better a few hours, or even a day, later. The veggies and sauce have time to marinate, and the crust will soak up the juices. If you can hold off, give it a try. Better yet, make extra so you'll have leftovers for the next day.

INSTANT PIZZA CRUST

MAKES 4 SERVINGS, OR CRUST FOR ONE 12-INCH PIE

To make this simple crust, mix the ingredients together, form the batter into your desired shape, and then add your favorite sauce and toppings. No dehydration required.

Seasoned with oregano, garlic, and olive oil, this is a moist, soft crust with a texture and consistency similar to that of a whole-grain, seeded, handmade tortilla.

You can form the batter into four individual pizzettes, or into one larger pizza crust.

> 1 cup sunflower seeds, ground into powder (about 1¼ cups, ground)
> 1 cup flax meal
> 2 teaspoons dried oregano
> ½ teaspoon salt
> 1 teaspoon minced garlic (about 1 clove)
> 2 tablespoons olive oil
> 5 tablespoons filtered water, plus extra if needed

Place the sunflower and flax meal, oregano, and salt in a mixing bowl. Toss to mix. Add the garlic, olive oil, and water, and mix well. You can add another tablespoon of water if needed to help batter stick together, but be careful not to add too much water so your crust doesn't get mushy.

If making individual pizzettes, scoop ⅓ cup lightly packed portions onto each of four serving dishes. Press each into a circle about 4 inches in diameter, with a raised edge around the circumference.

Or, on a serving tray, press the entire batter into one large pizza crust with a raised edge.

Scoop on your favorite sauce, cheeze, and toppings, and serve.

The crust alone will keep for 5 days in the fridge. An assembled pizza will keep for 1 to 2 days in the fridge, depending on the freshness of the toppings.

REMEMBER, THERE'S NO need to be extreme. So, if you prefer using an already baked whole-grain pizza crust, just top it with your favorite raw dairy-free cheeze and sauce, plus toppings. The raw ingredients won't require any additional cooking time, so you can still eat up right away.

AMBER WAVES OF GRAIN

WE ALL love our breads, bagels, pizza, pasta, breakfast cereals, and pancakes, which have become a staple in the American diet. But, as the book *Dangerous Grains* states, grains are at the root of many serious health issues. Wild grains are hard to eat and were never a part of our human diet until recent agricultural technology was invented. Grain farming requires more effort than hunting or gathering, but grains can be stored for long periods of time, making grains more reliable as a source of food. This enabled humans to settle into more permanent communities.

Most grains today are highly processed, have excessive amounts of sugar and carbohydrates, and are full of toxic pesticides and additives. Processing whole-grain wheat into white flour grinds away its nutrients and leaves behind pure starch devoid of vitamins, minerals, or fiber. Vitamins and minerals are later added back to the flour to make it "enriched."

Wheat is acid forming and slows down our metabolism. It contains a protein called gluten that creates inflammation in the body and contributes to bacterial imbalance, yeast overgrowth, and food allergies; depletes the immune system; and makes us feel and look bloated and swollen. Even organic whole wheat raises insulin levels, disrupts biochemistry, and impairs our body's ability to lose weight.

Dr. Joseph Mercola, author of *The No-Grain Diet*, says one in every thirty-three people exhibits symptoms of celiac disease, a severe from of gluten intolerance resulting in intestinal complications, and the numbers are continuing to rise. Gluten is an allergen protein in wheat, barley, and rye.

My friend Billy is an organic and permaculture farmer in Portland, Oregon, and he breaks it down for me like this: Grains are mass produced and mono-cropped, meaning the same crops are grown over large areas of farmland every year. This creates a breeding ground for pests because the crops aren't rotated. So, each year, stronger and stronger pesticides need to be used to combat stronger pests. Farming the same crops year after year depletes the nutrients in the soil, while the chemical pesticides and fertilizers provide no nutrients to the soil, nor to the crops grown in it. This is why nonorganic foods contain less nutrient value.

On the other hand, organic gardening and permaculture use broken-down plant materials, microorganisms, and compost to amend the soil, to replenish it, and to put nutrients back into it so the food grown is nutrient dense.

Michael Pollan, author of many books including *The Omnivore's Dilemma*, in his TED (Technology, Entertainment, Design) talk describes a farmer who calls himself a grass farmer, rather than a chicken or sheep or cattle farmer. This farmer moves chickens around his farm to help fertilize the soil. The chickens break down the cow manure and help to enrich the soil so it grows healthier grasses, which in turn feed his livestock. Pollan points out that we think that for us to get what we want, nature needs to be diminished. In this example of the farmer, there's actually more soil, more fertility, and more biodiversity created at the end of the season, not less. Says Pollan, "If we begin to take account of other species and the soil, we can take the food we need from the earth and heal the earth in the process. This is a way to reanimate the world." I couldn't agree more.

DEHYDRATED PIZZA CRUST

My pizza crusts are basically flatbread and cracker recipes that I think work well topped with pizza ingredients. When sauce and toppings are added, the crust takes on a texture and taste that to me is very baked pizza–like.

As with baked pizza that can be made on English muffins, baguettes, and sliced bread, you can also use whatever raw cracker or raw flatbread you may have on hand to make any pizza.

BUCKWHEAT PIZZA CRUST

MAKES 9 SERVINGS

The buckwheat makes this a light crust that's delicious when topped with marinara or pesto and your favorite pizza toppings.

If you don't have Buckwheat Crispies on hand, use ½ cup of dried buckwheat groats instead.

- ½ cup dried Buckwheat Crispies (page 63)
- 3 cups chopped celery
- 2 tablespoons olive oil
- ½ teaspoon sea salt
- 1 cup water
- 1 cup flax meal

Grind the Buckwheat Crispies into a powder, set aside.

Place the celery, olive oil, salt, and water in a high-speed blender. Blend until smooth. Add the flax meal and blend to mix well. Add the buckwheat powder and blend to mix well.

Scoop the batter onto a lined 14-inch-square Excalibur Dehydrator tray. Spread the batter evenly across the entire surface.

Dehydrate for 10 hours at 104°F. Flip and score into your desired shape, either a circular pie or nine slices. Dehydrate for another 4 to 6 hours, until the crust has your desired consistency.

TOMATO PIZZA CRUST

MAKES 9 SERVINGS

Made with both flax meal and flaxseed for additional texture and crunch, this pizza crust will add even more tomato flavor to your pizza. The tomato helps to keep this crust pizza dough–like, rather than too crispy.

- ½ cup flax meal
- 1½ cups seeded and chopped fresh tomato
- ½ teaspoon sea salt
- 1 cup filtered water
- 1 cup whole flaxseed

Place the flax meal, tomato, salt, and water in a high-speed blender. Blend until smooth. Add the whole flaxseeds, and pulse gently to mix.

Spread the batter evenly onto a lined 14-inch-square Excalibur Dehydrator tray.

Dehydrate for 6 to 8 hours at 104°F. Flip, score into nine slices, then dehydrate for another 4 to 6 hours, or until the crust has your desired consistency.

OREGANO PIZZA CRUST

MAKES 9 SERVINGS

This is a medium-thick crust with the soft texture of a baked pizza crust. Celery is blended with flax powder for a smooth texture and natural salt and spiced with oregano for Italian flavor.

1½ cups chopped celery

1½ cups flax meal

3 tablespoons dried oregano

1½ cups filtered water

Blend all the ingredients in a high-speed blender.

Spread the dough in a circle on a lined 14-inch-square Excalibur Dehydrator tray.

Dehydrate for 6 hours. Flip and dehydrate for another 6 hours, or until dry.

Mincing Garlic

I LOVE GARLIC, but it can be a pain to peel and chop when I don't have a lot of time. A simple way to peel garlic is to place a clove on your cutting board and press down with the flat side of your knife to smash it. Then peel off the skin.

To mince your garlic, use a fork. Place the peeled garlic on your cutting board. Use the fork's flat edge to press down, to mash and mince garlic.

BLACK OLIVE AND PESTO PIZZA

MAKES 4 SERVINGS

Start by choosing your favorite crust, either dehydrated or the quickie instant one. Top the crust with pesto, tomato, onion, bell pepper, black olives, and Rawmesan Cheeze.

If you can wait to dig in, try placing your assembled pizza in the dehydrator at 104°F for about an hour or two, to warm up.

CRUST

1 recipe Buckwheat Pizza Crust (page 213), Tomato Pizza Crust (page 213), Oregano Pizza Crust (page 214), or Instant Pizza Crust (page 209)

TOPPINGS

1 recipe Avocado-Pistachio Pesto (page 216)

1 tomato, sliced and seeded

3 tablespoons thinly sliced red onion

½ cup diced and seeded green bell pepper

¼ cup pitted, chopped black olives

1 recipe Rawmesan Cheeze (page 105) or Cheezy Sprinkle (page 106)

Olive oil or Herb-Infused Olive Oil (page 217)

To assemble your pizza, spread the pesto on the pizza crust. Top with the tomato and onion slices, then sprinkle with the bell pepper, olives, and Rawmesan Cheeze.

Drizzle a few tablespoons of olive oil over your pizza just before serving, to create that baked pizza greasy-mouth feel when you bite into it.

Will keep for a couple of days in the fridge.

AVOCADO-PISTACHIO PESTO
MAKES 1 CUP

A creamy, dreamy pesto with pistachio, fresh basil, and avocado, made in your food processor.

$\frac{1}{2}$ tablespoon crushed garlic (about 1 medium-size clove)

$\frac{1}{2}$ teaspoon salt

1 cup shelled pistachio nuts

2 cups fresh basil, lightly packed

1 tablespoon lemon juice

$\frac{1}{2}$ cup chopped ripe avocado

1 tablespoon olive oil

Place the garlic and salt in a food processor. Process into small pieces. Add the pistachio nuts, and process into small pieces. Add the basil, lemon juice, avocado, and olive oil, and process until mixed well.

This pesto is best made fresh and consumed within a few hours of making. The parts exposed to air will begin to oxidize and turn brown in time, so you'll want to scoop away the top brown layer before using.

FRIED ONION AND MUSHROOM PIZZA
MAKES 4 SERVINGS

Here, mushrooms are marinated with rosemary, then placed on your favorite pizza crust with marinara and Buckwheat-Battered "Fried" Onion Rings. If you want to avoid marinating in salty Nama Shoyu or Bragg Liquid Aminos, try using citrus juice and olive oil, or dehydrating. (See Marinating Mushrooms, page 80.)

If you can wait, let the pizza marinate at room temperature for an hour after it's assembled. The crust will soak up the sauce and marinade from the mushrooms. Another option is to put the assembled pizza into your dehydrator to warm up for an hour or two at 104°F before serving.

For a thicker marinara, add 1 tablespoon of chopped sun-dried tomatoes when blending your sauce.

TOPPINGS

2 cups sliced mushrooms (any type)

2 tablespoons Bragg Liquid Aminos or Nama Shoyu

2 tablespoons extra-virgin olive oil

½ teaspoon fresh rosemary, ¼ teaspoon dried, chopped

1 recipe Cherry Tomato Marinara (page 240)

1 recipe Buckwheat-Battered "Fried" Onion Rings (page 116)

Olive oil or Herb-Infused Olive Oil (page 217)

CRUST

1 recipe Buckwheat Pizza Crust (page 213), Tomato Pizza Crust (page 213), Oregano Pizza Crust (page 214), or Instant Pizza Crust (page 209)

Place the sliced mushrooms in a mixing bowl with the Bragg, olive oil, and rosemary. Toss to mix well, and set aside to marinate.

Assemble the pizza by spreading the marinara on your crust. Next, squeeze the liquid from the marinated mushrooms and discard the marinade. Add the mushrooms to your pizza. Lastly, sprinkle with your onions. Drizzle with several tablespoons of olive oil before serving.

SERVING SUGGESTION: Sprinkle with microgreens, arugula, and/or Cheezy Sprinkle (page 106).

Will keep for 1 to 2 days in the fridge.

Herb-Infused Olive Oil

YOU MAY HAVE noticed that I love to drizzle olive oil over my pizza just before serving. It's to create that greasy feel on your lips similar to when you're eating a baked dairy pizza.

A delicious idea is to pour about ¼ to ⅓ cup of olive oil into a small glass jar or bowl, and add fresh herbs and spices, such a tablespoon of torn fresh basil, thyme leaves, chopped rosemary, minced garlic, and/or diced chiles. Then, cover and set aside for an hour or more, to infuse and mix together all the flavors.

Use this infused olive oil to drizzle over your pizza. Don't bother to strain—include all the herbs and spices.

GARLIC MARGHERITA PIZZA

MAKES 4 SERVINGS

My raw version is very similar to the baked classic: marinara is spread over your favorite crust layered with sliced tomatoes, cheeze, fresh basil, and minced garlic.

CRUST

1 recipe Buckwheat Pizza Crust (page 213), Tomato Pizza Crust (page 213),

Oregano Pizza Crust (page 214), or Instant Pizza Crust (page 209)

TOPPINGS

1 recipe Cherry Tomato Marinara (page 240)

1 cup sliced and seeded tomato

1 recipe of your favorite Basic Cheeze (page 103)

¼ cup torn fresh basil

1 teaspoon minced garlic

Olive oil or Herb-Infused Olive Oil (page 217)

Make your marinara. For a thicker marinara, add 1 tablespoon of chopped sun-dried tomatoes when blending your sauce.

Assemble the pizza by spreading the marinara on the crust. Top with the tomato slices.

Drop dollops of cheeze from a spoon onto the pizza. Sprinkle with basil and garlic. Drizzle with olive oil before serving.

Will keep for 1 day in the fridge.

VARIATION: Mix it up by adding fresh herbs, marinated mushrooms, black olives, or other toppings.

HAWAIIAN PIZZA

MAKES 4 SERVINGS

Most of the flavor in Hawaiian pizza comes from the pineapple, with the bacon adding a salty, hearty mouthfeel. In my raw vegan version, the toppings are pretty much the same with marinara, cheeze, pineapple, plus my Coconut Bacon.

CRUST

1 recipe Buckwheat Pizza Crust (page 213), Tomato Pizza Crust (page 213), Oregano Pizza Crust (page 214), or Instant Pizza Crust (page 209)

TOPPINGS

1 recipe Cherry Tomato Marinara (page 240)

1 recipe Basic Cheeze (page 103)

1 cup diced fresh pineapple

1 recipe Coconut Bacon (page 76) or Eggplant Bacon (page 78)

Olive oil or Herb-Infused Olive Oil (page 217)

Make your marinara. For a thicker marinara, add 1 tablespoon of chopped sun-dried tomatoes when blending your sauce. The dried tomatoes will soak up excess tomato juice.

Assemble the pizza by spreading the marinara on the crust. Drop dollops of cheeze from a spoon onto the pizza. Add the pineapple and bacon. Drizzle with a few tablespoons of olive oil before serving.

Will keep for 1 day in the fridge.

NOODLES

Raw noodles are terrific for many reasons. First, they are made with vegetables, so they're wheat free, gluten free, and low-carb. Raw noodles are a great vehicle for enjoying delicious sauces (from Korean to Italian, and everything in between), but with less calories and no processed white flour.

An easy substitute for vegetable noodles are noodles made from kelp. Kelp is a sea vegetable that's full of minerals and iodine to feed our thyroid and helps regulate our metabolism. Kelp noodles only have 6 calories a serving. You read it right, 6 calories! The colder they are, the crunchier their texture. I like to warm them up by rinsing them in warm water to soften the noodles before using them in my noodle recipes. Kelp noodles originate in Korea and can be found in natural food stores, in Asian markets, and online.

To make any noodle dish, just choose your favorite noodles, then toss with the sauce you're craving. Explore toppings to add color and texture, such as fresh herbs, diced vegetables, or chopped nuts and seeds.

Making Noodles from Fresh Veggies

DIFFERENT TYPES of noodles can be made from such vegetables as zucchini or red bell pepper. Using a spiralizer, or spiral slicer, you can create angel hair–shaped noodles. No need to peel your zucchini, because the skin is soft and doesn't affect the noodle texture. Cut your zucchini into 3-inch-high rounds, and place securely into your spiralizer container, with the blade turned to the side with all the teeth, and then close the lid. It will take practice to master using the machine; a spiralizer can be tricky, but well worth the effort. Apply constant downward pressure onto the handle while turning slowly to slice your vegetables into long, angel hair noodles.

For flat, fettuccine-style noodles, slice vegetables into thin, long pieces on a mandoline slicer, then cut lengthwise with a knife to create a fettuccine shape.

If you don't have these tools, you can julienne or thinly slice veggies by hand or with a vegetable peeler.

Try adding sliced coconut meat to your noodles for extra texture and flavor. Or add long slices of dehydrated wrappers or crepes for another level of texture, color, and flavor.

FETTUCCINE WRAPPER NOODLES

When I'm in the mood to add a level of complexity and another layer of texture to my noodle dish, I'll mix the vegetable noodles half and half with wrapper noodles made by slicing wrappers into long strips shaped like fettuccine.

Tomato Wrapper or Apple Crepes are two flavors that work well in savory recipes, with all types of noodle dishes, dressing, and sauces.

KOREAN STIR-FRIED KELP NOODLES WITH VEGETABLES (*JAP CHAE*)

MAKES 4 SERVINGS

Jap chae is one of my favorite Korean noodle dishes, and it's traditionally made with rice noodles. This recipe was inspired by my mother, who pointed out how similar kelp noodles are to rice noodles. Mom helped me figure out how to season my noodles with pretty much the same ingredients as in the cooked version. I marinate my mushrooms and onions to get the same texture as if they were sautéed.

If you can't find kelp noodles, substitute your favorite vegetable noodles.

½ cup thinly sliced onion

1 cup sliced shiitake mushrooms

1 tablespoon Nama Shoyu or Bragg Liquid Aminos

½ cup julienned carrot

½ teaspoon minced garlic

1 teaspoon agave syrup

2 tablespoons toasted sesame oil

1 (12-ounce) package kelp noodles

1 cup spinach, washed well and packed

Place the onion and mushrooms in a large mixing bowl and toss with the Nama Shoyu until mixed well. Set aside for at least 15 to 20 minutes to marinate and soften.

Add to the marinade the carrot, garlic, agave, and sesame oil. Mix well. Add the noodles and spinach, and toss to mix well.

Will keep for 1 day in the fridge.

TERIYAKI NOODLES

MAKES 4 SERVINGS

A light sauce made by whisking together Nama Shoyu with tart vinegar, spicy ginger, savory garlic, and a splash of sweet agave syrup.

This delicious sauce makes a great dressing and dip for dumplings, vegetables, and wraps.

SAUCE

3 tablespoons extra-virgin olive oil

2 tablespoons Nama Shoyu or Bragg Liquid Aminos

3 tablespoons agave syrup

1 tablespoon apple cider vinegar

1 tablespoon grated fresh ginger

1 teaspoon minced garlic

NOODLES

4 cups spiralized zucchini noodles (4 to 5 zucchini)

Whisk together all the sauce ingredients, and toss with the noodles in a mixing bowl.

The sauce will keep for 4 to 5 days in the fridge. Noodles that have been tossed with the sauce will keep for a day or two in the fridge.

PAD THAI WITH KELP NOODLES

MAKES 4 SERVINGS

Although traditional peanut sauce can be complicated to make, my version is pared down to the basics. Because raw peanut butter doesn't taste very good, I use almond butter, seasoned with coconut oil, lemon, jalapeño, and coriander. Just blend and toss.

I recommend slicing your cabbage with a mandoline slicer, to get the thinnest slices. You can always use a knife. And, if you don't have kelp noodles, use spiralized zucchini or sliced coconut meat instead. Red bell peppers make tasty, pretty noodles, too.

"PEANUT" SAUCE
MAKES ABOUT 1½ CUPS

¼ cup almond butter

½ cup coconut oil

2 tablespoons Bragg Liquid Aminos or Nama Shoyu

¼ cup lemon juice

1 tablespoon seeded, chopped jalapeño, or to taste

1 teaspoon ground coriander

¾ cup filtered water

NOODLES

¼ cup sliced fresh basil

1 cup thinly sliced cabbage

2 (12-ounce) packages kelp noodles (or your favorite noodles)

Place the sauce ingredients in a 2-cup Personal Blender. Blend until smooth.

To serve, toss the sauce with the basil, cabbage, and noodles.

The sauce will keep on its own for up to 3 to 4 days in the fridge. Noodles that have been tossed with the sauce will keep for a day or two in the fridge.

SERVING SUGGESTION: Top with microgreens, Tamari Almonds (page 119), and wedges of lime.

SESAME NOODLES

MAKES 4 SERVINGS

This recipe calls for cashew and walnut butter, to make it easy to get a supersmooth texture. You can always grind your nuts into a powder first, or use whole nuts with a bit more water, only as needed, to blend into a smooth, rich sauce.

This sauce is flavored with toasted sesame oil, Bragg Liquid Aminos, vinegar, garlic, and ginger. Toasted sesame oil creates an authentic Asian flavor, but you can use raw sesame oil instead if you want to keep it truly raw.

SESAME SAUCE
MAKES 1 CUP

¼ cup cashew butter

¼ cup walnut butter

1 tablespoon toasted sesame oil

2 teaspoons Bragg Liquid Aminos

2 teaspoons apple cider vinegar

⅛ teaspoon cayenne, or to taste

1 teaspoon minced garlic (about 1 clove)

1 teaspoon minced fresh ginger

6 tablespoons filtered water

NOODLES

½ cup sliced and seeded red bell pepper

2 tablespoons thinly sliced green onion (about 1 stalk)

1 cup sliced coconut meat

1 (12-ounce) package kelp noodles (or your favorite noodle)

TOPPINGS

¼ cup coarsely chopped Tamari Almonds (page 119)

Place all sauce ingredients in a small Personal Blender and blend until smooth. (You can use a handheld blender as well.)

Place the noodle ingredients in a mixing bowl, and toss with the sauce.

To serve, distribute the tossed noodles among four plates. Top with the chopped almonds, and enjoy.

The sauce will keep for 3 to 4 days in the fridge. Noodles that have been tossed with the sauce will keep for a day or two in the fridge.

NOODLES WITH JULIENNED VEGETABLES, DAILY GREENS, TOSSED IN BASIC BLENDED DRESSING

MAKES 4 SERVINGS

I like tossing this dish with Basic Blended Dressing and zucchini squash in the summertime. For a sweeter salad, add 1 cup of fresh corn kernels to your mixture.

> 2 cups sliced white or cremini mushrooms (about 3.5 ounces)
>
> 1 tablespoon Nama Shoyu or Bragg Liquid Aminos
>
> 2 cups shredded green cabbage
>
> 2 cups torn romaine lettuce
>
> 1 cup julienned mixed carrots and broccoli stalks
>
> 1 recipe of your favorite Basic Blended Dressing (page 151)

First, toss the mushrooms with the Nama Shoyu, and set aside to marinate for at least 10 minutes.

In a large mixing bowl, combine remaining ingredients plus the marinated mushrooms with their marinade. Toss to mix well.

The tossed salad will keep for 1 day in the fridge.

AVOCADO-PISTACHIO PESTO NOODLE SALAD

MAKES 4 SERVINGS

I love tossing a bag of kelp noodles into my salad to create a new noodle recipe. Kelp noodles are combined here with a thick, rich, creamy pesto, and also a fresh herbed salad mixture for texture, more flavor, and color.

> 1 (12-ounce) package kelp noodles (or your favorite noodles)
>
> 4 cups herbed spring salad mixture, lightly packed
>
> 1 recipe Avocado-Pistachio Pesto (page 216)

Place all the ingredients in a mixing bowl and toss everything together well.

VIETNAMESE PHO NOODLE SOUP

MAKES 4 SERVINGS

Inspired by the Vietnamese broth called *pho*, made with aromatic ginger, cinnamon, cloves, and anise, this broth is poured over a bowlful of noodles, fresh herbs, bean sprouts, and lime. Star anise is beautiful, but if it isn't available, substitute ½ teaspoon of Chinese five-spice powder, aniseeds, or fennel seeds.

BROTH

½ cup thinly sliced yellow onion

1 teaspoon minced garlic

1 tablespoon minced fresh ginger

½ teaspoon ground cinnamon

⅓ cup Nama Shoyu or Bragg Liquid Aminos

4 pods star anise

4 cups filtered water

SOUP

2 (12-ounce) packages kelp noodles, rinsed and drained, or 4 cups of your favorite noodles

¼ cup thinly sliced green onions

1½ cups bean sprouts

½ cup whole fresh basil, mint, or cilantro leaves

1 lime, cut into wedges

1 red Thai chile (optional)

To make your broth, place onion, garlic, ginger, cinnamon, Nama Shoyu, and star anise in a large mixing bowl. Mix well, and set aside for at least 20 minutes to marinate. Then, add the water and stir well.

To serve, divide the soup ingredients among four bowls, and ladle your broth over the top. Make sure to include one star anise in each bowl, as garnish.

Pho will keep for 1 day in the fridge. The broth alone will keep for 2 to 3 days in the fridge.

CARROT ANGEL HAIR WITH SUN-DRIED TOMATOES IN CHEDDAR CHEEZE SAUCE

MAKES 4 SERVINGS

Beautiful orange carrots are spiralized into noodles that are tossed in a cheeze sauce with spicy arugula, topped with sun-dried tomatoes, pine nuts, and Rawmesan Cheeze.

> 4 cups spiralized carrots (about 8 carrots)
> 1 recipe Cheddar Cheeze Sauce (page 105)
> 2 cups baby arugula
>
> TOPPINGS
> ⅓ cup sliced sun-dried tomatoes
> ⅓ cup pine nuts
> 1 recipe Rawmesan Cheeze (page 105)

In a mixing bowl, toss together carrots, cheeze, and arugula to mix well.

To serve, distribute the noodles among four serving dishes and top with the tomatoes, pine nuts, and Rawmesan Cheeze.

SERVING SUGGESTION: Serve garnished with wedges of Kalamata Olive Crostini (page 114)

FETTUCCINE WITH LEMON, GARLIC, AND THYME-MARINATED MUSHROOMS

MAKES 4 SERVINGS

This beautiful dish is inspired by a classic Italian recipe. Dehydrated wrappers are cut into fettuccine-shaped noodle strips. If you want to lighten up this dish, mix dehydrated noodles half and half with zucchini noodles also sliced into long, flat strips.

4 cups finely sliced cremini mushrooms

⅓ cup extra-virgin olive oil

1 teaspoon sea salt

1 teaspoon minced garlic

2 teaspoons lemon juice

1 teaspoon lemon zest

1 teaspoon fresh thyme leaves, or ½ teaspoon dried

1 recipe Fettuccine Wrapper Noodles (page 222)

TOPPINGS

¼ cup chopped fresh parsley

1 recipe Rawmesan Cheeze (page 105)

Black pepper

Place the mushrooms, oil, salt, garlic, lemon juice and zest, and thyme in a mixing bowl, and toss well. Set aside for 20 minutes or more to marinate.

To serve, toss the noodles in a bowl with the marinated mushrooms. Distribute among four serving dishes, and top with the parsley, Rawmesan Cheeze, and black pepper to taste. Serve and enjoy immediately.

10

DUMPLINGS AND RICE

MANY DIFFERENT CULTURES have their own unique version of a dumpling, or a filled pocket typically made of wheat flour. Korea has their *mandu*, which is traditionally filled with vegetables or meat, pan-fried, steamed, or boiled in a soup. *Mandu* can be eaten on their own as a snack or appetizer with a soy vinegar dipping sauce. Similarly, you'll find gyoza in Japan and wonton in China. Italy has ravioli filled with cheese or other fillings and topped with marinara sauce; the Eastern European pierogi are laden with potato and cheese, among other savory fillings.

For my raw vegan versions of dumplings, I like to use my Spinach or Tomato Wrappers for the pocket, and fill them with vegetables and cheezes. Another easier and fresher way to make wrappers is to thinly slice beets, zucchini, daikon radish, or

turnip, and to then sandwich cheeze between two layers of the vegetables. If the circular slice is large enough, as with daikon, it can be folded to form a stuffed semicircle. The nice thing about these dumplings is that you don't have to wait for them to cook; they're ready to eat right away. They are wheat and gluten free, and super delicious!

My "rice" is made by mixing together small bits of pine nuts with turnips, and is used in the same way as cooked rice inside Japanese-inspired nori rolls and risotto. I sprout my quinoa and wild rice and use it to make delicious tabbouleh and wild rice recipes.

KOREAN DUMPLINGS

MAKES 4 SERVINGS

Traditionally, to make dumplings, a shredded vegetable filling is enclosed in a circular wrapper that's folded over the filling. It's easy to make, but making your filling, then stuffing all your wrappers, can take a bit of time. This is a fun thing to do with friends and kids, as extra sets of hands will speed up your process.

WRAPPERS

1 recipe Tomato Wrappers (page 173), dehydrated as directed, cut into 16 squares about 3½ inches across

FILLING

MAKES ABOUT 2 CUPS

½ cup Green Cabbage Kimchi (page 131), squeezed dry and sliced finely (if you don't have kimchi handy, see note below)

¾ cup finely chopped lettuce, such as iceberg, bok choy, or romaine

1¼ cups finely chopped bean sprouts, or your favorite sprout

2 tablespoons finely chopped green onion (about 1 whole green onion)

1 tablespoon toasted sesame oil, for flavor, or raw if you prefer

Place all the filling ingredients in a mixing bowl and toss to mix well. Squeeze out all excess liquid completely before using. Make sure the filling is drained well, otherwise your wrapper will get soggy quickly.

Place a wrapper square in the palm of your hand, shiny side up. (The side that dehydrated against the Paraflexx liner needs to be facing upward.) Scoop 1 tablespoon of filling into the center of your wrapper, and fold and seal a pocket in the shape of a triangle. Then fold so that the two far edges of the triangle meet, and pinch together. See Mandu Making, page 238.

Serve with Soy Vinegar Dipping Sauce (page 239).

KIMCHI SUBSTITUTE: If you don't have kimchi on hand, use ½ cup of shredded napa cabbage tossed with ½ teaspoon of Nama Shoyu or Bragg Liquid Aminos, a pinch of cayenne (to taste), 1 teaspoon of minced garlic, and 1 teaspoon of grated ginger. Set aside to marinate and soften for at least 5 minutes before using. Be sure to squeeze out all excess liquid before using.

Mandu Making

TO MAKE YOUR *mandu*, follow these easy steps:

- Make sure your wrapper is shiny side up. The side that was against the Paraflexx liner should face upward.
- Squeeze all excess liquid from your filling, the drier the better. Any moisture will damage your wrappers.
- Spoon a tablespoon of filling into the center of your square wrapper.
- Fold the wrapper in half to form a triangle, sealing in the filling, and secure the edges closed by pressing firmly.
- Join the corners of your triangle and secure into a ring shape by squeezing together. A drop of water on the corners will help to hold it together if needed.

Alternatively, instead of using dehydrated wrappers, which can tend to get soggy when filled with moist fillings, use very thinly sliced daikon radish. Set out at room temperature for 30 minutes to wilt and soften, then fill and fold over into a stuffed semicircle.

SOY VINEGAR DIPPING SAUCE

MAKES ½ CUP

A sauce to serve with your *mandu*, made with salty Nama Shoyu and tart vinegar, sesame, and fresh green onion. I like to use toasted sesame oil for a more authentic Korean flavor, but raw works, too. If you have a gluten allergy, substitute Bragg Amino Acid for the Nama Shoyu.

> ¼ cup Nama Shoyu
>
> 2 tablespoons apple cider vinegar
>
> 1 tablespoon agave syrup
>
> 2 tablespoons toasted sesame oil
>
> 1 teaspoon sesame seeds, raw or toasted
>
> 1 tablespoon chopped green onion

In a mixing bowl, mix together the Nama Shoyu, vinegar, agave syrup, and sesame oil. Add the sesame seeds and green onions and serve with your *mandu*.

Will keep for 3 days in the fridge. Without the green onions, the sauce will keep for 1 week in the fridge.

RAVIOLI

MAKES 4 SERVINGS

The easiest way I've found to make ravioli is to slice a beet of any color as thinly as possible. Then, use two slices to sandwich your favorite cheeze.

Chioggia beets, called the "Bull's-Eye Beet," have bright fuchsia and white rings that look impressive when sliced. You can also use turnip or zucchini if beets are not available.

Create your own variety of ravioli by mixing up your cheeze, vegetable "wrapper," and sauce to make your favorite recipe.

> 1 beet, washed and peeled, then sliced thinly, using a mandoline slicer
>
> 1 recipe of your favorite Basic Cheeze (page 103)
>
> 1 recipe Cherry Tomato Marinara (page 240)

To make your ravioli, sandwich about 1 teaspoon of cheeze between two slices of beets, depending on how big your slices are.

Divide the ravioli among four serving dishes, and drizzle with Cherry Tomato Marinara just before serving.

SERVING SUGGESTION: Garnish with julienned fresh basil, fresh thyme, or sliced black olives.

OPTIONS: Try adding marinated, diced mushrooms to the cheeze to make a mushroom ravioli, and top with Cheddar Cheeze Sauce (page 105) instead of marinara. Or, mix fresh thyme into your cheeze to make a ricotta-thyme ravioli; or add chopped Coconut or Eggplant Bacon to your cheeze to make bacon ravioli, and serve with Avocado-Pistachio Pesto (page 216).

CHERRY TOMATO MARINARA
MAKES 1 CUP

The easiest marinara sauce to make ever. Just blend tomatoes with a date for sweetness and herbs for flavor. The dried herbs will help to absorb excess tomato juice, and the date helps thicken the sauce, too. The oil helps smooth everything out to a rich consistency. Try making this using Roma tomatoes, as they are another lower-juice tomato, like cherry tomatoes.

> 1½ cups cherry tomatoes
>
> 2 teaspoons pitted Medjool dates (about 1 whole)
>
> 1 teaspoon dried oregano
>
> ½ teaspoon dried rosemary
>
> ⅓ cup olive oil
>
> ½ teaspoon salt

Place all the ingredients in a high-speed blender and blend until smooth.

Will keep for 2 to 3 days in the fridge.

PIEROGI

MAKES 4 SERVINGS

Pierogi are dumplings of Slavic origin and are semicircular or square in shape. My version is inspired from the Ukraine and is filled with cheeze plus Coconut Bacon and sauerkraut. For the wrappers, use either thinly sliced beets or Spinach or Tomato Wrappers.

FILLING

1 recipe Basic Cheeze (page 103)

¼ cup diced Coconut Bacon (page 76)

¼ cup Sauerkraut (page 121), squeezed dry and chopped

WRAPPER

1 beet, washed and peeled, cut square, and sliced thinly, using a mandoline slicer

or

1 recipe Spinach or Tomato Wrappers, dehydrated as directed, cut into 16 squares about 3½ inches across

GARNISH

1 recipe Miso Butter (page 98)

1 recipe Rawmesan Cheeze (page 105)

In a mixing bowl, combine the cheeze, bacon, and sauerkraut. Toss to mix well.

If using beets, sandwich about 1 teaspoon of filling between two square slices. If using Spinach or Tomato Wrappers, place about 1 teaspoon of filling in the center of each square. Fold the wrapper over the filling and pinch the edges together to form a rectangle shape. Wet the edges of the wrapper with your finger dipped in water, and press firmly to seal.

Serve drizzled with melted Miso Butter and sprinkled with Rawmesan Cheeze. To melt your Miso Butter, place in a small bowl. Then, place that bowl in a larger bowl filled with warm water. Set aside to melt into a liquid.

Enjoy immediately.

"RICE"

It's easy to make a mock "rice" by processing an autumn squash, turnip, and/or ji-cama into rice-size bits. All these vegetables are hard when whole but soften up when broken down into small pieces. Chopped pine nuts can be mixed in to create an even softer texture. The neutral flavors make for a rice that's easy to season and works well across many different recipes.

Also, raw seeds can be soaked and sprouted to make raw "rice." Wild rice and quinoa are both seeds rather than grains and can be soaked and sprouted. I like to soak wild rice for a day or two in filtered water. It will double in size and soften. The texture is chewy, hearty, and perfect on a cold day when I'm craving a heavier, starchier-tasting food. Following, you'll find tips for soaking and sprouting seeds.

These various rice bases are great with veggies or any of the sauces throughout this book. You can also use the rice with soups, as filling for wraps, or in sushi rolls.

Quinoa only needs to be soaked and sprouted for a few hours. To sprout it, I soak it for 3 to 4 hours, drain the soaked quinoa in a sieve, and rinse it well. I then set it aside in a covered bowl for anywhere from 4 to 8 hours, just until tails sprout and grow to $\frac{1}{8}$ to $\frac{1}{4}$ inch. Sprouted quinoa is a bit softer than sesame seeds, but still crunchy.

• • •

SUSHI "RICE"

MAKES 2 CUPS

Sushi rice is a glutinous short-grain rice that gets sticky when cooked. It's seasoned with rice vinegar, sugar, and salt. My version is made with turnips and pine nuts to add softness, apple cider vinegar for tartness, and a pinch of sea salt.

It's crumbly rather than sticky and will work best with a sauce that will help it hold together inside your nori rolls.

   $1\frac{1}{2}$ cups peeled and diced turnips
   $\frac{1}{2}$ cup pine nuts

¼ teaspoon sea salt

2 teaspoons apple cider vinegar

In a food processor, combine the turnips, pine nuts, and salt. Process into rice-size pieces. Add the vinegar and pulse gently to mix.

Will keep for a couple of days in the fridge.

If you don't have pine nuts, cashews are a good substitute here. And if you don't have turnips, you can also use jicama instead.

SOAKED WILD RICE

MAKES ABOUT 2 CUPS

Soaked wild rice is my favorite "rice." It's hearty and chewy and tastes great in salads, salsas, and soups. It takes a few days to soak but is easy to prepare. All you need to do is soak and rinse. You can sprout it, too, if you prefer, though I usually don't bother.

Wild rice is supposedly heated up during the manufacturing process. If you're concerned about this issue, I encourage you to do your own sleuthing to figure out what works for you. Truly raw sproutable wild rice is available online at my site at Ani-Phyo.com/store, and also at natural food stores and other Web sites.

1½ cups wild rice

3 cups filtered water

Place the wild rice in a bowl and cover with twice as much filtered water. Let it sit for at least twenty-four hours. I prefer to soak for 2 days when I have time. Rinse and change the water two to three times per day, making sure the new water covers the rice. Finally, rinse well before using.

To sprout, pour into a large sieve and rinse well. Set out on your counter top over a bowl, cover, and let sit for 2 to 3 days, rinsing a couple of times a day.

SPROUTED QUINOA

MAKES 2 CUPS

Quinoa, pronounced "keen-waa," is the seed of the goosefoot plant. It's rich in amino acids and protein and contains all nine essential amino acids. Quinoa contains lysine, which is essential for tissue growth and repair; it is also a great source of manganese, magnesium, iron, copper, and phosphorus and is said to help people with migraine headaches, diabetes, and atherosclerosis.

Quinoa only needs to be soaked and sprouted for a few hours. The texture of sprouted quinoa is similar to sesame seeds, and a bit softer. I choose red quinoa when available (though feel free to use the brown, black, or mixed varieties) and like to make a simple salad by tossing in some diced beets for crunch, and a drizzle of coconut oil.

> 1 cup quinoa
>
> 2 cups filtered water

First, wash the quinoa by immersing in a large bowl of water and rinsing several times until the water is clear. Next, soak the quinoa in a large bowl covered with the filtered water, for about 4 hours. Drain the soaked quinoa in a sieve and rinse well. Set the sieve on top of a bowl to catch the draining water, and cover it with a plate. Set aside for 4 to 6 hours, just long enough for the tails to grow to ⅛ to ¼ inch. Rinse well.

Use immediately, or within a few hours, for maximum benefit.

Can be stored for 1 day in the fridge.

NOTE: Quinoa is known to contain saponin, which protects the plant from insects and fungus. Saponin must be rinsed away before using, because it can have toxic effects. So, make sure to rinse your quinoa two or three times, until the water is clear, before using.

QUINOA TABBOULEH

MAKES 2 CUPS

In my Lebanese-inspired tabbouleh, I use quinoa instead of bulgur wheat. The quinoa is sprouted and mixed with cucumber, green onions, red bell pepper, fresh parsley, and mint. It's served with a light lemon dressing. Serve as the Lebanese do, and enjoy your tabbouleh with hearts of romaine leaves.

TABBOULEH

½ recipe Sprouted Quinoa (page 244)

½ cup diced cucumber

2 green sliced onions

½ cup seeded and finely diced red bell pepper

½ cup chopped fresh parsley

¼ cup chopped fresh mint

DRESSING

2 teaspoons fresh lemon juice

2 tablespoons extra-virgin olive oil

¼ teaspoon sea salt

To make the tabbouleh, place all the tabbouleh ingredients in a mixing bowl. Mix well.

To make the dressing, whisk together all the dressing ingredients. Set aside.

To serve, divide among four serving bowls, and serve with a side of the dressing.

PINE NUT–SHIITAKE RISOTTO WITH PEAS

MAKES 4 SERVINGS

A delicious creamy risotto made with Sushi "Rice" tossed in a rich cashew cheeze sauce, with green peas and marinated shiitake mushrooms, topped with pine nuts.

   2 cups sliced shiitake mushrooms

   2 tablespoons extra-virgin olive oil

   1 tablespoon Nama Shoyu or Bragg Liquid Aminos

   1 recipe Sushi "Rice" (page 242)

   1 recipe Basic Cheeze (page 103), made with cashews plus an extra ½ cup filtered water

   ½ cup peas

   ¼ cup pine nuts

Marinate the mushrooms in the oil and Nama Shoyu for at least 20 minutes.

In a mixing bowl, toss together the rice and the cheeze sauce. Add the mushrooms and their marinade; mix well. Lightly toss with the peas.

To serve, divide among four serving dishes and top each portion with pine nuts.

Will keep for 1 day in the fridge.

RISOTTO WITH CHERRY TOMATOES, BLACK OLIVES, AND JALAPEÑO CHEEZE

MAKES 4 SERVINGS

Sushi "Rice" is tossed with a spicy Jalapeño Cheeze to make a creamy risotto topped with sweet cherry tomatoes and salty black olives.

   1 recipe Sushi "Rice" (page 242)

   1 recipe Jalapeño Cheeze Sauce (page 104), plus an extra ½ cup filtered water

   1 cup halved cherry tomatoes

   ¼ cup pitted and chopped black olives

In a mixing bowl, combine the rice, cheeze, and tomatoes, and mix well.

To serve, divide among four serving dishes. Top each portion with chopped black olives, and enjoy.

Will keep for 2 to 3 days in the fridge.

CRANBERRY-CASHEW WILD RICE PILAF

MAKES 4 SERVINGS

Pilaf is traditionally rice cooked in a seasoned broth. My raw version uses Soaked Wild Rice and tosses it with sweet golden raisins, crunchy cashews, and fresh cilantro leaves to make a delicious, hearty dish that's delicious all year round.

> **1 recipe Soaked Wild Rice (page 243)**
> **1 cup cranberries**
> **1 cup cashews**
> **¼ cup chopped fresh cilantro leaves**
> **1 teaspoon sea salt**

Toss all the ingredients together and enjoy.

Will keep for 2 to 3 days in the fridge.

SERVING SUGGESTION: Enjoy with Indian Spiced Chutney (page 249).

MUSHROOM WILD RICE WITH ROSEMARY

MAKES 4 SERVINGS

Mushrooms and onions are marinated in rosemary and olive oil to soften, and then tossed with Soaked Wild Rice.

> **¼ cup diced red onion**
> **1 cup sliced mushrooms**
> **1 tablespoon olive oil**
> **1 teaspoon sea salt**
> **½ teaspoon fresh rosemary, or ¼ teaspoon dried, chopped**
> **1 recipe Soaked Wild Rice (page 243)**

Toss the onion and mushrooms in a bowl with the olive oil, salt, and rosemary. Set aside to marinate for at least 15 minutes. Add the rice and mix well.

Will keep for 2 days in the fridge.

SERVING SUGGESTION: Enjoy with Indian Spiced Chutney (page 249)

PARSLEY WILD RICE

MAKES 4 SERVINGS

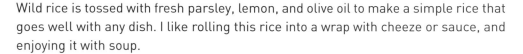

Wild rice is tossed with fresh parsley, lemon, and olive oil to make a simple rice that goes well with any dish. I like rolling this rice into a wrap with cheeze or sauce, and enjoying it with soup.

1½ cups chopped fresh parsley leaves

½ cup chopped yellow onion

1 teaspoon minced garlic

1 teaspoon lemon juice

3 tablespoons olive oil

Salt

1 recipe Soaked Wild Rice (page 243)

Place all the ingredients in a mixing bowl. Toss well and enjoy.

Will keep for 2 to 3 days in the fridge.

SERVING SUGGESTION: Enjoy with Indian Spiced Chutney (page 249).

INDIAN SPICED CHUTNEY

MAKES ABOUT 2 CUPS

Make this chutney with a fruit of your choice. Mulberries, which are sweet, and golden berries, which are tart, are both rich in antioxidants and create a great flavor. Fresh mango is sweet and works well, too. Mix with hints of Indian spices such as ginger, cilantro, chile, and onion. A delicious accompaniment to any dish.

1 teaspoon minced ginger

1 clove garlic, minced (about 1 teaspoon)

¼ cup chopped fresh cilantro

¼ cup chopped red onion

½ to 1 teaspoon chopped jalapeño

1 tablespoon olive oil

⅛ teaspoon cumin seeds (optional)

2 cups diced mango or 1 cup dried mulberries and
    1 cup dried golden berries

If using dried fruit such as mulberries and golden berries, first soak them in 1 cup of water for 3 hours or more, to hydrate before using.

Place the ginger, garlic, and soaked berries (if using) in a food processor. Pulse into small pieces. Add the rest of the ingredients, adding jalapeño to taste, and pulse to mix well.

NORI MAKI

The word *maki* means "roll" or "to roll," and *nori maki* are rolls made using a sheet of dried seaweed, or laver, called nori. Sea vegetables provide the broadest range of minerals of any food and contain almost all the minerals of the ocean—the same minerals as are found in human blood. Sea vegetables are a great source of iron, calcium, B vitamins, and lignans, which are antioxidants that have been found to protect us from cancer.

I'll show you how to make some seriously RAW king rolls, inspired by the Asian fusion of sushi restaurants here in Los Angeles. Most of the ingredients are the same as in cooked maki, such as avocado, cucumber, carrot, and nori.

The rice, of course, is not sticky as traditional sushi rice is and needs to be coupled with a sauce or avocado to help bind it together. The results are delicious rolls with the same texture and taste as their fishy counterpart, but even healthier for you, our animals, and our planet.

Throw a Make-Your-Own-Maki Party

HERE'S A GREAT way to enjoy clean, healthy, cruelty-free food that's fun to make, super healthy, eco green, and will cost less than going out to a sushi restaurant.

Ask guests to bring their favorite organic fillings and nori sheets. You can provide the Sushi "Rice," the rice-binding avocado or sauce, Nama Shoyu, and wasabi.

Show your friends how to roll the perfect maki, and invite them to make their favorite maki to share as it comes off the production line. Serve on platters, and skip the individual dinner plates and utensils, for easy cleanup. Maki is a great finger food.

CATERPILLAR NORI ROLL

MAKES 4 SERVINGS

Kale chips give this roll a sweet, chewy, crispy taste and texture that's surprisingly like the cooked version. Fill with avocado and cool, crisp cucumber. Enjoy with wasabi and Nama Shoyu or Bragg Liquid Aminos.

4 nori sheets

1 recipe Sushi "Rice" (page 242)

1 large ripe avocado, pitted and sliced into thin strips

1 small cucumber, sliced into long, thin strips

1 recipe Cheddar-Kale Chips (page 110)

Place a sheet of nori on a dry surface, such as a cutting board. Along the bottom third of the nori sheet, spread about ⅓ cup of Sushi "Rice" evenly. Press the rice down gently. Arrange one-quarter of the avocado slices evenly on top of the rice; it will help hold the rice bits together once rolled. Across the entire bottom edge of nori, place one-quarter of the cucumber, then the kale chips.

To make your maki, start with the edge closest to you. Lift the nori edge up and around the fillings, and roll tightly away from you. Repeat with the remaining nori sheets and fillings. See Rolling the Perfect Maki, page 254.

Enjoy whole, or slice each roll into four to six pieces with a dry, sharp knife. Eat immediately before the nori sheets get dampened by the ingredients.

SERVING SUGGESTION: Enjoy with Soy-Vinegar Dipping Sauce (page 239), or with Nama Shoyu and wasabi.

Rolling the Perfect Maki

NORI IS THE dried dark seaweed laver that's pressed into a flat sheet and used to roll rice and fillings into Japanese maki, or rolls. It contains almost 50 percent balanced protein; that's more than sunflower seeds or lentils. It's rich in iodine, iron, zinc, and calcium. Nori has high levels of vitamins B_1, B_2, B_3, B_6, B_{12}, A, C, and E, the "beauty vitamins," for building collagen and skin cells and is a low-fat food. Nori sheets are typically toasted, so you want to look for nori labeled "raw," which can be found at most natural food stores and online. Stored in a cool, dry place, dried seaweed will keep for several years in an airtight container.

Many people use a rolling mat made from strips of bamboo, to help make tight rolls; however, a rolling mat isn't necessary. I prefer just using my hands.

Start by placing nori sheet, shiny side down, on your rolling mat or on a dry surface, such as a cutting board or countertop. Some nori is thinner than others. Sometimes I double up thinner sheets for rolling.

Next, place your fillings all the way across the bottom edge of the nori. That's the edge that's closest to you. Typically, you want to put down the driest fillings first, to create a moisture barrier so your nori won't get soggy too quickly.

Starting at the edge closest to you, use your hands or the sushi mat to roll the nori to enclose the fillings as you roll upward toward the top edge of the sheet. Roll as tightly as you can, without squeezing the fillings out the sides.

Once your maki is completely rolled up, dab a little water along the top edge of the nori sheet, using your finger, and seal the roll closed.

You can enjoy as a handheld whole maki, or use a dry, very sharp knife to slice into four to six pieces.

Love Seaweed

SEA VEGETABLES provide a high level (38 to 50 percent) of complete protein and vitamin B_{12}. The chemical makeup of sea vegetables is similar to human blood, so they have a balancing, alkalizing effect on our blood. Seaweeds are known to reduce cholesterol, remove metallic and radioactive elements from the body, and prevent goiter. Seaweed also has antibiotic properties, which is why I like to use strips of nori instead of a Band-Aid on cuts.

MANGO–MACADAMIA NUT MAKI

MAKES 4 SERVINGS

The mango in this roll creates the fleshy texture, and the rich macadamia nuts add a soft crunch.

> 4 nori sheets
> 1 recipe Sushi "Rice" (page 242)
> 1 ripe mango, seeded, peeled, and sliced into thin strips
> 1 ripe avocado, pitted and sliced into thin strips
> ½ cup halved macadamia nuts

Lay a nori sheet on a dry surface, such as a cutting board. Along the entire bottom edge (the edge closest to you) spread about ⅓ cup of Sushi "Rice" evenly. Press down gently. Arrange one-quarter of the avocado evenly on top of the rice; it will help hold the rice bits together once rolled.

Across the entire bottom edge of the nori, place one-quarter of the mango and macadamia nuts, and roll up. Repeat with the remaining nori sheets and fillings. (See Rolling the Perfect Maki, page 254.)

SERVING SUGGESTION: Enjoy with Soy-Vinegar Dipping Sauce (page 239), or with Nama Shoyu and wasabi.

MAKI WITH MARINATED SPINACH AND "PEANUT" SAUCE

MAKES 4 SERVINGS

Spinach is marinated and softened, then rolled up inside maki with a peanuty sauce inspired by Thai spices.

- 4 cups spinach, well washed
- 2 tablespoons olive oil
- 4 nori sheets
- 1 recipe Sushi "Rice" (page 242)
- 1 recipe "Peanut" Sauce (page 259)
- 1 cup seeded red bell pepper, sliced into long, thin strips (about 1/2 whole pepper)
- 1/4 cup fresh cilantro leaves

Toss the spinach with the olive oil, and set aside for 5 minutes to soften.

Lay a sheet of nori on a dry surface, such as a cutting board. Along the entire bottom edge (the edge closest to you) spread about 1/3 cup of Sushi "Rice" evenly. Press down gently. Spread one-quarter of the "Peanut" Sauce evenly over the rice; it will help hold the rice bits together once rolled. Layer on one-quarter of the marinated spinach, then one-quarter of the red bell pepper strips and cilantro along the bottom edge. Roll up tightly. Repeat with the remaining nori sheets and fillings. (See Rolling the Perfect Maki, page 254.)

Enjoy whole or slice into four to six pieces with a dry, sharp knife.

Imaginative Nori Maki Making

THE PRECEDING recipes are just a few of my favorites. You'll want to experiment with your own combinations to re-create some classic rolls or to invent your own. Here's a basic maki cheat sheet:

For four rolls:

4 nori sheets
1 recipe Sushi "Rice" (page 242), or sprouted quinoa
2 cups of your favorite fillings

I like a combination of crunchy-crisp with soft and savory, for complex textures and flavors inside each roll. Sushi "rice" is softer and quinoa is crunchier. I like to use them both, depending on the texture I'm craving.

Try using some of the recipes from the wraps and burger chapters as fillings; the mock tuna salad/salmon burger pâté (page 195), undehydrated, can be the base for a spicy tunalike roll; or try marinated mushrooms and barbecue sauce to invent a new breed of *unagi*. Add spicy Jalapeño-Lime Kream (page 134). The options are unlimited!

Here are some additional tips for tasty maki:

- Use a thick sauce, cheeze, or avocado with the Sushi "Rice," to help keep the rice bits bound together.
- Create a moisture barrier by first placing a dry leaf (such as a whole romaine leaf, half a stemmed collard leaf, or ½ cup shredded romaine lettuce) along the bottom edge of the nori sheet. Then put the rice and toppings on top of the leaf. This will keep the nori from getting moist too quickly.
- Choose a combination of both soft and crunchy fillings, such as mango and macadamia nuts, or avocado and cucumber, to create a complex range of textures and colors inside your roll.
- Cut the fillings into skinny strips, rather than thick pieces. It's easier to roll up when using thinner pieces.

"PEANUT" SAUCE

MAKES ABOUT 1 CUP

A rich sauce inspired by Thai peanut sauce but made with almond butter (since raw peanuts don't taste very good) and whisked with lime juice, garlic, and Nama Shoyu. Use in your maki, wraps, on noodles, and as a dressing.

> ½ cup almond butter
>
> ¼ cup lime juice
>
> 2 tablespoons apple cider vinegar
>
> 1 tablespoon Nama Shoyu or Bragg Liquid Aminos
>
> 1 teaspoon minced garlic
>
> ½ to ⅔ cup filtered water, as needed

Whisk all the ingredients together in a mixing bowl, slowly adding only enough water to create a thick sauce.

MARINATED SHIITAKE MUSHROOM ROLL

MAKES 4 SERVINGS

Shiitake mushrooms have a rich, earthy flavor that lends itself well to Asian cuisine. They are softened and marinated in Nama Shoyu and sesame oil for a sautéed consistency. I like to use toasted sesame oil for the rich flavor.

> 2 cups sliced shiitake mushrooms
>
> 1 tablespoon Nama Shoyu or Bragg Liquid Aminos
>
> 1 tablespoon toasted or raw sesame oil
>
> 2 cups spinach, well washed
>
> 2 tablespoons olive oil
>
> 4 nori sheets
>
> 1 recipe Sushi "Rice" (page 242)
>
> 1 ripe avocado, pitted, halved, and sliced thinly
>
> 1 carrot, peeled and sliced into long, thin strips

Place the mushrooms in a bowl with the Nama Shoyu and sesame oil, and set aside for at least 20 minutes to marinate. Squeeze out the excess liquid before using, and discard the marinade.

Next, toss the spinach with the olive oil, and set aside for 5 minutes to soften.

Lay a sheet of nori on a dry surface, such as a cutting board. Along the entire bottom edge (the edge closest to you) spread about ⅓ cup of Sushi "Rice" evenly. Press down gently. Arrange one-quarter of the avocado slices along the bottom edge of the rice, which will hold the rice bits together once rolled.

Along the bottom edge, spread an even layer of one-quarter of the marinated spinach, then the mushrooms, then the carrot. Roll up tightly. Repeat with the remaining nori sheets and fillings. (See Rolling the Perfect Maki, page 254.) Enjoy whole or slice into four to six pieces with a dry, sharp knife. Serve immediately.

11
DESSERTS

DESSERT IS MY favorite part of every meal; in fact, one of these raw desserts can make a nutritious meal in and of itself for me. My desserts are a delicious, nutritious way to add healthy, whole foods into any diet—which is an easy way to get rid of unhealthy foods without even trying. The more nutrient dense foods we eat, the more *nutrified* we become, the healthier we feel, and the less room we have available to eat empty calories or less valuable foods. I find this approach to be less stressful than focusing on the elimination of certain foods out of our diet. Eating raw foods isn't about denial—it's about all the array of possibilities of the delicious, fresh foods your body will love.

By enjoying more of the delicious sweets in this chapter, you'll be displacing baked goods loaded with sugar, flour, eggs, butter, cream, and milk—ingredients that cause inflammation and swelling. Instead, you'll be eating superfoods such as nuts, seeds, and fruit—and the leaner you'll become. These desserts will help you achieve a tighter body full of valuable nutrients to build healthy bones, skin, fight age-accelerating free-radical damage, and create healthiness from the inside out. And, since our skin is our largest organ, health on the inside translates on the outside as a clear, radiant glow of health.

I start this chapter with an easy-to-make Basic Piecrust and Basic Fruit Pie Filling to which you can add ingredients to create new flavors and textures. Next are variations of a Basic Flourless Cake recipe that are simple yet sophisticated in presentation and flavor. I include two basic Ice Kream recipes, and several sweet sauces. Lastly are cookies that are really quick to assemble, using just a few ingredients, but require dehydration.

Yes, you can have your cake and eat it, too . . . and get a healthy glow on.

Vanilla

EARLIER IN this book, I offer a recipe for making your own vanilla extract in organic vodka (see page 99). If you want to avoid alcohol, use alcohol-free extract, but realize it usually contains glycerin.

The best bet is to always go directly to the whole food source, in this case, to use whole vanilla beans. They can be expensive, but the flavor is worth it.

Use one tablespoon extract to one vanilla bean pod, seeded, or use the whole pod if blending in a high-speed blender.

PIES

My pies are usually made in two parts, first a crust and then a filling.

Pie filling can be made with fruits or with nuts. I'll show you a really simple Basic Fruit Pie Filling, to which you can add other ingredients you have on hand, to mix up the flavors and textures.

You can make a kream pie or tartlets by filling your crust with Whipped Cashew Kream, made by blending cashews with a bit of coconut oil and vanilla, and topping with your favorite fruits.

• • •

BASIC PIECRUST
MAKES 1 PIECRUST

This is the simplest way to make a fast piecrust. It's made with chopped nuts that are bound together, using sticky dates. I recommend lightly chopping the nuts for texture, but you can also grind them into a powder for a smoother crust texture.

Try using different varieties of dates and nuts to change up the flavor and texture. You can swap out the dates for raisins, cranberries, and other sticky dried fruits, and the nuts for seeds, coconut, and other dry ingredients.

> 2 cups nuts, such as almonds, pistachios, pecans, or walnuts
>
> 1 teaspoon sea salt
>
> 2 cups pitted dates (any type, preferably semisoft, such as Medjool)

NOTE: If using drier dates, soak them first in filtered water for 15 minutes or more to hydrate before using.

Pulse the nuts into small bits with salt in a food processor. Make sure not to over-process nuts into a powder; you want small chunks for texture.

"Flour" the bottom of your pie dish with some of the finer nut powder to keep the crust from sticking to the pan.

Add the dates to the food processor with the nuts and pulse to bind into a dough. If the dough is too crumbly, add a few more pitted dates. Process until you get a dough that stays together.

Press the dough evenly into the bottom of your pie dish.

Fill with your favorite filling.

OPTIONS: Some of my favorite combos include chunky almonds bound together with Medjool dates; pecan pieces held together with cranberries; and for a smoother crust that works well for small tartlets, I like to use an almond meal bound with Medjool dates.

 ## BASIC FRUIT PIE FILLING
FILLS 1 PIE

Here's an easy way to make a fruit pie. Choose your favorite in-season fruit, and slice thinly. Then toss in agave syrup, or your favorite syrup, to sweeten.

Try adding a cup of dried fruit, such as raisins or cranberries, for color, texture, and flavor, along with such flavorings as a tablespoon of alcohol-free vanilla extract or a couple of teaspoons of ground cinnamon.

For other delicious variations, try tossing fruit with your favorite Fresh Fruit Jam (page 96), Vanilla Butter (page 98), Lavender Butter (page 98), or Chocolate Butter (page 100).

> 4 to 5 cups sliced fruit, such as apples, persimmons, strawberries, or peaches
>
> ¼ cup agave syrup

Place the fruit and syrup ingredients in a mixing bowl. Toss to mix well. If you have time to spare and are using firmer fruit such as apples, set your filling aside for a few hours to release water, soften, and marinate. This will give your filling more of a cooked fruit texture.

Spread in your piecrust, and enjoy.

Will keep for a couple of days in the fridge.

OPTIONS: Some of my favorite combinations include apple slices with a cup of raisins and a tablespoon of alcohol-free vanilla extract; blueberries tossed with agave syrup and a teaspoon each of ground cinnamon and grated nutmeg, for a spiced flavor; and sliced peaches tossed with agave syrup and Lavender Butter.

STRAWBERRY KREAM PIE

FILLS 1 PIE

Fill your favorite Basic Piecrust with Whipped Cashew Kream, and top with beautiful strawberries.

> 1 recipe Basic Piecrust (page 263)
> 2 recipes Whipped Cashew Kream (page 266)
> 2 cups halved strawberries
> 2 tablespoons agave syrup

Spread the whipped kream in your piecrust, in a single, even layer.

Toss the strawberry halves in the agave syrup, then arrange the strawberries, sliced side down, on top of the kream.

Will keep for 2 or 3 days in the fridge.

SERVING SUGGESTION: Serve with Chocolate Fudge Sauce (page 282) or Strawberry Sauce (page 280).

WHIPPED CASHEW KREAM

MAKES 1½ CUPS

A white, rich kream to enjoy on top of your pie, ice kreams, and as a dip for berries and sliced fruit.

> 1 cup cashews
> ½ cup coconut oil
> 1 tablespoon alcohol-free vanilla extract (see Vanilla, page 262)
> ½ cup filtered water

Place all the ingredients in a high-speed blender and blend until smooth. Transfer to a small bowl and place in the center of a serving tray or platter.

Will keep for 4 to 5 days in the fridge.

SERVING SUGGESTIONS: Serve with 1 pound of strawberries, blackberries, or sliced peaches or apples. Spread the kream inside your piecrust, then top with the fresh fruit to make a kream pie.

CUSTARD TARTLETS

MAKES ABOUT 6 TARTLETS

To make tartlets, which are traditionally small pastry crusts, divide and press Basic Piecrust into the compartments in a tartlet pan to make individual mini pies. These tiny pies are filled with Whipped Cashew Kream, and topped with a variety of fruits for a beautiful display.

> **1 recipe Basic Piecrust (page 263), made with almond meal**
> **2 recipes Whipped Cashew Kream (page 266)**

Your favorite small fruits for topping each tartlet, such as 1 blackberry, 3 blueberries, 1 raspberry, or cacao nibs

Line the compartments of a tartlet or multiple brioche pan with plastic wrap first, then press the piecrust firmly into the pan. Remove by gently lifting up the plastic wrap.

Next, spoon the whipped kream into each tartlet. Top each tartlet decoratively with one type of fruit or the cacao nibs.

Serve immediately, or keep in the fridge.

Will keep for 2 or 3 days in the fridge.

CAKES

The cakes in this book are inspired by the texture of baked flourless cake. It's a dense, moist, and gooey consistency similar to that of fudge or a brownie. The cake tastes guilt laden, but in reality, is packed with antioxidants that are healthy and good for you, our animals, and the planet.

• • •

BASIC FLOURLESS CAKE

I like to leave small bits of nuts in my cake mix for more texture visually and for a more interesting mouthfeel. If you prefer a smoother cake mix, you can process your nuts into a powder first, before adding dates to bind it all together.

My recipe calls for Medjool dates because they have a higher moisture content and are soft and sticky. If you use a drier date, soak them in warm water for 20 minutes or more before using to add moisture.

To make your cake, nuts are bound together with the stickiness of the dates. If your cake is too crumbly, just add a few more dates to the mix. You can even add a tablespoon or two of water or agave syrup, to add more moisture that will help bind, if needed.

> 3 cups nuts, such as walnuts, almonds, or Brazil nuts
>
> ¼ teaspoon sea salt
>
> 1 cup pitted Medjool dates, packed
>
> 1 tablespoon alcohol-free vanilla extract (see Vanilla, page 262)
>
> 1 to 2 tablespoons agave syrup (optional)

Place the nuts and salt in a food processor and break down the nuts into chunks. Add pieces of dates, rather than one large lump, and the vanilla. Process until the nuts bind together with the sticky dates to form a cake batter.

Test the batter by grabbing a handful and squeezing to make sure it holds together. If it's not sticky enough, add a few more dates, or 1 to 2 tablespoons of agave syrup, and process until it holds together.

OPTION: To add crunch, mix in ½ cup of Buckwheat Crispies (page 63) to your batter. To make more complex cakes, alternate layers of different flavors, such as vanilla with chocolate cake.

ORANGE-ALMOND CAKE

MAKES 1 CAKE

A two-layer cake filled with orange sauce and segmented oranges. The top of the assembled cake is finished off with a dusting of white coconut powder.

> 1 recipe Basic Flourless Cake Mix (page 268), made with almonds
> ½ recipe Basic Fruit Sauce (page 280), made with oranges
> 1 orange, pitted and segmented (remove all peel and pith)
> ¼ cup dried coconut, ground into a powder

Divide the cake mix into two equal parts. Form two cake rounds by hand. Or, line a small cake pan with plastic wrap first, then press one portion of the dough inside to form the shape. Flip the formed cake out of the pan and peel off the plastic. Repeat with the second portion of dough.

Place the first round onto a plate and top with orange fruit sauce and segmented orange slices. Top with the second cake round. Use a wire sieve to dust the top of the cake with the coconut powder.

Will keep for 3 to 4 days in the fridge.

RASPBERRY-LEMON DREAM

MAKES 1 CAKE

Two layers of a moist, flourless cake sandwich a tart lemon sauce and bright, fresh, red raspberries.

> 1 recipe Basic Flourless Cake Mix (page 268), made with your favorite nut
> ½ recipe Basic Fruit Sauce (page 280), made with lemon
> 1½ cups raspberries

Divide the cake mix into two equal parts. Form two cake rounds by hand. Or, line a small cake pan with plastic wrap first, then press one portion of the dough inside to form the shape. Flip the formed cake out of the pan and peel off the plastic. Repeat with the second portion of dough.

Place the first round on a plate and top with lemon fruit sauce and 1 cup of the raspberries. Top with the second cake round and the remaining raspberries.

Will keep for 3 to 4 days in the fridge.

STRAWBERRY SHORTCAKE

MAKES 1 CAKE

Fresh red strawberries and sweet whipped kream are layered between a moist flourless cake.

> 1 recipe Basic Flourless Cake Mix (page 268), made with your favorite nut
>
> 1 batch Whipped Cashew Kream (page 266)
>
> 1½ cups sliced strawberries

Divide the cake mix into two equal parts. Form two cake rounds by hand. Or, line a small cake pan with plastic wrap first, then press one portion of the dough inside to form the shape. Flip the formed cake out of the pan and peel off the plastic. Repeat with the second portion of dough.

Place the first round on a plate and top with whipped kream and half the strawberries. Top with the second cake round, remaining kream, and remaining strawberries.

Will keep for 3 to 4 days in the fridge.

COCONUT CAKE WITH NUTELLA HAZELNUT SAUCE

MAKES 1 CAKE

Vanilla flourless cake is filled with a rich hazelnut chocolate sauce, vanilla whipped kream, and chopped almonds. It is frosted with vanilla kream and topped with shredded coconut.

> 1 recipe Basic Flourless Cake Mix (page 268), made with your favorite nut
>
> 1 recipe Whipped Cashew Kream (page 266)
>
> 1 tablespoon alcohol-free vanilla extract (see vanilla, page 262)
>
> 1 recipe Nutella Hazelnut Sauce (page 282)
>
> 1 cup coarsely chopped almonds
>
> ½ cup shredded dried coconut

Divide the cake mix into two equal parts. Form two cake rounds by hand. Or, line a small cake pan with plastic wrap first, then press one portion of the dough inside to form the shape. Flip the formed cake out of the pan and peel off the plastic. Repeat with the other portion of dough.

Mix the whipped kream with the vanilla extract.

Place the first cake round onto a plate. Top with the chocolate hazelnut sauce, then half of the vanilla whipped kream, and then the chopped almonds. Top with the second cake round, remaining vanilla kream, and shredded coconut.

Will keep for 4 to 5 days in the fridge.

CHOCOLATE-CHERRY CAKE

MAKES 1 CAKE

Cherries, cherry jam, and whipped kream are layered between two cake rounds. Ideally, you want to use fresh cherries, but frozen will work, too.

> 1 recipe Basic Flourless Cake Mix (page 268), made with your favorite nut
> ⅔ cup cacao or carob powder
> 1 recipe Fresh Fruit Jam (page 96), made with cherries
> 1 cup pitted halved cherries
> 1 recipe Whipped Cashew Kream (page 266)

Add the cacao to your cake mix and mix well. Divide the cake mix into two equal parts. Form two cake rounds by hand. Or, line a small cake pan with plastic wrap first, then press one portion of the dough inside to form the shape. Flip the formed cake out of the pan and peel off the plastic. Repeat with the other portion of dough.

Place the first round on a plate. Top with the cherry jam, half of the cherries, then half of the whipped kream. Top with the second cake round, remaining kream, and remaining cherries.

Will keep for 3 to 4 days in the fridge.

VARIATION: Make bite-size brownies with just the Basic Flourless Cake Mix and cacao powder. Frost with Nutella Hazelnut Sauce or Chocolate Fudge Sauce.

ICE KREAM

I'll show you how to make two types of ice kream. The first is nut-free and is made by processing frozen bananas. You can enjoy it immediately, or freeze it again for a couple of hours to stiffen up the consistency.

The second type of ice kream is made by blending nuts into a rich cream and then freezing it overnight. I've figured out how to mix ingredients that won't freeze, such as agave syrup, with nuts and water, so that my ice kream remains scoopable straight out of the freezer. My recipes don't require an ice-cream maker, but you can use one if you want.

Your favorite flavors, such as fruit, chocolate, and vanilla bean, can be added to your ice kream to make different variations.

• • •

  ## BASIC BANANA ICE KREAM (NUT-FREE)
MAKES 4 SERVINGS

When you have superripe bananas that need to be eaten right away, use them to make banana ice cream. Peel and freeze the bananas for at least 8 hours. Then process the frozen bananas to make your ready-to-eat ice kream.

6 ripe bananas, peeled and frozen
¼ cup agave syrup
Water, if needed

Place the frozen bananas in a food processor and process into a smooth ice kream.

Enjoy immediately with your favorite toppings, such as chopped nuts and fruit, sauces, and syrups. Or, transfer to a container and place in the freezer to firm up for an hour or two, to your desired consistency.

Will keep for weeks in the freezer. Remove and let sit at room temperature for 10 minutes, to soften before scooping.

SERVING SUGGESTION: Serve with sliced strawberries and Chocolate Fudge Sauce (page 282).

CHOCOLATE-BANANA ICE KREAM WITH HAZELNUTS

MAKES 4 SERVINGS

Bananas are flavored with cacao powder for chocolate ice kream. Hazelnuts are added for flavor and crunch. Make a sundae with your favorite sauce, such as Berry Compote (page 281) topped with Lavender Extract (page 99).

> 6 ripe bananas, peeled and frozen
>
> 2 tablespoons agave syrup
>
> ¼ cup cacao powder
>
> ½ cup coarsely chopped hazelnuts

Place the frozen bananas and agave syrup in a food processor and process until smooth. Add the cacao and process to mix well. Add the hazelnuts and pulse lightly to mix.

Enjoy immediately, or transfer to a container and place in the freezer to firm up for an hour or two, to your desired consistency.

Will keep for weeks in the freezer. Remove and let sit at room temperature for 10 minutes, to soften before scooping.

BASIC ICE KREAM
MAKES 2 CUPS

Start with this basic recipe, then add your favorite flavors to create endless flavor combinations.

If you don't have a high-speed blender, first grind nuts into a powder. Then, put into the blender, and blend with the remaining ingredients. This will help you achieve a smoother texture.

I've discovered a way to keep my ice kream scoopable straight out of the freezer. The water is in a delicate balance with the syrup, which doesn't freeze solid when frozen. If you're finding your ice kream too icy or hard, try decreasing the amount of water next time. And, if it's not freezing hard enough for you, add another tablespoon or two of water to find the exact balance for the consistency you love.

> 1 cup nuts, such as cashews, Brazil nuts, hazelnuts, or almonds
> ¼ cup agave syrup
> 4 to 6 tablespoons filtered water, as needed

Blend the nuts with the agave syrup, adding only enough water to make a thick cream. The less water you use, the less ice crystals will form in your final frozen recipe.

OPTIONS: Add 1 tablespoon alcohol-free vanilla extract or the seeds from 1 vanilla bean pod for a traditional Vanilla Ice Kream flavor. Or, replace the water with fruit juice, such as orange. Or, lightly swirl in a syrup or sauce (pages 280 to 283) before freezing. The combination of flavors are endless!

MEXICAN CHOCOLATE ICE KREAM
MAKES 2 CUPS

Inspired by Mexican hot chocolate, which is a blend of chocolate with cinnamon mixed with an optional bit of the Mayan-influenced spice, cayenne.

> 1 recipe Basic Ice Kream (page 277)
> ¼ cup cacao powder
> 1 teaspoon ground cinnamon powder
> ⅛ teaspoon cayenne (optional)

Blend together all the ingredients, including the cayenne, if desired. Transfer to a container, cover, and place in the freezer overnight.

LAVENDER ICE KREAM

MAKES 2 CUPS

An aromatic ice kream with the flavor of lavender. I prefer using lavender extract, for a smoother texture. But you can also use straight, pulverized flowers to avoid the alcohol in the extract.

> 1 recipe Basic Ice Kream (page 277)
>
> 1 tablespoon lavender extract, or 2 tablespoons pulverized culinary lavender buds (do not consume any lavender sold for potpourri)

Blend together all the ingredients. Transfer to a container, cover, and place in the freezer overnight.

SERVING SUGGESTION: Serve with your favorite sauce.

LÚCUMA ICE KREAM

MAKES 2 CUPS

A gelato-like ice cream popular in South America, *lúcuma* is a fruit with a flavor reminiscent of caramel. You don't need an ice-cream maker to enjoy this recipe. Just blend and freeze.

  You can also make this ice kream without a high-speed blender by first grinding up your cashews into a powder, then blending with the remaining ingredients. This will help you achieve a smoother final product.

NOTE: If you don't have yacón syrup, just replace it with agave syrup. You may want to add 1 tablespoon of blackstrap molasses, which is not raw but will richen the flavor.

Lúcuma powder is available at natural food stores and online, and in my e-store, at www.aniphyo.com/store.

> 1 recipe Basic Ice Kream (page 277), made with cashews and yacón syrup instead of agave, if available. (See Note above.)
>
> 1/2 cup lúcuma powder
>
> 1 tablespoon alcohol-free vanilla extract (see Vanilla, page 262)
>
> 1/2 cup filtered water

Place all the ingredients in a high-speed blender. Blend slowly at first, increasing the speed gradually to get the smoothest consistency possible.

Transfer to a container and place in the freezer overnight. Enjoy straight from freezer with your favorite sauces and syrups (pages 280 to 283).

SWEET SAUCES

Sauces are a great way to add an extra level of flavor and visual complexity to any sweet treat. So, sauce it up from simple to sophisticated with easy-to-make sauces. Just process your favorite fruit and agave syrup together. Now, that's even faster and easier than walking down a grocery aisle to find a jarred sauce.

Use these sweet sauces to make ice-kream sundaes with your favorite ice kream, drizzle over your pies or pancakes, and even to dip your cookies into.

• • •

 ## BASIC FRUIT SAUCE
MAKES 1½ CUPS

Make your favorite sauce with whatever fruit is in season and whatever you happen to have on hand today. Adding a brightly colored syrup is a great way to bump up the sophistication of your presentation and flavor profile.

I always prefer fresh fruit when it's in season, but you can use frozen if fresh isn't available. Just thaw before using frozen fruit in this recipe.

This basic sauce is similar to the Raspberry Sauce from *Ani's Raw Food Desserts*, but the recipe in this book will help you to create your own varieties and flavors.

> **2 cups fruit, such as pineapple, mango, or peaches**
> **½ cup agave syrup**

Place the ingredients in a high-speed blender and blend until smooth to make a beautiful colored sauce.

Will keep for 3 to 4 days in the fridge.

AGAVE BLUEBERRY SAUCE

MAKES 1½ CUPS

Blueberries are processed with agave syrup to create a chunky sauce that's beautiful in color, and tastes great with every dessert.

1 recipe Basic Fruit Sauce (page 280), made with blueberries

Place the sauce ingredients in a high-speed blender. Blend smoothly to make a bright purple sauce that looks amazing and tastes delicious.

MAPLE-STRAWBERRY SAUCE

MAKES 1½ CUPS

This recipe calls for maple syrup, which isn't raw but adds a great flavor. Medjool dates also have a maple flavor. So if using agave syrup instead, add two or three Medjool dates, too.

2 cups strawberries

½ cup maple syrup, or ¼ cup agave syrup and 2 to 3 Medjool dates with 2 tablespoons water

If using dates, place in a food processor, and chop into small bits first.

Place the strawberries and your syrup of choice in a food processor, and pulse into sauce. If using dates, add with the water and pulse.

Will keep for 4 to 5 days in the fridge.

BERRY COMPOTE

MAKES 1½ CUPS

Compote is fruit in syrup. I use red wine with fresh fruit, sweetened with agave syrup.

2 cups raspberries

¼ cup red wine

2 tablespoons agave syrup

1 tablespoon lemon zest (optional)

Place all the ingredients in a food processor. Pulse lightly to mix.

NUTELLA HAZELNUT SAUCE

MAKES 1 CUP

Inspired by the Italian jarred sauce, Nutella, a delicious chocolate-hazelnut sauce that's used for dipping fruit, on sandwiches, and in crepes with sliced bananas. Use my uncooked version in exactly the same way, drizzled over cake, pie, and crepes, and as a dip for cookies. It's delicious!

1 cup hazelnuts

2 tablespoons agave syrup

2 tablespoons coconut oil, warmed at room temperature until liquid

1 tablespoon cacao powder

2 to 4 tablespoons filtered water, as needed

In a food processor, process the hazelnuts until they have formed a butter, scraping down the sides and mixing those nuts with the butter that forms at the bottom. Next, add the agave syrup and coconut oil and process to mix well. Add the cacao powder and as much water as needed to create your desired consistency.

Will keep for 4 to 5 days in the fridge. Can also be frozen for a few weeks. Defrost back into a syrup consistency before using.

CHOCOLATE FUDGE SAUCE

MAKES 1 CUP

A delicious sauce that's supersimple to make. Just place agave syrup and cacao powder in a small blender, and add a splash of olive oil to add body. Blend and eat right away. If using a larger blender, you may want to double this batch so it blends better. It keeps for a couple of weeks anyway, so it's a good idea to keep some on hand.

You can substitute maple syrup for the agave, if you prefer. Maple is darker in color than agave, but the chocolate powder will hide that. Choose Grade B maple syrup; it's less processed and contains more minerals.

   This is similar to the chocolate sauce in *Ani's Raw Food Desserts*, but I'm including this variation here because I can never have too much chocolate sauce for topping cakes, pies, ice-kream sundaes, and cookies.

½ cup cacao powder

¾ cup agave syrup

4 teaspoons extra-virgin olive oil

Blend all the ingredients together and enjoy.

Will keep for a couple of weeks in the fridge.

SERVING SUGGESTIONS: Use Chocolate Fudge Sauce (page 282) to make a sundae by topping your favorite ice kream, and drizzle over slices of cake or cookies before serving.

COOKIES

Inspired by cookbooks that make 101 cookies starting from just one base recipe, I decided to also start from one base recipe created using just four ingredients. From there, you can add whatever you happen to have on hand in your pantry, to create endless combinations of cookie flavors.

• • •

BASIC COOKIE DOUGH
MAKES ABOUT 16 COOKIES

Almond meal is sweetened with your choice of syrup and a pinch of salt. Add fillings and flavorings to make a variety of cookies. It doesn't get much easier than this.

2½ cups almond meal

½ teaspoon salt

½ cup agave, maple, or rice syrup

¼ cup filtered water

1½ to 2 cups of your favorite fillings, such as dried fruit, cacao nibs, chocolate chips, or chopped nuts

Mix the almond meal with the salt. Add the syrup and water; mix well. Add your favorite flavorings and fillings.

Use a 2-tablespoon scooper to portion the dough directly onto the mesh screen of your 14-inch-square Excalibur Dehydrator trays. Dehydrate at 104°F for 4 to 6 hours, or to your desired consistency.

NOTE: You can buy finely ground almond meal. To make your own, just process almonds into a powder in your food processor or grinder.

GOJI BERRY–CHOCOLATE CHIP COOKIES

MAKES ABOUT 18 COOKIES

Splashes of beautiful red goji berries and dark chocolate chips make these my all-time favorite cookies. I like to use organic dark chocolate chips, which are hard to find sugar-free. I figure in this one instance, the joy these cookies bring me offsets any negative effects of a tiny bit of sugar. For a completely raw and sugar-free cookie, use cacao nibs instead.

> **1 recipe Basic Cookie Dough (page 284)**
> **1 cup goji berries**
> **½ to 1 cup dark chocolate chips or cacao nibs**

Mix all the ingredients together in a large mixing bowl.

Use a 2-tablespoon scooper to portion the dough directly onto the mesh screen of your 14-inch-square Excalibur Dehydrator trays.

Dehydrate at 104°F for 4 to 6 hours, or to your desired consistency.

Will keep in the fridge for one week. Will keep in the freezer for several weeks; thaw for 10 minutes before eating.

ORANGE-CRANBERRY CHOCOLATE CHIP COOKIES

MAKES ABOUT 18 COOKIES

Delicious orange and chocolate combine with tangy cranberries for a powerful antioxidant blast. These cookies fight age acceleration and free-radical damage.

> **1 recipe Basic Cookie Dough (page 284)**
> **1 tablespoon orange zest, or ½ teaspoon alcohol-free orange extract**
> **1 cup dried cranberries**
> **1 cup semisweet dark chocolate chips or cacao nibs**

Mix all the ingredients together in a large mixing bowl.

Use a 2-tablespoon scooper to portion the dough directly onto the mesh screen of your 14-inch-square Excalibur Dehydrator trays.

Dehydrate at 104°F for 4 to 6 hours, or to your desired consistency.

Will keep in the fridge for one week. Will keep in the freezer for several weeks; thaw for 10 minutes before eating.

BROWNIE CACAO CHIP COOKIES

MAKES 16 COOKIES

Moist, rich, dark chocolate brownies as bite-size cookies. Cacao powder is mixed into your cookie dough with raisins for added sweetness and cacao nibs for crunch. Adjust the amount of nibs to your liking. They are bitter and taste like coffee beans. You may prefer to use only ½ cup for crunch. But if you like cacao nibs, bump it up to 1 cup.

> 1 recipe Basic Cookie Dough (page 284)
> 1 cup raisins
> ½ to 1 cup cacao nibs
> ½ cup cacao powder

Mix all the ingredients together in a large mixing bowl.

Use a 2-tablespoon scooper to portion the dough directly onto the mesh screens of your 14-inch-square Excalibur Dehydrator trays.

Dehydrate at 104°F for 4 to 6 hours, or to your desired consistency.

Will keep in the fridge for at least one week. Will keep in the freezer for several weeks; thaw for 10 minutes before eating.

WALNUT BROWNIE COOKIES

MAKES ABOUT 18 COOKIES

The texture of this cookie is very similar to that of a traditional baked brownie. This version has chunks of walnuts, plus raisins for added moistness and sweetness. The texture of dehydrated cookies are very different from nondehydrated cookies, whose nuts are bound together using sticky dates.

> 1 recipe Basic Cookie Dough (page 284)
> ½ cup cacao powder
> 1 cups walnut pieces
> ½ cup raisins

Mix together the Basic Cookie Dough and cacao powder. Add the walnuts and raisins and mix well.

Use a 2-tablespoon scooper to portion the dough directly onto the mesh screen of your 14-inch-square Excalibur Dehydrator trays.

Dehydrate at 104°F for 4 to 6 hours, or to your desired consistency.

Will keep in the fridge for one week. Will keep in the freezer for several weeks; thaw for 10 minutes before eating.

BANANA-CHOCOLATE CHIP COOKIES
MAKES 16 COOKIES

Inspired by chocolate-covered bananas, dried banana and chocolate are mixed into the Basic Cookie Dough. To make these cookies even more decadent, serve with Chocolate Butter.

> 1 recipe Basic Cookie Dough (page 284)
> ³⁄₄ cup chopped dried bananas
> 1 cup semisweet dark chocolate chips or cacao nibs

Mix all the ingredients together in a large mixing bowl.

Use a 2-tablespoon scooper to portion the dough directly onto the mesh screen of your 14-inch-square Excalibur Dehydrator trays.

Dehydrate at 104°F for 4 to 6 hours, or to your desired consistency.

SERVING SUGGESTION: Serve with a side of Chocolate Butter (page 100) or Chocolate Fudge Sauce (page 282) for dipping.

ALMOND COOKIES

MAKES ABOUT 20 COOKIES

This recipe, inspired by Chinese almond cookies, is a slight variation of the Basic Cookie Dough recipe. I still use almonds for flavor and add additional buckwheat for a light crunch. These cookies look pretty with a whole almond pressed into the center.

> 1 cup dried buckwheat groats
>
> 2 cups almond meal
>
> 1 tablespoon almond extract
>
> $^2/_3$ cup agave syrup
>
> 1 cup filtered water
>
> 20 whole almonds

Grind the buckwheat into a powder, and place in a medium-size mixing bowl. It may help to grind a half cup at a time. Add the almond meal, almond extract, agave syrup, and water. Mix well.

Use a 2-tablespoon scooper to portion the dough directly onto the mesh screen of your 14-inch-square Excalibur Dehydrator trays.

Press one almond into the top of each cookie.

Dehydrate at 104°F for 4 to 6 hours, or to your desired consistency.

Will keep in your fridge for one week. Will keep in the freezer for several weeks; thaw for 10 minutes before eating.

OPTION: Fold in 1 cup slivered almonds to add more texture.

FRUIT MACAROONS

MAKES ABOUT 16 COOKIES

Make your favorite fruit macaroons by mixing up the fruits you use in this recipe. Try banana, blueberry, strawberry, mango, or pineapple. The sticky fruit will bind your coconut together. If you like your macaroons a bit sweeter, add an additional tablespoon or two of agave syrup.

> 1$^1/_2$ cups whole strawberries, diced pineapple, blueberries, sliced bananas, or your favorite fruit
>
> 3 tablespoons agave syrup
>
> 2 tablespoons alcohol-free vanilla extract (see Vanilla, page 262)

½ cup almond meal

2 cups dried shredded coconut

Place the fruit, agave, and vanilla in your food processor. Process into a puree. Add the almond meal and coconut, and pulse to mix well.

Use a 2-tablespoon scooper to portion the dough directly onto the mesh screen of your 14-inch-square Excalibur Dehydrator trays.

Press one almond into the top of each cookie.

Dehydrate at 104°F for 3 hours, or to your desired consistency.

Eco Gift

YOUR FRIENDS AND family will love you for gifting them with homemade, delicious, healthy cookies. I like to package them in a jar with a ribbon and custom labels made from recycled stickers. A great way to avoid the busy mall during holiday season.

12
SAMPLE MENUS

BREAKFAST

Weekday mornings can be rushed, especially when getting children off to school. A quick, easy cereal with nut mylk and toast are a great way to start the day, and they can all be prepared once at the start of the week.

My weekend mornings, which I try to make more leisurely, are when I'll have time to savor pancakes, crepes, scrambles, biscuits and gravy, and quiche.

WEEKDAY BREAKFAST

Dried Fruit, Pecan and Coconut Rawnola, page 62
Vanilla Almond Mylk, page 41
Toast with Jam and Butter, page 91

WEEKEND BRUNCH, PANCAKES

Matcha Shake, page 43
Brazil Nut–Banana Pancakes, page 75
Berry Compote, page 281
Coconut Bacon, page 76, or Eggplant Bacon, page 78

WEEKEND BRUNCH, RANCHEROS

WEEKEND BRUNCH, SCRAMBLE

LUNCH AND PICNIC

My workday lunches are usually leftovers from my dinner the night before, or even brunch from the weekend.

I love bringing my own lunch. It saves money. Plus, it ensures I eat healthy so I stay my ideal weight, feel great, and remain productive for the rest of the day, without the postlunch slump. My co-workers have always been more interested in my raw lunches than in what they were eating.

Soups, pizzas, wraps, noodles, and burgers all keep and travel well, making terrific lunch options. These lunches can be enjoyed outside in the sun on a nice day, and on a blanket for a picnic, too.

Any of the following lunches can also be enjoyed as dinner menus.

WEEKDAY LUNCH, THAI INSPIRED

WEEKDAY LUNCH, AMERICAN INSPIRED

WEEKDAY LUNCH, ITALIAN INSPIRED

Basic Kreamy Fruit Smoothie, page 34
Tomato and Tarragon Bisque, page 137
Garlic Margherita Pizza, page 219
Custard Tartlets, page 267

DINNER

I like to prepare weekday dinners with recipe items that can be made ahead and stored, then assembled quickly before serving for minimal effort and time after a long day.

Even on weekends, I find myself busy catching up on things left over from the week. The bottom line is, I prefer the fastest and easiest recipes always. Unless, for a special occasion, making dinner for someone I want to impress.

If necessary, components of burger, bread, rice, pizza, salad, soup, and noodle recipe can all be prepared days ahead of time and stored separately, and then assembled quickly before serving.

Most of these items keep and travel well and are great to carry with you for lunch the following day. So, make extra so you'll have leftovers.

DINNER, KOREAN INSPIRED

Persimmon Smoothie, page 34
Wontons in a Light Sesame-Soy Broth with Peas, page 141
Korean Stir-Fried Kelp Noodles with Vegetables (*Jap Chae*), page 224
Napa Cabbage Kimchi, page 126
Spicy Korean Cucumber Slices, page 127
Chocolate-Banana Ice Kream with Hazelnuts, page 271

DINNER, JAPANESE INSPIRED

Ginger-Lemon Martini, page 47
Yin and Yang Salad with Jalapeño-Tahini Dressing, page 162
Mango–Macadamia Nut Maki, page 255
Marinated Shiitake Mushroom Roll, page 259
Coconut Cake with Nutella Hazelnut Sauce, page 271

DINNER, MEXICAN INSPIRED
Muddled Strawberries in Coconut Kefir, page 49
Nachos, page 109
Tortilla Soup with Jalapeño-Lime Kream, page 134
South-of-the-Border Wraps, page 180
Mexican Chocolate Ice Kream, page 277

DINNER, AMERICAN INSPIRED
Pomegranate-Mint-Cucumber Fizz, page 49
Caesar Salad Boats with Coconut Bacon and Rawmesan Cheeze, page 166
Chickenless Burger with Aioli Mayonnaise, page 197
Battered Zucchini Sticks, page 116
Sun-Dried Tomato Ketchup, page 205
Sliced Cucumber Pickles, page 123
Strawberry Kream Pie, page 266

FOODS TO GO

I carry snacks with me when I travel and when I'm away from home, to ensure that I fuel myself with nutrient-rich foods that power me through my day.

Easy-to-carry travel foods that don't need refrigeration include cereals and dehydrated crackers, breads, nuts, onion rings, wrappers, and bacon. Traveling with breads and crackers makes it easy to assemble a sandwich or toast with fresh avocado and tomato when you arrive at your destination. And onion rings and bacon spruce up any salad you may order at a restaurant.

Prepared foods that travel well and can stay out of refrigeration for a few hours include drinks, collard wraps, pizza, burgers, sandwiches, soups, and breads.

Shelf stable, no refrigeration required
(ordered from the longest to shortest time at room temperature):

CEREALS
Buckwheat Crispies, page 63
Dried Fruit, Pecan and Coconut Rawnola, page 62
Super Chia Cereal, page 66

CRACKERS, FLATBREADS, PIZZA CRUST, CHIPS, CROUTONS
If fully dried, will keep for at least a couple of weeks at room temperature.

SEASONED NUTS
If fully dried, will keep for at least a couple of weeks at room temperature.

BUCKWHEAT-BATTERED "FRIED" ONION RINGS
If fully dried, will keep for at least a week at room temperature.

WRAPPERS
When stored on their own and fully dried, wrappers will keep for at least several days at room temperature.

BACON
When fully dried, will keep for many days at room temperature.

CAKES AND COOKIES
Basic Flourless Cake (page 268) will keep for days at room temperature when stored on its own, since all its ingredients are shelf stable to begin with. Assembled cakes last a few hours, depending on the fruit and sauces. Cookies will keep for several days at room temperature or longer, depending on how long they were dehydrated.

Can stay out of refrigeration for several hours or longer
(ordered from the longest to shortest time at room temperature):

SUN BURGERS
All dehydrated burgers will keep for a day or longer out of the fridge, stored on their own, without sauces.

DRINKS
Smoothies, Mylks, Shakes, Sun Teas, pages 31 to 51

CULTURED DRINKS
Can stay at room temperature for a day or more, but beware of pressure that builds up inside your bottle when opening.

QUICHE
Spinach Quiche, Asparagus-Mushroom Quiche, Broccoli-Cheddar Quiche with Coconut Bacon, pages 86 to 88

CHEEZES

All, except Coconut Kefir Cheeze.

RICE AND QUINOA

Will keep for several hours or more when stored separately. Assembled recipes will keep for a couple of hours out of the fridge. The wrappers on nori maki rolls get soggy quickly once assembled but still taste good and will keep several hours at room temperature.

SOUPS

Will keep several hours out of the fridge.

WRAPS

Wraps rolled in lettuce leaves and collard will keep for several hours out of the fridge.

RAVIOLI

Assembled ravioli with wrappers made from such vegetables as sliced beets will keep for a few hours out of the fridge.

PIZZA

All assembled pizzas will keep for at least a few hours out of the fridge.

NOODLES

All noodles will keep for several hours or more when stored separately from sauces. Liquid will begin to release, so these are best enjoyed immediately. I don't mind extra juice in my noodles, though.

SANDWICHES

All sandwiches will keep for a few hours out of the fridge when assembled, and longer when their components are stored separately.

PIES AND SWEET SAUCES

Pies will keep for a few hours at room temperature, depending on the fruit filling. Sweet sauces will also keep for several hours.

Eating on the Road

BEFORE I TRAVEL, I research to locate local co-ops, health food stores, and farmers' markets at my destination. Most restaurants have fresh vegetables available, usually as salads. Most will use conventional produce, so remember to have gratitude and to do the best you can.

I pack my crackers, cereal, bread, seasoned nuts, wrappers, cake, cookies, and sheets of nori. I use avocado and vegetables to make sandwiches with my bread, wraps with my wrappers and nori sheets, and snack on seasoned nuts, cake, and cookies. I sprinkle on my bacon and Buckwheat-Battered "Fried" Onion Rings to spruce up a boring salad, or munch on them as snacks.

13
RAW FOR DOGS

I MAKE KANGA a birthday cake every year to celebrate the day I found and rescued her. Or rather, the day she rescued me.

KANGA, MY DOG

Dogs help to relieve our stress. Kanga, my Rhodesian Ridgeback, makes me laugh all the time. She reminds me to take breaks to walk her and hug her and acts as my compost bin, eating all my leftovers. Kanga loves everything I make.

Dogs should not eat onion, macadamia nuts, or chocolate (all are poisonous to them in even small amounts), and sweets. The following recipes are good to use to make your pooch treats that he or she will love you for.

Basic Nut Mylk, no sweetener, page 41
Mineral Green Mylk, page 42
Buckwheat Crispies, page 63
Crackers, pages 112 to 114 and Flatbreads, pages 123 to 124 (shape into dog biscuits)

PART 3

RESOURCES

In this section, I'll offer some tips and inspiration for helping to lower our carbon footprint when traveling and while in our homes. I list several Web sites, including my own, AniPhyo.com, where you can find uncooking videos, recipes, kitchen tools, appliances, organic ingredients, and water kefir grains. And, I'll recommend a few of my favorite films that'll hopefully change the way you view our world. They did for me.

REDUCING YOUR CARBON FOOTPRINT

I do as much as I can every day to reduce my carbon footprint. Although these suggestions aren't doable for everybody, here's a list of ideas to help you tread more lightly on the planet:

TRANSPORTATION

▸ Walk or bike whenever possible.

▸ When available, take public transit on local trips.

▸ If you have a car, limit its use as much as possible, even if you have a Prius or other energy-efficient vehicle.

▸ Take a bus or train rather than short airplane trips.

SAVING ENERGY AND MONEY IN YOUR HOME.

▸ Install compact fluorescent bulbs in all your light fixtures, and dispose of bulbs safely as they contain mercury.

▸ Weatherproofing your home is a good idea, as is insulating your water heater or switching to a tankless heater that heats water as you need it.

▸ In cold months, wear more layers indoors and keep your thermostat low.

▸ When you are ready to replace your appliances, buy energy-efficient appliances.

▸ Wash clothes only when your machine is full.

▸ Dry your clothes on a clothesline when possible.

▸ Defrost your fridge and freezer regularly.

▸ Unplug electronics when not in use; they still suck power even when off.

▸ Hand wash your dishes as they get dirty.

▸ Compost instead of using a garbage disposal.

▸ Take shorter showers.

As you can guess from my recipes, I eat as much local, seasonal foods as possible, buy in bulk to reduce packaging and waste, and shop at farmers' markets. Planting a garden and cutting back on animal products has a huge impact on our planet. This is from my book *Ani's Raw Food Desserts*, and I'm repeating it here again: switching to a totally local diet saves 1,000 miles of driving per year. Replacing red meat and dairy with vegetables just one day per week saves resources equal to 1,160 miles of driving per year. And, switching to a completely vegan diet is the equivalent of driving 8,100 fewer miles per year! What we choose to eat has a huge impact on our environment.

REDUCE, REUSE, RECYCLE

Not only were my parents early raw fooders, they were also the first recyclers I knew. I've been trained by my folks to conserve by using and buying less, which saves money. I replace items only when needed, reuse and recycle, compost, and buy recycled products, including clothes and furniture. Remember, it takes resources and energy to recycle, make recycled products, and package, warehouse, and distribute them.

Visit www.myfootprint.org—take the quiz at this Web site and estimate the size of your ecological footprint. You may be surprised at how big your footprint is. I was.

RECYCLING AND ECO DISPOSAL

It's important to dispose of toxic substances properly to keep them from contaminating our ground water and environment. The U.S. Geological Survey found medications such as antibiotics, birth control hormones, and antidepressants in more than 80 percent of the rivers they tested.

Visit www.Earth911.com—type in your zip code and what you want to recycle, such as paint or compact fluorescent lightbulbs, to find nearby drop sites.

MORE RESOURCES

ANI'S RECIPES AND UNCOOKING VIDEOS

http://www.aniphyo.com/category/recipes/
http://www.aniphyo.com/category/videos/
http://www.youtube.com/aniphyo
Visit my Web site, SmartMonkey Foods, where I offer recipes and inspiration—
http://www.smartmonkeyfoods.com/.

INGREDIENTS

AniPhyo.com/store—organic food and ingredients such as cacao, nuts and butters, sea vegetables, sweeteners, pet care
GoldMineNaturalFood.com—cultured vegetables, raw nori
PremierOrganics.org—Artisana nut butters
UltimateSuperFoods.com—superfoods such as cacao, goji, spirulina
LivingTreeCommunity.com—Nuts and butters, oils, grains, and seeds
Nutiva.com—hemp, coconut oil
KelpNoodles.com—kelp noodles

KEFIR GRAINS

I buy my water kefir grains from Cheree, and you can also buy kombucha culture from her store at http://www.stichingtime.com on eBay, or http://www.bonanzle.com/booths/stichingtime, or e-mail at chereepaula@rocketmail.com.

If Cheree's temporarily out of stock, here's another source:

http://happyhealthybalance.blogspot.com/2009/07/get-your-kefir-on-
water-kefir-grains.html

And Dom's site is packed with information on water kefir, kefirkraut, and other fermented foods and drinks:

www.kefir-grains.com

KITCHEN TOOLS

AniPhyo.com/store—kitchen tools such as dehydrators, blenders, ceramic knives, spiralizers, and my cooking DVDs

ExcaliburDehydrator.com—dehydrators and Paraflexx liner sheets

www.Tribest.com—Personal Blender, juicers

MOVIES TO WATCH

The Future of Food
Investigation into the disturbing truth behind the unlabeled, patented, genetically engineered foods that have quietly filled U.S. grocery store shelves for the past decade.
http://www.thefutureoffood.com/ or watch online at
http://www.hulu.com/watch/67878/the-future-of-food

Food, Inc.
How industrial food is making us sicker, fatter, and poorer, and what you can do about it.
http://www.foodincmovie.com/

Flow
Our world water crisis, and the growing privatization of the world's dwindling fresh water supply with an unflinching focus on politics, pollution, human rights, and the emergence of a domineering world water cartel.
http://www.flowthefilm.com/

Justicia Now!
> Chevron Texaco's toxic legacy in the Northern Ecuadorian region of the Amazon rainforest—and a courageous group of people called Los Afectados (The Affected Ones) who are seeking justice for the ensuing cancer, sickness, and death in the largest environmental class-action lawsuit in history.
> http://www.mofilms.org/justicianow/index.html

METRIC CONVERSIONS

The recipes in this book have not been tested with metric measurements, so some variations might occur.

Remember that the weight of dry ingredients varies according to the volume or density factor: 1 cup of flour weighs far less than 1 cup of sugar, and 1 tablespoon doesn't necessarily hold 3 teaspoons.

GENERAL FORMULA FOR METRIC CONVERSION

Ounces to grams	multiply ounces by 28.35
Grams to ounces	multiply ounces by 0.035
Pounds to grams	multiply pounds by 453.5
Pounds to kilograms	multiply pounds by 0.45
Cups to liters	multiply cups by 0.24
Fahrenheit to Celsius	subtract 32 from Fahrenheit temperature, multiply by 5, divide by 9
Celsius to Fahrenheit	multiply Celsius temperature by 9, divide by 5, add 32

VOLUME (LIQUID) MEASUREMENTS

1 teaspoon = ⅙ fluid ounce = 5 milliliters
1 tablespoon = ½ fluid ounce = 15 milliliters
2 tablespoons = 1 fluid ounce = 30 milliliters
¼ cup = 2 fluid ounces = 60 milliliters
⅓ cup = 2⅔ fluid ounces = 79 milliliters
½ cup = 4 fluid ounces = 118 milliliters
1 cup or ½ pint = 8 fluid ounces = 250 milliliters
2 cups or 1 pint = 16 fluid ounces = 500 milliliters
4 cups or 1 quart = 32 fluid ounces = 1,000 milliliters
1 gallon = 4 liters

VOLUME (DRY) MEASUREMENTS

¼ teaspoon = 1 milliliter

½ teaspoon = 2 milliliters

¾ teaspoon = 4 milliliters

1 teaspoon = 5 milliliters

1 tablespoon = 15 milliliters

¼ cup = 59 milliliters

⅓ cup = 79 milliliters

½ cup = 118 milliliters

⅔ cup = 158 milliliters

¾ cup = 177 milliliters

1 cup = 225 milliliters

4 cups or 1 quart = 1 liter

½ gallon = 2 liters

1 gallon = 4 liters

WEIGHT (MASS) MEASUREMENTS

1 ounce = 30 grams

2 ounces = 55 grams

3 ounces = 85 grams

4 ounces = ¼ pound = 125 grams

8 ounces = ½ pound = 240 grams

12 ounces = ¾ pound = 375 grams

16 ounces = 1 pound = 454 grams

LINEAR MEASUREMENTS

½ in = 1½ cm

1 inch = 2½ cm

6 inches = 15 cm

8 inches = 20 cm

10 inches = 25 cm

12 inches = 30 cm

20 inches = 50 cm

OVEN TEMPERATURE EQUIVALENTS, FAHRENHEIT°F AND CELSIUS°C

100°F = 38°C

200°F = 95°C

250°F = 120°C

300°F = 150°C

350°F = 180°C

400°F = 205°C

450°F = 230°C

ACKNOWLEDGMENTS

Thank you, Jae Phyo, my mother, and Max Phyo, my brother, for your endless supply of unconditional love and support. Thank you for this life I am blessed to live. Thank you, Ruben Cartegena, for taking great care of Mom, for continued medical discussions, and for photography advice.

Tyler Golden, thank you for the delicious food photographs and your meticulous attention to detail. Andre Schnyder, thank you for your creativity, patience, and for the beautiful lifestyle photos. Antonio Sanchez, my dear friend and family, thank you for continuing to grace my books with your beautiful illustrations. You are the world's best illustrator.

Carol Conforti, thank you for being gorgeous in every way, and for your excitement to help with everything from location scouting, to production assisting, to styling, to testing and prep. So Young Lee, my friend and family, Korean recipe consultant, and beautiful supermodel, thank you and Jennifer Kang and Sean Kang for your support and for jumping in to join my production.

Chris Elwell and Kory Odell, thank you for hosting me at the Odellwell Manor and Retreat Center, for being my eager testers, for believing in me all these years, and for being my good friends. Christopher Autry, my cosmic twin, thank you and Grant Nvision for loving my food. I miss having you both here in L.A. Joe Arancio, thank you for being my biggest fan. Kato Banks, thank you for your bright energy and love.

Shadi Azarpour, dear friend and fellow doggie mommy, you are a gift. Thank you and Eric Weissler for believing in me, for your valuable legal advice, and guidance. Tina Wexler, thank you for taking great care of me and my books. George Ruiz, thank you for being my champion, and for introducing me to Tina. Bill Ahmann, thank you for continuing to protect my SmartMonkey IP, you're an angel.

Thank you to Shauna Verkade and Excalibur Dehydrators for your love and support. *VegNews Magazine* and publisher Joseph Connelly and Colleen Holland, thank you for standing up for the truth, and for believing in me. Bryant Terry, thank you for being an inspiration and good friend.

Phillip Schenkler, Leandra Yahola, Martin Libich, and Stephanie Person, thank you for being my models and testers, and for showing up for me the way you do. Thank you, Barry Jan, for taking photos of my demo at the SF Ferry Building Farmers' Market, and for letting me use them in this book. David Daugherty, my old friend, thank you for connecting me back to organics so many years ago. I couldn't have guessed I'd end up here.

A special thank you to my team at Da Capo. Renee Sedliar and Wendie Carr, it's been a joy and honor to work together with you both over the past four years. Kevin Hanover and Lindsey Triebel, thank you for believing in me and my books.

And, of course, Kanga, thank you for endless hours of snuggles, licks, and tail wags.

INDEX

Brazil Nut–Banana Pancakes with Blue-
berry Syrup and Sliced Bananas, 75
Chocolate-Banana Ice Kream with Hazel-
nuts, 275, 295
Band-Aid, nori used as, 255
Basic Cheeze, 219, 220, 241, 247
Basic Fruit Smoothie, 31
Basic Green Smoothie, 32
Basic Kreamy Fruit Smoothie, 34, 295
Basic Nut Mylk, 41, 45, 302
Battered Zucchini Sticks, 116, 297
BBQ Burger, 201–202
BBQ Sauce, 201
Beauty and fashion, xxi, xxvii, 36
Beets, 239
Bell Peppers, "Roasted," 118, 203
Berry Compote, 281, 293
Biscuits, 93–95
Black Olive and Pesto Pizza, 215
Blended Dressing, Basic, 151, 160
Blender, 3, 4, 29, 31
BLT Club, 190
Bowls. *See* Mixing bowls
Bragg Liquid Aminos, 11, 76, 78, 80
Brazil Nut–Banana Pancakes, 73, 293
Brazil Nut–Banana Pancakes with Blueberry
Syrup and Sliced Bananas, 75
Bread, 187, 209
Brewer's yeast, 10
Broccoli, Kream of, with Red Bell Pepper
Kream, 138
Broccoli-Cheddar Quiche with Coconut Bacon,
88–89, 294
Brown rice syrup, 10
Brownie Cacao Chip Cookies, 288
Brunch, 294
Buckwheat Batter, Basic, 115, 116
Buckwheat Battered "Fried" Onion Rings, 116,
203, 217
Buckwheat Biscuits, 93–94
Buckwheat Crispies, 63, 93, 268, 302
Buckwheat groats, 114
Buckwheat Pizza Crust, 212, 215, 217
Burger turned Inside Out with Sun-Dried
Tomato Ketchup, 205
Burgers, 194–205
BBQ Burger, 201

Burger turned Inside Out with Sun-Dried
Tomato Ketchup, 205
Chickenless Burger with Aioli Mayonnaise,
197–198
Hemp Sun Burger with Mustard, 199
Portobello, 203
Sloppy Joe, 202–203
Burrito, Wet, 175–176
Butenko, Victoria, 32
Butters, 11, 91, 98–100

C

Cabbage
Cabbage Salad with Fresh Mint, Viet-
namese, 156
Chinese Chickenless Salad, 161
Green Cabbage Kimchi, 131, 237
Green Cabbage Sauerkraut, 121–122
Napa Cabbage Kimchi, 126, 295
Red Cabbage and Grapefruit, 164
Vietnamese Cabbage Salad with Fresh
Mint, 156
See also Sauerkraut
Cabbage Kimchi, 131
Cabbage Salad with Fresh Mint, Vietnamese,
156
Cacao, 23
Brownie Cacao Chip Cookies, 288
Chocolate Mylk, 41
Super Cacao-Coconut Energizer, 39
Caesar Salad Boats with Coconut Bacon and
Rawmesan Cheeze, 166, 186, 297
Caesar Salad Wrap, 186
Caffeine, 39, 43
Cakes and cookies, 268–273, 284–292, 298
Calories in raw foods, 30
Caraway, 23
Carbon emissions, 103
Carbon footprint, 306
Carob, 9, 23
Carrot Angel Hair with Sun-Dried Tomatoes in
Cheddar Cheeze Sauce, 233
Cashew Gravy, 93, 94
Cashew Kream, 70, 94–95, 266, 271
Caterpillar Nori Roll, 253
Celery, 23, 24

stocking the fridge, 13
See also Salads; *specific vegetables*
Vietnamese Cabbage Salad with Fresh Mint, 156
Vietnamese Pho Noodle Soup, 232
Vinegar, 11

W

Wakame, 153
Walnut Brownie Cookies, 288–289
Water Kefir, 56
Watercress with Cranberries and Almonds, 158
Watermelon Cooler, 48
Watermelon Punch, 46
Weight loss, xxvii
Wet Burrito, 175–176
Wheat
    effect of processed grains, 210–211
    gluten intolerance, 210–211
Whipped Cashew Kream, 94–95, 266, 271
Whisk, 5
Whisked Dressing, Basic, 149
Wigmore, Ann, 59–60
Wild rice, 243, 248, 249
Wild Rice, Soaked, 243
Wine, 47, 48
Wontons in a Light Sesame-Soy Broth with Peas, 141, 143, 295

Wrapper, Tomato, 173, 175, 176, 186, 237, 298
Wraps, 170–186
    Caesar Salad Wrap, 186
    Cheeze Enchilada with Ranchero and Mole Sauce, 176
    Corn Tostada, 171
    Garden Wrap, 180–181
    Mediterranean Wrap with Red Pepper Hummus, 181, 184
    South-of-the-Border Wraps, 180
    Tahini Zucchini Rolls, 175
    Tomato and Olive Quesadillas with Mango-Cucumber Salsa and Sour Kream, 177–178
    Wet Burrito, 175

Y

Yacón, 10, 38
Yeast, 10
Yin and Yang Salad with Jalapeño-Tahini Dressing, 162, 295

Z

Zucchini Bread, 23, 190, 192
Zucchini noodles, 225
Zucchini Sticks, Battered, 116

Eat Well and Live Long

I'm grateful to live a life I love, doing what I enjoy, for people I care about. Every day, I make sure to spend time with my family and friends, play with my dog, sweat, stretch, study, eat good food, live eco-green, practice patience and kindness, and work and play hard. I meditate, contemplate, and remember to focus on what I want and try not to think about the things I don't want,

Eat up, be blissful, and live long. Happiness is a reflection of your health. Yum!